OWNERSHIP:
EARLY CHRISTIAN
TEACHING

CHARLES AVILA

OWNERSHIP: EARLY CHRISTIAN TEACHING

ORBIS BOOKS
Maryknoll, New York 10545

Sheed and Ward
London

The Indexes were prepared by Marilyn Barr

Copyright © 1983 by Charles Avila
Published jointly by Orbis Books, Maryknoll, NY 10545, and Sheed and Ward
Limited, 2 Creechurch Lane, London EC3A5AQ

Library of Congress Cataloging in Publication Data

Avila, Charles
  Ownership, early Christian teaching.

  Includes bibliographical references and index.
  1. Property—Religious aspects—Christianity—History.
2. Fathers of the church.   I. Title.
BR115.E3A94   1983   261.8'5   83-8330
ISBN 0-88344-384-8 (pbk.)

Sheed and Ward ISBN 0-7220-6316-4

To

EUGENIO AND ELEANOR AVILA
my parents and first teachers

and to the memory of

VERNA GOLAMCO-AVILA

with gratitude and love

Contents

Preface   *xi*

Chapter 1
The Concept of Ownership   *1*
    Two Approaches   1
    The General Notion   3
    Origins of Private Property   4
    An Ancient Notion Prevails   8
    Exploring Patristic Thought   10

Chapter 2
Roman Law Theory and Practice of Ownership   *14*
    Influence of Roman Law   14
    Beginnings   16
    Nature of Ownership and Property Distinctions   19
    From Land Ownership to Slave Ownership   22
    Socioeconomic Conditions in the Patristic Age   25
    Resistance, Resignation, Decline   30

Chapter 3
Clement of Alexandria: The Koinonic Goal   *33*
    The Texts   35
        1. Autarkeia, *or Self-Sufficiency, As a Purpose of*
            Property   *35*
        2. Koinōnia *As a Purpose of Property*   *37*
        3. Limits of the Use of Wealth   *42*
        4. All Wealth a Gift to All   *43*
    Summary   45

Chapter 4
Basil the Great: Robbery by Any Other Name . . .   *47*
   The Texts   49
     1. The Rich Are Thieves   49
     2. The Injustice of Usury   56
     3. The Injustice of Luxury in the Midst of Poverty   56
   Summary   57

Chapter 5
Ambrose: Born Naked   *59*
   The Texts   61
     1. The Natural Equality of All in Womb and Tomb   61
     2. The Wealthy Few Cause the Many to Groan in Misery   64
     3. The Earth Belongs to All: The Wealthy Few Have a Duty of Restitution   66
     4. Helping Others Places God in Our Debt   69
     5. The Most Excellent Christian Quality   70
     6. We Lose Things That Are Common When We Claim Things As Our Own   71
     7. Nature Is the Mother of Common Right, Usurpation of Private Right   73
     8. His Sun Rises for All, His Rain Falls on All, and He Has Given the Earth to All   76
     9. It Is Idolatrous of the Rich to Usurp God's Absolute Dominion   78
   Summary   78

Chapter 6
John Chrysostom: You Are Possessed by Possessions   *81*
   The Texts   83
     1. Not to Share One's Resources Is Robbery   83
     2. The Meaning of "Mine" and "Not Mine"   85
     3. To Possess and Not Be Possessed by One's Possessions   87
     4. The Many Poor Are Not Slothful: The Huge Inheritance of a Few Is Unjust   88

5. *The Few Who Are Rich Are Accountable to All: Their Manner of Accumulating Wealth May Class Them with Murderers*   *91*
6. *The Root of Accumulated Wealth Must Be Injustice: Private Ownership Causes Antagonisms, As If Nature Itself Were Indignant*   *94*
7. *Where Is the God-Given Dignity of All, When the Poor Rank Beneath the Dogs of the Rich?*   *98*
8. *The Dispersion of Property Is the Cause of Expense and Waste, and So of Poverty*   *100*
Summary   102

Chapter 7
Augustine: What You Have Is Not Your Own   **105**
The Texts   108
1. *Some Terms Defined:* Frui, Uti, Pecunia   *109*
2. *Theocratic "Communism"? Law Should Be Ruled by Ethics*   *110*
3. *Superfluities Are Others' Property*   *113*
4. *Do Not Think You Are Giving from What Is Yours*   *115*
5. *Private Property Is Loss*   *116*
6. *Do Not Entrust Your Children to Your Patrimony Rather Than to Your Creator*   *119*
7. *Private Ownership Begets Manifold Miseries*   *119*
Summary   122

Chapter 8
The Patristic Response: Attack on an Ideology, and an Alternative Program   **125**
The Christian Movement   127
The Patristic Philosophy of Ownership   131
Wealth in Itself Is Good, but the Wealthy Are Thieves   *131*
Individual Ownership of the Koina *Is Robbery*   *134*
Inheritance: Transmission and Accumulation of Stolen Goods   *136*
Restitution   *137*

Condemnation of Private Ownership   138
Private Ownership As Idolatry   140
Affirmation of Human Equality: Common Origin,
    Common Nature, Common Destiny   141
Twin Goals of Ownership: Autarkeia and
    Koinōnia   144
Chrysostom's Practical Program   146
The Christian ''Social Dropout'' Movement   148

Conclusion   151

Notes   156

Appendix: Original Texts   171

Index of Biblical References   207

General Index   209

Preface

The research and writing of this book was begun in the Philippines almost twenty years ago. As a Catholic seminarian who had become an organizer in the resurgent Filipino peasant movement, I found myself in two different worlds at once. At times these worlds simply ignored each other. At other times they were overtly antagonistic.

First there was the world of the seminary, with its Latin and its Greek, and the various branches of philosophy and theology. It was a world of books and study-periods, symposia and term papers, sports and retreats—a secure world of five meals a day and multiple options for development in the liberal arts and the sciences. One was constantly challenged to "excel," during a twelve-year "formation process" designed in view of a "total development of the whole person," with the ambitious, perfectly serious—if amusing in retrospect—aim of becoming, at the end of this long training, "what a priest should be: all things to all people."

In the context of Philippine society, then and now, this world was without any doubt a world of privilege—as symbolized by the imposing, costly seminary buildings and extensive grounds, surrounded by a string of *barrios*, or rural villages, inhabited by sharecroppers who were, for the most part, poor because they were economically and culturally deprived and politically oppressed. These formed the nation's vast majority and constituted the "other world" of Philippine society. This world was perceived by the privileged few as composed of people who were poor because they were "ignorant, lazy, superstitious, and resistant to change." In the privileged view, which was the unquestioned orthodox doctrine, by and large, of the mass media, the Churches, and academia, the poor majority had "always been that way" (poor), and this was certainly thought to be no fault of those who were presently rich, privileged, and powerful.

One often heard, "So few have so much *and* so many have so little," or "The few rich become richer *and* the many poor become poorer and poorer." The undeniable facts of wealth and poverty were cited, but mention of a possible causal relationship between the two was assiduously avoided.

The dominant view emphasized that poverty was nothing new. The peasants had always been poor, and the chances were that they would remain poor for a long time to come, given the slow-but-sure nature of general economic development. We were a developing country, according to the orthodox view: in the long run, we would become a developed country, and have a chance to eradicate mass poverty. Of course one must not forget that Jesus himself recognized that the poor would always be with us. In the meantime, the Christian challenge to the rich was to engage in ever more philanthropic and charitable works. "Social justice" was occasionally urged as the progressive thing—but always with a caveat against "fomenting class struggle" and a stern reminder of the sacred character of private property.

Communists, socialists, and other radicals were simply written off as power-hungry exploiters of the poor, who wanted to use peasants to conduct a violent revolution against lawfully constituted authority. In the eventuality of a radical victory, one was warned, the poor would become poorer than ever because radicals advocated the abolition of private property. Moreover, according to the established view, Christianity taught love and harmony between classes, not hatred and class antagonism. Christianity essentially upheld the "sacred right" of private property as a fundamental means of defending human dignity—even if the broad majority of people had no such concrete right to be defended because they did not own any property.

Thus, Christian leaders, both hierarchical and lay, cooperated in and roundly applauded the military defeat of the Communist and Socialist-led *Huk*s, or armed peasant rebels, in the early 1950s by the U.S.-backed Magsaysay administration. In the wake of the *Huk* defeat, reform-oriented Catholic activists, scarcely enthusiastic at the prospect of a communist Philippines, began to organize in field and factory, lobbying in the halls of Congress for the promise of "social reforms." Concerned Christians seeking to "do something about the poor" were now divided between charity-oriented projects on one side and power-oriented efforts at organizing the poor on the other.

But now these social-justice oriented Catholic organizers were labelled "warmed-over Marxists," and the suggestion was made that they might be even more insidious than the imprisoned communists and socialists, because they claimed to be Christian-inspired, while they were equally guilty of "promoting class conflict" and trying to set limits on "the moral, constitutional, and legal right of private ownership." It is true that they were not yet advocating armed struggle, as the Marxist radicals had done, but according to the prognosis of the privileged view, it was just a matter of time before they would do so.

In any case, the Philippines in the early 1960s saw a great deal of discussion in the establishment press of the need to alleviate the poverty of the majority, if only to dampen the fiery unrest of a peasantry who seemed always on the verge of rebellion despite the crushing of the *Huk*s a decade earlier.

A certain Filipino professor in the Divine Word Seminary at this time, Father Jose Vicente Braganza, S.V.D., used to interrupt his lectures in philosophy and theology and digress into a lively and provocative discussion of politics and the Philippine economy, with the accent on the plight of the poor. A deeply spiritual person, whose excellence in varied intellectual pursuits was local legend, Braganza constantly criticized the Church's utter lack of identification with the poor. To him, Christianity had to pass the test of Matthew 25—by feeding the hungry, visiting the sick and the imprisoned, and so on down the list of clearly "secular" tasks. Before long he succeeded in persuading some of his students to accompany him in his regular visits to prisoners in various Philippine jails. It was an uplifting change of pace for us to be allowed to break out of the closely sheltered world of the seminary and learn from new teachers of another milieu—the prisoners of Quezon City jail and the National Penitentiary.

Listening to the stories of the prisoners was a practical course in Philippine sociology. I saw the pattern of ex-tenants migrating to the cities because they had been evicted from the farms they did not own. The landlords were mechanizing these farms and gradually evicting the tenants, even if these families had tilled those lands for many generations. But the cities, more often than not, only offered the ex-tenants unemployment, and the opportunity to commit the petty crimes (thefts, typically) for which they were now in jail. I became a messenger from many prisoners to their relatives, to inform the latter of their loved ones' whereabouts.

But one jail we began to visit held political prisoners—the captured socialist leaders of the notorious *Huk* movement, which had so nearly succeeded in toppling the Philippine government in the early 1950s. I became fast friends with the famous leaders of the movement who had been condemned to death, commuted to life imprisonment, for the crime of "rebellion compounded with murder, robbery, arson, and kidnapping." This crime was non-existent in the legal statutes, however, and this circumstance helped secure their release from jail a little less than a decade later.

The socialist leaders did not look to me like the monsters the establishment media had made them out to be. They impressed me as highly intelligent, gentle people of strong convictions. Each time I went back to the seminary to discuss with my confreres the new information I had learned in my "new university," I would be warned of the "clever brain-washing tactics" that could be used with me by these "die-hard communists." "Once a communist," I was reminded, "always a communist."

One political detainee, in particular, was first and foremost a peasant leader and, perhaps sensing a basic open-mindedness in this new student of his, wanted to help him to a deeper knowledge of the peasant situation. But he was in a government jail, and I was in my own glorified jail of a school. So, using little notes from him in the form of letters of introduction, I began to pay visits to peasant families in Central Luzon, the traditional rice-bowl of the Philippines.

Braganza, meanwhile, had invited the leader of the Federation of Free Farmers (FFF), a successor peasant organization to the *Huk* movement, to hold a summer course on social justice at the seminary. The socialist prisoners advised me that, while the FFF leader was "reactionary," it was not a bad idea to stay close to the movement he led because at least it was genuinely composed of the peasantry.

Thus, while I continued to live and study in the seminary, I used every chance I could find, "legal and illegal," to leave the grounds and participate in the educational/organizational activities of the legally resurgent peasant movement, now under the aegis of the FFF.

The peasants lived in thousands of small villages dotting the whole country, in houses made of bamboo and coconut leaves. Many of them fished the seas and rivers, but most farmed the land, whose ownership, for centuries now, had been concentrated in the hands of a few *hacenderos*, or landlords. Some of their children went to school, but would be very fortunate to finish even the elementary grades: more urgent economic considerations demanded that, like their parents before them, they take the plow and the water buffalo early in life and devote themselves to the labor of the land.

It was not that they particularly disliked this life and work. They loved their life close to nature, watching plants grow and bear fruit and contemplating the water buffalo as she lay resting in the mud from the sun's scorching heat. But feudal landlordism annoyed them beyond endurance, and they detested it. Somebody else owned the land they tilled.

When harvest time came, no matter how hard they had worked, no matter how much they had invested in the land, the landlord got the lion's share of all the crops. The rent was not a capitalist rent taken from the surplus of the worker's average profit, but a feudal, pre-capitalist rent based on the landlords' ownership of the land and the peasants' dependence on them for the privilege of tilling it. The peasants were left with only a meager part of the harvest, and invariably with more debts than they had had the year before.

If they were farm workers—say, in the sugarlands—they would be lucky indeed if their wages amounted to forty cents a day for eight to twelve hours of back-breaking work. And the sight of their pregnant women working in the fields for even less mortified them with sorrow and rage. When their children fell ill, their anguish was compounded—not just with the thought of larger debts, but above all with the knowledge that another death in the family might very well be imminent.

In all their trials and sufferings, the peasants knew that if only they could own their land—if landlordism were extinct—then surely, instead of nothing but debts and constant penury, there might be some savings and the opportunity for decent food, clothing, and shelter. And so, out of sheer necessity, the Filipino peasants, in different parts of the country and at various times, began to ask the basic moral question: *What is just with regard to the land?* Their question was primarily moral-philosophical rather than legal. They were not so naive as to doubt that what was legal was simply what the rich power-holders permitted. Through the painful experience of trying to do what they thought was right, the peasants had learned that what was provided by the law did not necessarily reflect what was just. And in the Philippines, the mighty were the big landlords who also became the big capitalists: middlemen, moneylenders, bureaucrats, and industrialists. Ownership of land led to ownership of varied kinds of capital. Because of the agrarian nature of the economy, land wealth was the prime source of all wealth and privilege, and the basic status of the deprived and oppressed was landlessness.

Wherever I went in the countryside, whenever there were peasant meetings, informal seminars in barrio chapels, story-telling sessions under a mango or coconut tree, or any other "self-education" courses promoted by the peasant movement, the same basic question arose and was endlessly discussed: "Why can we not own the land we till, which our ancestors tilled before us? The land was there before you and I were born. When the landlords and we shall die, the land will still be there. Whose is the land really? When we were drafted as soldiers during the last war, we thought we were fighting for 'our Philippines.' Now that the war is over, where is *our* Philippines? All of us, rich and poor, sometimes pray to God, whom we have been taught to call 'Our Father.' If it is true that God is our Father, then shouldn't all the goods God has created be considered family goods? Why should they be monopolized by a few rather than be shared by all?"

I was beginning to understand why the peasant movement was despised, feared, or hated, as the case might be, by those who espoused, by interest or indoctrination, the view of the privileged few. I had begun to realize that what writers often referred to as "the Peasant Question" was literally that—the question the peasants asked. It was a question hardly found in the halls of academia, hardly heard in the pulpits of the churches, hardly treated in the reams of newsprint and flood of airwaves of the mass media, hardly asked on the floors of Congress, and hardly discussed in the judicial courts of the land. It was a question on the level of "first principles," which are very rarely subjected to review, but which form the threshold of all our thinking. To cross that threshold was both dangerous and impractical. Thus the absolute conception of ownership was taken for granted as fact and right. It was implicit in every legislative and judicial debate, even on the rare occasions when peasant rights were under discussion, and functioned as the final touchstone of all arguments. It was implied in the Catholic priest's stern advice to tenants who asked their question about the land: "Thou shalt not covet thy neighbor's goods." The tenants knew, of course, that the local church had most of the goods.

The Church as a moral institution offered anything but a warm welcome to the moral question posed by the peasantry. Its heart lay where its treasure was—in the contributions of the landlords and in the wealth accumulated through centuries of sword-and-cross methods of grabbing the lands of the peasants. The very few exceptions in the Church of identification with the struggles of the poor only proved the general rule of institutional identification with the rich. Even the social encyclicals of the popes remained locked in the vaults of abstraction, unrelated and unapplied to the Philippine setting—when they were not completely ignored as if they had never been written.

A few apparently well-meaning bishops and priests received a great deal of publicity in the establishment media for engaging in an "action, and not merely talk-oriented" approach to the problems of the poor. They had urged the establishment of model farms and the extension of modern methods of production to tenants. "Development" had now become a new name for paternalistic charity. However, this new "answer" to the peasants' problem of poverty carefully avoided the peasant question—the troublesome issue of ownership. And so, predictably, the beneficiaries of "development" remained the same old beneficiaries of everything—not the tenants, but the landlords, whose only "contribution" to production was ownership of the land.

The peasants who asked the hateful question of ownership did so with trepidation and misgivings. They knew the question meant trouble. As one peasant leader used to say, "A way to salvation without crucifixion has not yet been found." There was bound to be trouble when people who were accused of being resistant to change began asking for the most fundamental change of all—a change in the theory and practice of land ownership. The people accused of being superstitious were suddenly the most skeptical of all when it came to the powers of "miracle rice," chemical additives, and new production methods to solve their problem of poverty. The so-called lazy continued to work long, hard hours under the burning sun or heavy rains in order to survive the certain deprivation they would suffer from the fact that other people owned the land they tilled. And they who were accused of ignorance knew better than the experts that the moral, philosophical, and political question could not be answered by whatever number of relief projects and technological innovations might be imposed on them by Church and government. They knew they needed to evolve a clearer concept of what was just with regard to ownership. They knew they needed to evolve a tenacious praxis of struggle. All of this meant trouble, class conflict, and a thankless battle with the basic cleavage in society between rich and poor, haves and have-nots, until a more just dispensation prevailed. The peasants knew that because they believed God did not will an unjust order they would be denounced as "godless communists," simply because they were struggling to bring about a more just and more humane social order.

And so I participated in the strategy sessions of the peasant movement. I agreed with those who proposed, among other things, to take the battle to the country's "moral leaders," opinion-makers, and otherwise well-meaning but establishment-indoctrinated do-gooders.

In the seminary, which had now become my "other" world, I was under great pressure to begin my dissertation "in partial fulfillment of the requirements for the degree of Master of Arts in Philosophy." I had learned from the leading lawyer in the peasant movement, who had shared a few of his law books with me, that the philosophy of ownership which was at the basis of property laws and practices in the Philippines, as well as of most modern legal systems, actually went a long way back in history—

all the way back to Roman law. It was Roman law which had developed the ownership concept which legitimized the accumulation of wealth by a few at the expense of the impoverishment of the many. As I had to do that dissertation, I started wondering whether there might be any philosophers of the period of the Roman Empire who had anything significant to say about the ownership concept. Church History classes had introduced us to the "fathers of the Church," and I had noted some of their criticisms of usury. I wondered whether they had more to say on that subject, as well as on the matter of ownership in general. If they did, I would make their thought the topic of my dissertation.

Most of the faculty warned me that I would be wasting my time pursuing a topic of so little interest to thinkers of the patristic period. These, it was pointed out to me, discussed the "big" theological questions—the Trinity, the Divine Nature of Christ, Mary's Divine Motherhood, and of course moral questions like virginity. Braganza, however, predictably said to me that the only sure way to find out whether my idea was worthwhile was to dig into the Latin and Greek originals. Austrian Father Manfred Mueller, S.V.D., whose doctorate was in Church history, kindly agreed to assist me in the evaluation of my research, to help me with the German books which were sure to be necessary secondary sources, and to serve as my moderator, a task which would entail so many hours of consultation together. Father Frederick Scharpf, S.V.D., showed me the kindness of being strict with me about my Greek, as did Father Peter Michel, S.V.D., with my Latin.

So I scoured the four volumes of indices to Migne's monumental 383 volumes of Latin and Greek *Patrologiae Cursus Completus* for references to "property," "ownership," and so forth. I had not gone far when it became clear to me that the research would indeed be well worth my while. The early Christian philosophers—Clement of Alexandria, Origen, Cyprian, Lactantius, Basil the Great, Gregory of Nazianzus, Gregory of Nyssa, John Chrysostom, Ambrose, and Augustine, especially—all dealt with the question of ownership in Roman law times.

My fellow seminarians Noel Mondejar, Cesar Mascariñas, Florencio Lagura, and Arturo Bastes were as excited by the idea of bringing our two worlds together as I was, and they helped me a great deal in the year-long page-by-page survey of all the works of the Latin and Greek philosophers I am about to treat in this volume, locating the pertinent passages and copying them out for use in their original languages. Another seminarian, Edicio de la Torre, helped me much in our constructive critical discussions. The librarians of the University of the Philippines and Ateneo de Manila University were also very helpful in many ways.

Even before the dissertation was finished, the spokespersons and leaders of the peasant movement were able to use many of its ideas and patristic citations in the numerous seminars we conducted for priests, nuns, students, and other opinion-makers in order to gain more support for the cause of the peasantry.

The occasions have been many, these past sixteen years, when friends have urged me to rewrite my dissertation as a "regular book." I have always gladly agreed with them—but somehow the project was always "bumped" from my priority agenda by so many more urgent tasks in the liberation movement. Moreover, the actual ideas of my unpublished dissertation had already enjoyed so much propagation in so many seminars, conferences, meetings, and shorter writings by people in the movement, that it often seemed to me that the effect of a published book had practically been attained. But at last, in 1981, while visiting Maryknoll, New York, headquarters of an American missionary order many of whose members in the Philippines eventually became some of the staunchest supporters of the peasant movement, I met John Eagleson, editor of Orbis Books. John was in a position to do something concrete about actual publication. The timing of our meeting could not have been better. Within a few months I would again be driven underground, this time by the combined persecution machines of both the Philippine and U.S. governments, for alleged "terrorism"—meaning revolution—against the U.S.-sponsored Marcos dictatorship, which had imprisoned and murdered thousands of peasant organizers over the previous ten years. Ironically, I now had time to make a second journey to the past—to the Roman Empire and the early Christian social critics—for a better understanding of so many issues of the present.

Needless to say, without the help of these dear friends—and others in various places whose names must remain unmentioned for now, brave friends who have offered a fugitive shelter and protection, food and drink, access to reference books and type-writers, fruitful discussions and suggestions, and much deep affection—the present volume could never have been written. Immense thanks to them all. I am specially grateful for a grant from Morgan Associates in Ardsley, New York; for the assistance of the St. Robert Bellarmine Newman Foundation at Illinois State University, Fathers Louis Vitale and Bruno Hicks, and the Franciscans of California; and, above all, for the tremendous support given by Jennifer Morgan, Maureen Morgan, Father Joseph J. Kelly, and Rosie Kelly, without whose material assistance and moral support this book may have remained in the realm of perpetual possibility.

Finally, as this volume goes to press, the news is fresh of more martyrs like Edgar Jopson and Father Zacharias Agatep, who were gunned down by a regime intent on suppressing the good news of ideological change in the Philippine ownership structures. Militant advocates of change like Gerry Esguerra, Karen Tañada, Fathers Conrado Balweg, Nilo Valerio, Nic Ruiz, Cirilio and Bruno Ortega, and thousands of others continue the struggle underground, many of them carrying bounty prices on their heads. Furthermore, the number of political detainees like Doris Baffrey, Boyet Montiel, Mar Canonigo, Gerry Bulatao, and hundreds of others has not appreciably decreased in recent years. It has only increased with the recent arrest of the Philippines' apostle of nonviolence, Aquilina Nene Pimentel, Jr. The hope, however, grows stronger that their sacrifices for the advent of a new political order will one day find vindication, when the democratic power of an aware populace will finally seize the opportunity to bring about a transformation in society's theory and practice of ownership. The dormant seeds of change sown by the early Christian philosophers fifteen to eighteen hundred years ago may then come to historical fruition in the last two decades of the twentieth century.

Chapter 1

The Concept of Ownership

> But what is the meaning of "mine"
> and "not mine"? . . . chilly words
> which introduce innumerable wars
> into the world.
> —John Chrysostom

> By human law, one says, "This es-
> tate is mine, this house is mine, this
> servant is mine." This is therefore by
> human law—by the law of the Em-
> perors.
> —Augustine of Hippo

TWO APPROACHES

There are two fundamentally different approaches to the understanding of ownership. Ordinarily, people speaking of ownership refer to its factual legal arrangements and discuss matters of
documentary and ascertainable record. They talk of ownership-
as-it-is: ownership as a sociological phenomenon, changing in
form with the different stages of development in the actual means
of subsistence and division of labor down through history. This
phenomenon, in turn, is governed by positive human laws, which
regulate, tolerate, or forbid transactions and relations among individual persons. Thus it is laws and customs that define the

1

methods of acquiring and maintaining ownership—again, in function of the ways a society produces wealth, whether by a slave-based economy, or a feudal, or a capitalist one. It is also laws and customs that define the rights and duties of legal ownership, including civil liability and criminal responsibility, the remedies for wrongs, and proper procedure in case of allegations of abuse.

This purely factual or socio-legal view of ownership, however, is not the only one. There is another approach, which might be termed the philosophical and moral one. When John Chrysostom, in the late fourth century, asked, "But what is the meaning of 'mine' and 'not mine'?" and said these were "chilly words which introduce innumerable wars into the world," he was taking the moral-philosophical approach to the understanding of ownership. This is what the Third World peasant of the twentieth century is beginning to do. He or she is not just meditating facts, but asking questions and searching for meaning. The peasant's question, too, is moral-philosophical in nature: "When the landlord claims, 'This land is mine,' does it mean he rightly owns the whole of that land absolutely and forever just because his great-great-grandparents came on the land a year or two ahead of any of my own forebears?"

Without a doubt, both the twentieth-century peasant and the fourth-century moral leader are not asking primarily about ownership as a factual and legal phenomenon. They are not asking about ownership in practice, or ownership-as-it-is. They know all that only too painfully well. Rather, the peasants, and John Chrysostom, are searching for the meaning of the concept of ownership-as-it-ought-to-be. They want to discover the living soul, the essence and purpose, the "within," the innermost meaning, of ownership. Their viewpoint is not merely factual, it is ethical. They are searching for a moral-philosophical theory, one either logically realized or grossly betrayed by current practices and institutions. Indeed, their question seeks to investigate the deeper reasons behind even this foundational idea, as they search for a model of how this powerful right enjoyed by some individuals really ought to be regarded. They are asking whether there is an ethic, a moral philosophy, of ownership.

THE GENERAL NOTION

The general notion of ownership is familiar to everyone. In a dictionary or an encyclopedia, a history manual, or a scientific journal, the term simply signifies what ordinary parlance conveys by "yours," "mine," "his," "hers," "theirs," and "ours." It denotes the right to an exclusive free disposition over material goods—now therefore termed "property," "something owned." Ownership is understood as "the right of the individual to enjoy exclusive possession of material goods with the right of free use and non-use."[1] Some define ownership as "the dominion of a thing real or personal, which one has the right to enjoy and to do with as he pleases, even to spoil or destroy it as far as law permits, . . . the right by which a thing belongs to a particular person to the exclusion of all others."[2] In this common understanding of the term, ownership is a relation, but not so much a relation between a person and the thing owned as between the owning person and other people, whom the owner excludes from, or to whom the owner concedes, possession.

Thus ownership is understood as "the exclusive right of disposing of a thing as one's own,"[3] that is, as reserved to oneself, as belonging to oneself to the exclusion of all others. "Disposing of" means "keeping, changing, giving away, selling, using, consuming, or even destroying."[4] Of itself the ownership right is unlimited, though limitation may come from an external source, like civil law, or the demands of a higher order, like charity. But it is essentially an "exclusive" right, so that, where there is no one to exclude, the right, as commonly understood, cannot and does not exist.[5] Thus when I say, for example, "This chair is mine," or "This land is mine," I declare and mean it to be "mine" in the sense that it is not yours, nor hers, nor his, nor theirs, nor ours-in-common, but simply mine alone. And because it is mine, I can do with it whatever I wish: I can use it, abuse it, or, if it is consumable, consume it. If it is land, I can let others work it, or leave it idle, as I desire—because it is "mine."

Exclusiveness and unlimited disposition, then, are the chief elements of ownership as the term is commonly used.

ORIGINS OF PRIVATE PROPERTY

The Filipino Tasaday tribe, living in the rain forests of Minda-nao, whom anthropologists and ethnologists consider the oldest human tribe in existence, are reported to have a remarkably lim-ited vocabulary. For instance, while they have a word for love, they have none for hatred or for war. Neither do they have a word for property. And yet historians know of no age when the concept of ownership has not been known among "historical" peoples. It seems that, once human beings began to produce their means of subsistence, they immediately began to have a concept of owner-ship corresponding to their way of livelihood—that is, corre-sponding to the way they divided among themselves the labor nec-essary to produce whatever was required to sustain life: food, clothing, shelter, and other necessities.

Very early, then, in Asia as in other parts of the world, as peasants organized themselves in villages, adopting a communal way of producing their life necessities, possession of the land was collective. Rather than the individual person or the immediate family, the basic unit of production was the village, with leader-ship dictated by kinship ties. Thus no one ever thought or said of land, their basic means of subsistence, "This is mine." Rather, everyone understood that the land was "ours," for everyone to use.

Many Asian cultures had two distinct terms for "ours." In Fili-pino, for instance, one could use the term *ámin*, meaning "exclu-sively ours," and refer to village lands as collectively belonging to a given village to the exclusion of others; or one could use the term *átin*, meaning "ours" in an inclusive sense, comprehending liter-ally everyone, both within and without that particular village or *baranggay*. Thus some lands were *ámin* ("ours" exclusively), while rivers were *átin* ("ours" inclusively).

In many places, the village units might pay tribute to some king or emperor, whether relatively nearby or far away. (In some places, however, like the Philippines, the people did not even know what tribute meant until the age of colonization forcibly schooled them in the practice.) But originally, in exchange for tribute, the outside power provided economic, political, or religious service—in the building of irrigation tanks as in Sri Lanka, providing defense against banditry by invading forces, or the establishment and maintenance of religious centers and other symbolic legitimations of a given society, as in South America. However, in keeping with the collective manner of producing the necessities of life, the tribute was not an individual tax, but the whole village unit's responsibility. As ownership of the means of subsistence was collective, so was taxation.

The concept of individual private ownership must have developed after, and at first alongside, the dominant view of collective ownership or possession of the means of subsistence. Doubtless no historian will ever be able to assign an exact date to the development of human consciousness regarding one's right to oneself and the use of one's own faculties. One may conjecture that it accompanied the development of the human capacity to produce certain tools and ornaments. Whenever it occurred, however, it cannot have been long before the corollary idea developed of one's right to the enjoyment of the fruits of one's own exertions or the produce arising from the exercise of one's own faculties. If I am my own, and my labor power belongs to me, then what I make is "mine." The objects around me belong to me as my own, either because I made them, or because the one who made them transferred them to me—in the latter case, either directly as a gift, or in exchange for something that I had made, and either directly from his or her own hands or indirectly through the hands of others in various places and times. At all events, the labor or exertion of individual human beings gave them, in their mind, the right to "own" the products of their labor.[6]

A corollary to this ethical basis of individual property, in turn, was the early idea among most peoples that, precisely in order to safeguard the individual's right to the produce of his or her own exertions, no one might monopolize things that no one had made. Things that are just "there"—due to no one's merit, effort, or origination—the things of nature's bounty or the natural elements of production like land and water and other similar resources, could not be justly monopolized by anyone. Among food-gathering tribes, land could not be sold, exchanged, or given away, because it was simply not considered subject to private ownership.[7] There was no question of individual ownership of the land on which and from which *all* must live.

According to a study by the Belgian political economist, M. Emile de Laveleye:

> In all primitive societies, the soil was the joint property of the tribes and was subject to periodical distribution among all the families, so that all might live by their labor as nature has ordained. The comfort of each was thus proportioned to his energy and intelligence; no one, at any rate, was destitute of the means of subsistence, and inequality increasing from generation to generation was provided against.[8]

The development of agriculture should logically have necessitated the recognition of the individual right to own land in order to secure for oneself the exclusive enjoyment of the results of cultivation. Nonetheless, the ethical view continued to prevail among primitive communities that land, like the rest of nature's bounty, should be held in common for the use of all.

Sometimes land was divided among the productive units as a matter of practical consideration, corresponding to a particular stage of development in a given manner of production. Nonetheless, the right over the land enjoyed by the productive units—whether these units were individuals, families, or extended families—was limited purposefully: either by the prohibition of alienation, as in the Mosaic law, or by a periodic redivision, as among the Teutonic peoples.

Hilaire Belloc, the English historian, once remarked that the human being is, quite inescapably, "a land animal": without land the human being simply cannot live. All that one consumes, and every condition of one's being, is ultimately referable to land. "The very first condition of all, viz. mere space in which to extend his being, involves the occupation of land."[9]

The injustice of individual ownership of land seems to have been recognized quite instinctively by the earliest human beings, both at the food-gathering stage, and when they first graduated to the production of their means of subsistence. The appropriation by some individuals of the land on which and from which all must live was seen as a condemnation of the producers of wealth to deprivation, while non-producing owners would be pampered in luxury at their expense. The producers would be denied the right to either a part or the whole of their own produce. Some persons would be able to appropriate the produce of other persons' labor as the price of permission to work the land—which no one had made but was simply "there," a free gift of nature. In the end, it was feared, ownership of the land would give the landlords ownership of the labor power on the land. And of course, ownership of that on which and from which all people must live would be little different from owning the people themselves.

Thus, in his reflections on the history of property, Henry George unequivocally stated that private property in land must necessarily lead to the enslavement of laborers, for the essence of slavery is that it takes from the worker the products of his or her labor without further compensation than what may be required for a level of subsistence that will enable the worker to keep on working, essentially as a water buffalo is maintained in life in order to be able to continue drawing the plow. Ownership of land by some individuals would therefore simply rob the others, the producers, of their produce.

Patristic thought—the thought of the fathers of the Church, the early Christian philosophers—concurs, as we shall endeavor to establish in this book. Ownership of the land compels the non-owners to slave it out for the owners in order to survive.

Quite understandably, then, all tribes and peoples, in all countries and continents of the globe, *originally* viewed the right to land as a common right, upholding the individual's exclusive right to the produce of his or her labor.[10] They recognized that ownership must be determined by the nature of the thing owned, admitting a real and natural distinction between things which are the product of labor, and those which are not due to any human exertion or merit but which simply constitute a free gift of nature. In effect, the product of labor was clearly distinguished from the free field or environment of labor. It was distinguished from the raw material on which, and the natural forces with which, one's labor can act—the storehouse from which one's needs must be supplied.

How, then, can the fact of individual ownership in land be explained? The fathers of the Church already held what political economists twelve to thirteen centuries later would learn from their researches and analyses. Historically, they said, whenever private ownership of land prevailed, it was always the result of usurpation, arising by violence and force, war and conquest, or outright robbery. In time these violent acts of deprivation would be reinforced by the clever use of superstition, religion, and the law.

The concentration of property in private hands began very early in Rome and was indeed based on the foundational and legitimizing idea of absolute and exclusive individual ownership in land. This was the same idea which would now come to form the basis of the slave-owning, the feudal, and the capitalist (including the pseudo-socialist, or state-capitalist) economic systems successively. Modern civilization has not yet discarded this antiquated ownership concept, which was originally derived from ancient Rome. In fact, it seems to us, this is one of the main roots of the present global crisis, in which the rich become richer because the poor become poorer.

AN ANCIENT NOTION PREVAILS

It is true that modern legal systems preserve a few relics of the older common right. The ancient "commons" of England are a case in point, as is the concept of "eminent domain," which is also found in Islamic law, and even in some socialist systems, which, at least in theory, make the sovereign state the representative of the collective rights of the people. The distinction in legal terminology between "real" and "personal" property is the survival in words of an ancient real distinction between property held in both theory and practice as common by its very nature, and property which was the fruit of one's labor.

All these things, however, are today nothing more than relics which have lost their vitality. On the other hand, principles of Roman law embodying the concept of private ownership have remained the great source of modern jurisprudence regarding the theory and practice of ownership—not only ownership in land, but also in the subsequent forms of wealth, originally accumulated through the appropriation of the produce of the laborers when these had to give up what was rightfully theirs as the price of survival on and from the land.

Thus, a former Justice of the Provisional Supreme Court of Shanghai told law students that "one cannot really know the human law without taking account of its sources."[11] For, in the words of the late Supreme Court Justice Benjamin Cardozo, "implicit in every decision where the question is, so to speak, at large, is a philosophy of the origin and aim of law, a philosophy which, however veiled, is in truth the final arbiter. It accepts one set of arguments, modifies another, rejects a third, standing ever in reserve as a court of ultimate appeal. . . . Neither lawyer nor judge, pressing forward along one line or retreating along another, is conscious at all times that it is philosophy which is impelling him to the front or to the rear."[12]

Thus the legislature and supreme court of a Third World country may declare a "radical" land reform program to be unconstitutional because the legislators' and justices' implicit philosophy of ownership compels them to interpret the constitutional right to property in the manner of the Roman law conception—an absolutist and thoroughly exclusivist conception. "Reformist" philosophers—from Herbert Spencer and John Stuart Mill to numerous other social thinkers of this century, including pious and militant church leaders—will advocate the promotion of "social justice" without stopping to think that individual ownership of nature's bounty might be socially unjust in itself. And yet patristic thought insisted long ago that there can be no real justice, or abolition of poverty, if the *koina*, the common natural elements of production, are appropriated in ownership by individuals.

Under the heading of "just compensation to landowners," Spencer, Mill, and others would simply have landlords paid through government taxation of workers' produce what those landlords used to appropriate for themselves in rent. By contrast, according to the early Christian philosophers, the theft of nature's bounty by usurping owners is not like the robbery of a plough or an ox, that ceases with the act. It is a continuous plunder, fresh every day, robbing the workers of both their past and present produce. By definition, rent collected on nature's bounty is unowed—as it is due to nothing the owners have contributed. Because the workers were robbed last year and the year before, patristic thought did not see why they should be robbed this year and next year. Worst of all, in the mind of the fathers of the Church, law and ethics now proclaimed that these usurping owners had acquired, by the fact of ownership, a vested right to rob those whom they had robbed before without that right.[13]

The unarticulated philosophy of a property-dominated society finds curious acceptance not only among the haves, but also among the have-nots. All one need do is occasionally drag out and dust off the pat slogan, "Property is sacred," and critical thinking is stifled. This idea, derived from Roman law, is deemed to be best for everyone, indeed even necessary for the proper use of resources, the production of wealth, and the requirements of freedom. Because this sacrosanct nature of property in the hands of a few is confirmed by law and sanctioned by state power, even the dispossessed majority tends to accept it—but only up to a certain point: for, eventually, courageous and enlightened moral voices are heard, and a politically conscious movement gathers sufficient momentum among the deprived and the oppressed.

EXPLORING PATRISTIC THOUGHT

Even in the historical period of the Roman Empire, there were such courageous and enlightened moral leaders to be found—prophets, frankly—who gathered up the bitter cries of thousands of the dispossessed and hurled them into the hostile world of the propertied classes. Now they challenged, now they persuaded, but always they strove to foster a deeper and stronger appreciation of the ethical conflict between Christianity as they understood it and the predominant theory-and-practice of property ownership.

These thinkers and leaders, however, traditionally called fathers of the Church, seem to have been honored for everything but this. In the rest of philosophy and theology they have been honored as giants, down through the centuries, not only by Christians, but by others as well. The British historian of Western philosophy, Bertrand Russell, for instance, has said of Ambrose of Milan and Augustine of Hippo that "few men have surpassed these in influence on the course of history." It was not "until nearly a thousand years later that Christendom again produced men who were their equals in learning and culture."[14]

It is strange, then, that the fathers of the Church have not been remembered for their remarkable work in the theory of ownership. This, for centuries upon centuries, has remained the well-kept secret of the very Churches that have revered them as saints and of the civilization that has been so grateful to them for their diverse contributions in other areas of investigation and achievement. Nothing, in fact, could be more striking than the extent to which the Roman law theory-and-practice of ownership, which the fathers attacked and sought to replace, has retained the ascendancy all through the Christian centuries that have elapsed since their thundering critical voices fell silent. Patrology manuals which seek to apprehend ''as a unity all those writers of Christian antiquity whom the Catholic Church calls to bear witness to her doctrine, treating them according to the methodical principles of the science of history,'' have for the most part as yet simply found no room for patristic thought's moral philosophy of ownership.[15]

It is true that most early Christian philosophers were not directly and ex professo concerned with ''social theory,'' and that it is only by analyzing relevant passages scattered throughout their extensive writings that one can arrive at a philosophical unification of their vision on property and wealth and what they think ownership, as concept and practice, ought to be. In fact, they were not purely philosophers, in the sense that for them, as for so many ancient thinkers, since religion preceded philosophy in social life, naturally religion had to be taken into principal consideration in their writings, and they stressed the points of a faith-vision which they sought to realize in society.[16] They were preachers, moral thinkers, and dogmaticians. Imbued with Greek ideas, they nevertheless considered profane philosophy as incidental and secondary. They were pastors, concerned with leading people to a way of life, and not merely to an intellectual discussion of life. But the massive volume of major declarations, side remarks, whole homilies or sermons, and essays, on wealth, poverty, almsgiving, and the ethical conception of property, which we find scattered throughout their writings, leaves no room for doubt as to the importance they attached to their treatment of the ownership idea-practice-and-institution for the lives of the people of their time.

The urgent question of ownership in the last quarter of our twentieth century is essentially the same as the question faced by these Christian philosophers in the era of the late Roman Empire. The idea of ownership was already fully developed. Only the concrete historical forms of ownership differ today, corresponding to a different stage in the development of the means of production and the division of labor. Thus a sociohistorical exploration of what these moral philosophers taught about ownership, using the principles of the science of philology and the findings of historical socioeconomic research as ancillary tools for a philosophical analysis of the relevant passages in context, will be no merely academic pursuit, and no mere journey to the past. The question of ownership that faced our early Christian philosophers is as real today as ever, and just as urgently asked—only, this time, it is being asked by millions of people all over the world, and not just by a handful of great philosophers in the Mediterranean basin.

From the latter half of the eighteenth century, socialist writers had begun to invoke the authority of the fathers of the Church in support of their theories of communal ownership.[17] This prompted Catholic authors like John A. Ryan, writing just after the turn of the twentieth century, to react, saying that patristic teachings must be interpreted in a way consistent with the actual practice of private ownership.[18] Similarly, in 1908 Otto Schilling published a study of the doctrine of property according to patristic thought. Like Ryan's study, Schilling's represented the dominant capitalist position of our modern day. But two decades later, Matthias Laros questioned the reliability of Schilling's work and was joined in 1963 by Franz Klueber, who denounced Schilling's study as a "misinterpretation" arising from an "anti-socialist hate complex," which had inclined Schilling to succumb to "the tendency to soften the traditional Catholic doctrine on property and to dilute it individualistically." Following Laros, Klueber concluded that a study of patristic literature on the ownership question had to be done again.[19]

A 1980 study by L. W. Countryman discussed at length the history of the literature over the last century devoted to early Christian views on wealth and property.[20] Unfortunately, however, Countryman's survey, which is otherwise extensive, and while mentioning Schilling's work, omitted any reference to the works of Laros and Klueber. Countryman does show that many of the works on the patristic age tell us less about the early days of

Christianity than about the political struggles of the nineteenth and twentieth centuries, and he concludes with Shirley Jackson Case that "the [proper] function of interpretation is, at all costs to modern wishes, to allow the life of the ancients to throb afresh through the veins of the historical documents."[21]

Fortunately, our knowledge of the socioeconomic and political conditions of the ancient world has increased tremendously in recent years, thanks to the major contributions of a growing number of genuinely scientific historians.[22] Their work has made it possible concretely to situate the writings of the early Christian philosophers in both their sociocultural and their political-economic contexts. Availing ourselves of the new tools provided by these authors, then, and motivated by the shortcomings of the works on the subject that have just been cited, we shall undertake, in the following pages, to ascertain what certain of the greatest fathers of the Christian Church held with respect to the theory and practice of private ownership in the Roman law context of their times, a context that has so little changed from their times to ours.

Among the patristic writers who have dealt with the question of ownership, five especially stand out as having made the greatest extant contribution, quantitatively at least, to the discussion of property, wealth, labor, justice, mercy, almsgiving, and social relations. The five represent both the Western and Eastern Roman Empire and span the period from the later second to the mid-fifth centuries A.D. They are Clement of Alexandria (Titus Flavius Clemens Alexandrinus), who lived ca. 150–211/16; Basil the Great (Basilius Magnus of Caesarea in Cappadocia), ca. 330–379; Ambrose of Milan (Ambrosius Mediolanus), ca. 333–397; John Chrysostom (Ioannes Chrysostomus), ca. 344–407; and Augustine of Hippo, ca. 354–430.

Chapter 2

Roman Law Theory and
Practice of Ownership

The great estates ruined Italy.
—Pliny

In Italy, the wild beasts have their
holes and their lairs where they can
rest, but you who fight and die for
Italy's power have nothing but air
and light, which are about all you
cannot be robbed of. You roam with
your wives and children without
house and home.
—Tiberius Gracchus

INFLUENCE OF ROMAN LAW

To refer to "Roman law" is to refer to a most cumbersome, only partially extant bulk of legal and juristic materials, which even in antiquity could not have been well known to the majority of the populace.[1] Probably the most familiar part of the law, functionally at any rate, as far as both the owning minority and the peasant and tenant majority were concerned, was the law of property, with its principle of absolute and exclusive individual ownership. That principle—and this is what is important for our purposes—has survived almost intact right down to the present day.

The influence of Roman law on today's world is a routine matter of study by practically every law student in the West, hence by the majority of the law students of the world.

> Roman law forms the basis of all the legal systems of Western Europe with the exception of England (but not of Scotland) and Scandinavia. Outside Europe, the law of places so diverse as Louisiana and Ceylon, Quebec and Japan, Abyssinia and South Africa is based firmly on Roman law. Even in England and the countries of Anglo-American law in general, the influence of Roman law is considerable.[2]

When the State of Louisiana found it necessary to legitimize and regulate its practice of slavery, it turned to Roman law for guidance. Thus the Louisiana civil code of 1824 and its earlier digest of 1808 are pure Roman law.[3]

Before the advent of colonialism, most of the villages of South America and the Philippines exercised *collective* authority over their lands, which the people were considered to own in common. It was not until the coming of the Spaniards that the notion of legal title to the land was introduced and the Roman law concept of individual ownership propagated. Thus ownership by Spaniards of large tracts of land seized from the natives came to be recognized as legal.

Seeing the advantages conferred by individual ownership of land, many village leaders began imitating the conquering foreigners and registered the village's communal lands in their own names. Thus the Roman law idea of ownership consolidated the earlier military success of colonialism by uniting the colonizers and local leaders in a common project: many of these leaders found it convenient to collaborate with a regime which enabled them to appropriate the produce of their people's labors by the simple expedient of acquiring a title of individual ownership in land. Backed by the might of the invaders, village leaders could now tell their people: "According to law, these lands no longer belong to the village. They are now mine. Do you see this document in my hands? It is called a 'title' to the land, and it proves that I now own all these farms. However, I shall permit you to continue working them if you will give me regular payments as the price of my permission. We must have order. We must follow the law.''

BEGINNINGS

Looking back at the Rome of antiquity, however, we learn that there was a time when land, or at least the greater part of it, could not be owned privately. According to tradition, at the foundation of Rome, Romulus distributed a *heredium*, or lot, of two *iugera* to every citizen. But two *iugera* were little more than an acre of land—not nearly enough to support a family, unless there were to be some additional form of communal cultivation. The *heredium,* then, must have served merely as a little homestead plot which was inalienable, supplementing the public domain which was for common use. In the words of the ancient Romans, ''The cornland was of public right.''[4]

Through war and conquest, this public domain was now extended. Then patrician families, illegally at first (contrary to custom), succeeded in carving out their landed estates from it. The patricians were the aristocrats or nobles of ancient Rome. In the beginning, however, it was not nobility of birth or aristocracy that entitled them to the land. It was the simple appropriation of the public domain which elevated certain families to the status of nobility and aristocracy.

Private ownership and possession of land originally belonging to all in common enabled the patricians to exact services and rents in money or kind from plebeians who had had to stay within the limits of their original homesteads. Now, whenever these plebeians needed to use the land, they found they had to pay a price to new owners for permission to use what was originally of common domain.

Some scholars hold that there was originally a racial difference between plebeians and patricians. According to this hypothesis, the plebeians were the original Latin inhabitants, and the patricians their Etruscan conquerors. Others say that the plebeians were simply those who had become the dependents or clients of the original land seizers—the ''great families,'' as they were called—without distinction of racial origin.[5] What is unquestioned, however, is that the distinction and struggle between the two orders centered on the question of land ownership. In other words, the class conflict was originally socioeconomic in nature, and only subsequently political as well.

To be sure, the two classes formed one nation. The plebeians, as small owner-tillers, surely had a stake in the country—if not as great a stake as the patricians, who were now the large land-owners—and the plebeians made up the large patrician-led armies which enabled Rome to carry through its enterprise of world conquest—one which began early enough, in 396 B.C., with the subjugation of the Veii. From the first, then, patriotism was an emotional bond strong enough to unite two conflicting classes.

However, this unity in time of war only led to more class conflict in time of peace, for the new public lands, too, the spoils of conquest, tended to be monopolized by the patrician power holders, instead of being kept as public domain to which the poorer plebeians could have free access.

The Roman state, from very early times, was governed by elements especially favorable to patrician interests: the king, whose role was subsequently taken over by the magistracy; the council of elders, which became known as the senate (from *senex*, "elder"); and the assembly of the people (or *concilium plebis*). The people—the plebs—had hardly anything to say in matters of moment, for instance regarding decisions to go to war. They were the soldier-farmers. They were not political decision-makers. Each time they returned from war, they might find their little farms ruined through neglect or devastated by the enemy. The patricians, on the other hand, had slaves to carry on the farm work in their absence. Wars impoverished the plebeians, then, and they were often forced to borrow from the patricians in order to begin all over again. But the patricians were enriched by war, for they had the money to lease or buy the large tracts of land conquered by the Roman state. They could also acquire as many slaves as they liked, and these were not only cheaper to use than free labor, but could not be drafted for military service, and therefore would be available to tend the farms continuously. The plebeians were thus progressively buried in debt and reduced to ever more dire poverty and greater dependence.

According to tradition, which some historians say is history with an admixture of legend, the plebeians organized themselves into an association or corporation, held meetings, and elected officers called *tribuni*. Their discussions clarified for them what economic and political demands they should make on the patrician-dominated state. In the economic sphere, their demands centered on the question of public lands and the debtors' laws. The plebeians sought access to the public lands, which were increasingly monopolized by powerful patricians. They also wanted to remove the threat of slavery, which hung over their heads like a sword as they sank into ever deeper debt. Correspondingly, in politics, the plebeians denounced the patrician monopoly of the magistracy (that is, the offices of consul, emergency dictator, quaestor, who was a consul's assistant, and priests). They demanded that their assembly's resolutions be recognized by the state as having the force of law in their regard. Finally, they denounced the prohibition of marriage between patricians and plebeians, which only helped to concentrate ownership in the patrician order.[6]

The First Secession of the Plebs took place in 494 B.C. The plebs left Rome as a body, to return only after some concessions were granted. Land on the Aventine Hill was distributed to poorer citizens, and the plebeian tribunes were recognized, together with the union or association of the whole plebs. The tribunes had the right of *auxilium*—the right to shield and protect plebeians, especially against abusive punishments by the magistrates.

The absolute nature of the right of ownership, however, remained unquestioned. It was accepted by both small and large landowners, who were thus distinguished from the conquered slaves. And so the strife between plebeians and patricians continued, until it was temporarily alleviated by the enactment of laws known as the Twelve Tables. The prohibition of inter-class marriage was removed, and plebeians became theoretically eligible to hold a magistracy in the Roman state: military tribunes could be elected from among their numbers, with consular power. In practice, however, only two plebeians had been elected by 400 B.C., and only seven followed, between 400 and 367 B.C., when the office of tribune was abolished. There is no record of how many inter-class marriages occurred to bring about a greater diffusion of land ownership.

In 367, following a decade of violent agrarian unrest, the Licinian Laws were enacted, which were a kind of limited land reform. While the right of ownership remained absolute in nature, now the right was conceded to more people. Further private occupancy of public lands was limited to 500 *iugera* (approximately 320 acres) per investor—for investors already wealthy enough to afford it. Finally, the large landowners were now legally obliged to employ a certain proportion of free laborers or dispossessed peasants on their farms, instead of using only cheap slave labor as in the past.

NATURE OF OWNERSHIP AND PROPERTY DISTINCTIONS

Through all these struggles, Roman law was dominated by what is commonly called the absolute conception of ownership, and by the action (called *vindicatio*) through which that absolute right was asserted. According to this concept, ownership is "the unrestricted right of control over a physical thing, and whosoever has this right can claim the thing he owns wherever it is and no matter who possesses it."[7]

Ownership was sacrosanct. Although there were a few restrictions in practice (for instance, as provided in public law) on the power of ownership, philosophically and in theory this power, called *dominium* or *proprietas*, was nearly unrestricted. Anyone who could say of anything, whether corporeal or incorporeal (such as debts and servitudes), "Meum est—it is mine," had the power over it "to have, to hold, to use, to enjoy, to do as one pleased—*habere, possidere, uti, frui, licere.*"[8]

In Roman law, property, or something owned, was an economic and not merely a physical conception. It denoted an element of wealth, an asset. Thus slavery was regulated not by the law of persons, but by the *ius rerum*, or law of things, because slaves were an asset, or economic thing.

Roman law did hold the commonsense ethical notion that sea and air were *res communes*, things common to all. It regarded the seashore as common, as well, and generally no one might build a shelter there. If someone did, by government license, one could own only the shelter, not the part of the shore on which it was built. However, in keeping with the practice of land appropriation, other land was not included in the legal category of *res communes*. Thus the ideological conception, in early Roman times as in our own, only tended to mirror the actual economic power relations prevailing in society. In turn the ideological conception reinforced those power relations. What patristic thought called outright robbery—beginning with the land seizures of the earliest patricians, and continuing down to the *latifundia,* or great estates, of the late Roman Empire—was securely legitimated by the Roman law conception of *dominium*, or ownership. *Dominium* was the ultimate right, the right which had no right behind it, the right which legitimated all others, while itself having no need of legitimation. At times, to be sure, it was a mere *nudum ius*, a naked right devoid of practical effect. But it was still *dominium.*[9] It was the *right* "of using, enjoying, and abusing—*ius utendi fruendi abutendi.*"[10]

Roman law provided many different modes of acquisition of the right of absolute ownership over a thing. There was the solemn *mancipatio*—or the equivalent *in iure cessio*—whereby transferor and transferee appeared before a magistrate, and the transferee claimed the thing, while the transferor refrained from making a counter-claim.[11] There was the mode of *occupatio*, or first possession of a previously unowned thing (land, wild animals, gems on the shore, and so on), including goods seized from the enemy. *Specificatio*, or the creation of a new thing (like my making wine from your grapes), and *accessio*, or the irrevocable joining of a smaller object to a larger one (like painting on a board), were still other methods of legal acquisition. Finally, *usucapio*, or prescription, occurred when a person had enjoyed uninterrupted possession of something, land, for instance, over a given number of years.

The concept of possession became highly refined. Originally it had meant physical control of a thing, and this was what had been legally protected. However, a person who possessed something could do so either personally or through a proxy of some kind. Thus possession often meant absentee tenure of land by an owner acting through his or her tenants, who stayed on the land by the owner's permission.[12]

Corresponding to these various modes of acquisition, there were various distinctions of property in ancient Rome. The main property distinction was that between *res mancipi* and *res nec mancipi*. *Res mancipi* were things whose ownership, or *dominium,* by an individual was solemnly recognized by society. These could be transferred only by the solemn ceremony of mancipation, which included the gesture of physically grasping the property, whereas *res nec mancipi* were things that could be transferred by mere delivery (*traditio*). From the ceremonial of mancipation itself, some scholars have concluded that, originally, land could not have been categorized as a *res mancipi*, because "the grasping of land is an impossible, or at least undignified gesture . . . [and] the reason why land was not originally included among the *res mancipi* was that it was not capable of private ownership."[13]

Once the Twelve Tables had been codified, during the class struggles of the plebeians against the patricians, *res mancipi* included land, slaves, beasts of draft and burden, including cattle, and rustic servitudes attaching to the land, while *res nec mancipi* were all other things. By the time of the patristic period in the Roman Empire, the distinction between these two types of possessions had died out. What remained was the concept of absolute ownership in almost everything one could conceivably possess, without distinction of manner of possession.

Why did the plebeians not seek to change this state of things? The reason seems to have lain in the belief of small landowners that the concept of *dominium* would guarantee them the little that was theirs—an attitude not unlike that of incipient peasant movements in the twentieth century. Small landowners seemed to think that the right of ownership would be sufficient protection from the clever and insatiable land seizures of the larger landholders. Thus we have no evidence of any plebeian movement to revert to very early custom, which, as we have seen, generally refused to recognize private property in land.

Centuries later, Julius Caesar, and still later, the Roman general Tacitus, encountered Germanic tribes who acknowledged individual occupation of land only as a homestead, while the land itself was owned by the community as a whole and redistributed every year for cultivation.

By the time Roman law was fully developed, Romans lived mainly in settled communities, which were both agricultural and military. Thus they accorded special status in law to particular classes of things which were vital to this particular way of living and producing: "the land, the slaves and beasts with which it is worked, and the rights of way and water without which, if it is away from the public road or has no water on it, it cannot well be farmed; and the horses used in battle."[14]

FROM LAND OWNERSHIP
TO SLAVE OWNERSHIP

Throughout Roman antiquity, the basic means of subsistence and production of wealth was agriculture. Crafts and trading existed, but were secondary. Food production for the self-sufficiency of the family was far more important than production for sale. The aim of the family farm was to provide food for the kitchen, flax and wool for clothes, leather and wood for furnishings and tools, and other immediate products for immediate needs. Only a small surplus remained and could be sold.

However, the appropriation of greater portions of land by a few changed the situation. The large landowners could now realize a greater surplus for sale to craftsmen, who produced other useful objects, and to merchants, whose business it was to make goods and materials available in places where they were lacking. The larger surplus now enjoyed by the great landowners was, of course, the result of mere ownership. "To the owner of the land belong the fruits thereof"; thus the surpluses acquired but not produced by the large landowners led to the rise of crafts and trade, which in turn led to new inequality by favoring the landowners who lived near the market centers.[15]

But the ownership of land, especially large tracts of it, was useless unless one disposed of the labor power to work it. The first labor force is the family. When the family is not equal to the requirements of extensive property holdings, wage laborers come next, usually in the form of temporary and exceptional help at harvest time. In the beginning, however, the supply of free labor tends to be extremely meager. Laborers have their own families, and their own little lands. Only compulsion can generally supply the permanent labor force required by a family that owns much more than it can till. Thus the ownership of increasingly huge portions of lands inevitably led, in Roman antiquity, to the acquisition and ownership of slaves.[16]

Initially, most slaves were domestic, and not generally subjected to severe mistreatment. They were additions to the master's *familia*, his *famuli*, or personal servants, and originally included his wife and children. As early as the regal period of Rome (753 to 509 B.C.), the head of the family, or *paterfamilias*, actually owned his wife and children.[17] However, productive work was done by all together, including the master, for the needs of family self-sufficiency, which were still limited. Daily association between the master and all the members of the family, including the domestic slaves, raised the latter to the dignity of human beings. These slaves were "properly motivated" in their work. They worked knowing that it was in their own interest to contribute to family prosperity, for they thereby contributed to their own prosperity as well.

With the continued appropriation of larger tracts of land on the part of a few, however, the need for war and conquest grew apace. Now more slaves were needed, and more lands as well. The core of the Roman army, of course, was a free peasant militia. It was the owner-tillers, the citizens, who went to war for the homeland. When they returned to ruined farms, many of them fled to the towns, to become either craftspeople or *Lumpenproletariat*—the "rabble." Of the latter, a goodly number turned to banditry and petty crimes, often for sheer survival. These were hunted as criminals, and when caught, were either crucified or enslaved.

But this new kind of slavery was different from the old, relatively benign domestic slavery. Slaves on the great estates and in the mining industry worked to produce profit in the form of *money* for their masters. Their purpose was no longer to produce objects for immediate family consumption. They were no longer part of the *familia* at home. Their numbers, and the separation of their workplace from the master's residence, ruptured all personal relations between master and community-slaves. Slavery was now for pure profit. Thus as much work was obtained from the slaves as these could possibly produce, and they were fed and clothed only as well as necessary for their physical survival. Indeed, often only the expense of buying a new slave motivated the master to spare the old one.

True enough, slave labor of the commodity kind had to be performed without "proper motivation" and was never as productive as the labor of free peasants had been. But slaves were cheap and could be sweated to near death without second thought; hence they actually produced a greater surplus for their absolute owners than the free peasants had. On the large estates, the slaves were put to work not only in agriculture, in season, but in industry during the agricultural off-season. They did weaving and tanning, they made plows and pots. Often the surplus they produced in these industries yielded profits even at exceedingly low market prices. This did a great deal of economic harm to the free peasants and arrested the development of strong free crafts. The growing surpluses produced on expanding landholdings by more and more slaves were not applied to the development of new means of production. New, more advanced tools could not have been used in any case: slaves lacked the incentive industriously to apply even the work methods that had already been developed and were very far from being inclined to assimilate new technology. They mistreated one another and vented their anger on work animals or fine tools. Often savagely abused, they had for their masters nothing but hatred. Only the crudest tools could be put into their hands.[18]

Thus the only object of the owners' drive for even greater wealth was an increase in the capacity for luxury, pleasure, and various forms of extravagance. The crafts and trades that developed among free workers were in luxury items like slaves and pomades, paintings and statues, lavish and showy construction projects, and whatever else the large landlords required for the new competition in pleasure, luxury, and ostentation.

The profitability of a slave economy based on the notion of absolute ownership meant a new pressure to extend the field of exploitation by seizing neighboring peasants' lands. At the same time, the growth of slavery and the diminution in the numbers of free peasants impaired Roman military capacity. Slaves were not conscripted. They remained behind, to till the lands of the rich. All the while, of course, the wars were depleting the ranks of the soldier-farmers.[19] Survivors returned to till their old farms only with extreme difficulty: low harvests would raise the price of food they needed for their own subsistence, while a better harvest the next year could send prices so low that small farmers would be unable even to recover their costs. Thus, in growing numbers, they were driven to towns and cities and reduced to beggary.[20]

The absolute power of ownership brought the landlords of ancient Rome to an exclusive world of privilege that seemed "to sweat riches at every pore." And yet, at its very height that society was doomed to death. A decline in the slave economy followed the decline in Roman military success, which was in turn the direct result of the decline in the condition of the free peasantry. One would have expected this decline in the slave economy to have brought about a renaissance of a stronger free peasant economy, dictated by a nation's enlightened self-interest. Yet it did not. The owners of the *latifundia* simply had no intention of giving up their absolute ownership of the land. To do so would have been tantamount to parting with their power and privileges voluntarily, and this is something which no large economic sector of society seems ever to have had the foresight to do.

SOCIOECONOMIC CONDITIONS IN THE PATRISTIC AGE

Agriculture continued to hold its privileged position in the economy of the Roman Empire. It provided the greatest part of the national income by far, and the vast bulk of state revenue. Of all the surpluses that went to corporations, like cities and churches, to the senatorial and curial orders, and to all the professional classes, nearly ninety percent came from agricultural land rents, and only a little more than ten percent from urban property of all kinds—houses, gardens, warehouses, baths, and bakeries.[21]

Senators who took an active part in government had salaries, in addition to their vast agricultural incomes from mere ownership of land. Newcomers to the senatorial order made their fortunes by means of salaries and other office perquisites, then invested in land, increasing their holdings by land grants from the crown to ensure that their descendants would be large landlords themselves.

Estates, both great and small, were often scattered, so that they consisted of a number of separate farms of all sizes. There was a strong tendency, however, for large landowners to try to consolidate their estates by buying up adjacent farms. The older and wealthier the family, the larger the farms comprising its estates. Some of these estates were larger than the territory claimed by many cities. The biographer of one Melania, a generous benefactor of the Christian community, describes how one of her many estates stretched "from the sea to the forest," and included a magnificent villa, with sixty-two hamlets of some 400 slaves each. Melania endowed many churches with large estates, and, with a sacred indifference to wealth, as her biographer tells us, sold vast properties to wealthy purchasers in order to bestow the proceeds upon the Church. She is not known to have favored her tenants, however, with any of her benefactions.[22]

Now, in the patristic age, as it had been in the beginning, land ownership conferred nobility, and nobility consolidated the ownership of land, hence wealth and power. After the great persecutions had passed, many Church officials came to be numbered among the landholding class. Churches began to acquire property as early as the third century. At first they acquired only places of worship and burial grounds, probably in the legal personality of a loose mutual-aid association. In the primitive Church, the clergy had had to earn their livelihood by other employment, in addition to their sacred tasks. By mid-third century, however, following upon greater and greater donations by landlord Christians, bishops and priests had begun to consider themselves full-time workers in the service of the Church and had begun to take salaries from their benefices. The fourth century found the churches acquiring far-flung estates indeed, as a result of bequests and donations from the emperors and other benefactors. Church estates were to be found in over twenty-five cities in Italy, in two large groups in Sicily, in seven in Africa, two in Achaea, and a number in Antioch, Tarsus, Alexandria, Tyre, Cyrrhus, and elsewhere, all belonging to the Roman Church. By the time of Pope Gregory the Great, at the close of the sixth and beginning of the seventh century, the Church had extensive landholdings in Sardinia, Corsica, Gaul, and Dalmatia. The greater Church of Constantinople eventually established an Estate Office, divided into departments corresponding to its suffragan dioceses in Thrace, Christian "Asia" (today's Turkey), Pontus, and the Near East. Constantinople had still other lands in Egypt.[23]

Once the status of the clergy had become that of a class and profession, many of the clergy became landowners. Indeed, all the professions, in the agricultural society of that time, drew largely on the landowning class: landowners entered the civil service, the law, the Church, medicine, teaching, and the army. Successful professionals, moreover, who wished to provide for their old age, sought to do so by investing in land, which was the only secure investment of the time. It also enabled them to acquire wealth without actual labor, since the concept of absolute ownership ensured that mere ownership was title to a great part of the fruits of the labor of those who rendered the land productive. Legislation from the year 433 eventually provided that the estate of any cleric who died intestate passed to the Church. In 470, an imperial decree banned the alienation of Church property, thus ensuring the landed wealth of the institutional Church for all foreseeable future time.[24]

Land, however, becomes unproductive when left to itself. It has to be worked. Landowners, then, were always seeking permanent workers, whose exertions would ensure the landowners' income. After the second century A.D., as the Roman Empire entered its military and hegemonic decline, slaves began to be more difficult to come by, and, like any commodity in short supply, more expensive. Sometimes still, it is true, barbarian prisoners would be thrown on the market at bargain prices. But generally, slave-owning became an expensive proposition. Nonetheless, landowners were not inspired to renounce the right they claimed to the land. Some retrenched operations; but the prevailing trend was to lease the estates to free tenants. Of course, the strongest landlords could maintain their stock of slaves by breeding them, since agricultural slavery was hereditary. Still, even here, in time male slaves married the daughters of free tenants and owner-tillers, and the offspring of these unions commonly rose to the status of serf-tenants.

As slaves rose in their status, freeholders, or owner-tillers, declined in theirs, to the slave-like status of the *coloni*, or serfs. Technically serfs were not slaves. But they were bound to the land; their tenancy was not a matter of choice. From the time of Diocletian, peasants were registered in their villages, to facilitate the state's levy and collection of taxes. Tenants, for their part, were registered by farm and landlord, consistent with the spirit of absolute ownership prevailing in a landlord-dominated state. Thus the fiscal motives of the state combined with the ownership interests of the propertied classes to cause the registration of "free" tenants as something very much like the property of their masters and mistresses. With agricultural labor in decreasing supply, landholders of course welcomed this legislation that forbade tenants to abandon their farms.

Still later, even after the original fiscal motive of the state was no longer a factor, Valentinian and Theodosius both ruled that bound tenancy should continue. They decreed:

> [The *coloni*, or serfs] shall be bound by the rule of origin, and, though they appear to be freeborn by condition, shall nevertheless be considered as slaves of the land itself to which they are born, and shall have no right of going off where they like or of changing their place, but that the landowner shall enjoy his right over them with the care of a patron and the power of a master.[25]

There was never any question whose economic interests were served by most political decisions. The members of the ruling aristocracy belonged to the landlord class.[26] Even a superficial analysis of any of this legislation readily reveals that the interests of the peasantry, who formed the majority of the population, are conspicuous by their absence. Peasant proprietors received almost no attention at all, and the *coloni*, or bound tenants, were treated entirely as suited the interests of the landlord. Thus it was the absolute right of ownership that dominated all proprietary legislation, direct and indirect. Even the law that freed *coloni* from their landlords' claims after thirty years' prescription admitted in its own preamble that it was being enacted because Palatine officials were being blackmailed as descended from *coloni*.[27]

The peasantry as a whole, in all its sectors and sub-sectors, had almost no forum for making their grievances known, let alone felt, by the government. The power of ownership was not theirs—hence they had no political power at all. By contrast, the landlord class, not only that of the senatorial aristocracy, who had a direct influence on government policy, but even the middle and smaller landlords in the provinces, enjoyed a direct influence on government policy. They filled the city councils and provincial assemblies with their own best choices, from among their own number, and fine indeed was the line, as they viewed it, dividing the status of slavery from that of the bound *colonus*, or serf-tenant. A serf, for example, had no right to sue in the courts. From A.D. 396, even tenants were debarred from taking legal action against their landlords. A slave, who in earlier times could actually become Bishop of Rome, now could not even be ordained a priest without the consent of his master or mistress. In the year 409 this prohibition was extended to tenants as well.[28]

Tenants paid a high price for the privilege of being allowed to maintain themselves and their families on and from land they did not own. Tenants who worked vineyards were commonly required to pay their landlords two-thirds to three-fourths of their produce. Most other landlords demanded a 50 percent share of the harvest. Work was hard. We are still a long way from the scientific and industrial revolutions of the eighteenth and nineteenth centuries. As simple a tool as the wheelbarrow was still unknown. The horse-harness had not yet been invented, so that the ox, a much slower animal than the horse, had to be used for plowing. Watermills existed, but were not yet very common. Harvesting was done by hand, with sickle and scythe. Primitive reaping machines, drawn by oxen and very wasteful of grain, were employed only in Gallic provinces, where weather was a special problem, and faster reaping a very high priority. With the exception of the Nile basin, in Egypt, which was irrigated by annual flooding and hence could be harvested annually, most farmlands of the Empire were dry-farmed, and harvested biennially. Soil could be broken up, and weeds kept down and moisture conserved, only by laborious plowing and hoeing.

In addition to paying rents, tenants of the great estates performed services of labor (*operae*) on the landlords' home farms. This is what John Chrysostom is alluding to when, in his Homily on Matthew, he attacks the landlords of Antioch:

> [They] impose increasing and intolerable payments on [the peasants] and require of them laborious services. . . . What sight can be more pitiable than when, having toiled the

whole winter through in frost and rain, spent with work, the peasants, returning with empty hands, and even in debt, dread and fear more than this ruin and more than hunger, the torments inflicted by the bailiffs, the seizures, the demand notes, the arrests, and the inescapable forced labor.[29]

RESISTANCE, RESIGNATION, DECLINE

Peasant resistance sometimes occurred, but it was usually futile, for the well-organized armed forces of the state were in the service of the landlord class. Libanius, A.D. 386, wrote that military assistance was easily had by landlords when there was question of subduing tenants:

> Some treat them too like slaves, and if they do not approve of their extortionate demands upon them, a few syllables are spoken and a soldier appears on the estate with handcuffs and the prison receives them in chains.[30]

For that matter, large landholders often maintained their own armies, or bands of armed retainers called *bucellarii*, and had prisons on their estates.

Still, peasant resistance was not totally unknown. If the name of Spartacus symbolized the spirit and reality of the slave revolts of the past, peasant resistance was epitomized in the sustained, widespread revolts among the Bacaudae of Gaul and Spain, which lasted from the late second to the mid-fourth century. Two of the leaders of the Bacaudae, Aelianus and Amandus, enjoyed enough success to be called "usurpers" by the state. In some places Roman officials were expelled and lands expropriated. Not only did the peasants have an army, they set up courts of justice. Full-scale military operations were mounted against them, and *Bacauda* (probably a Celtic word) came to mean "brigand" in state jargon. It is a pity that so little is recorded of the character, goals, and organizational politics of this tenacious peasant movement.[31]

Mid-fourth-century "Africa," too—Roman, northern Africa—saw a peasant resistance movement against the landlords and money-lenders. Here, Donatist-inspired peasants rose up against Catholic landlords.

What seems to have been common to all these movements, even more common than armed rebellion, is an attitude of fatalism, or, where possible, flight. Peasants fled the rural scene altogether, and became beggars, or *Lumpenproletariat*, in the towns and cities. Remaining in the countryside as tenants, they saw, did not necessarily entail access to food. Indeed, oppressed in so many ways by taxes, land rents, forced service, and bondage to the land, those who produced the food but did not own the food-producing resource—the land—often had no access to their own produce. During lean months, when many of them were reduced to eating grass, wheat was available in the cities, stocked by large landholders or kept in government granaries. And so the hungry tillers flocked to the towns to beg food—the food they themselves had produced, but of which they had been deprived with ruthless efficiency by landlords and tax-collectors. Ambrose of Milan bitterly protested this state of affairs to the wealthy aristocrats who wanted to expel all non-residents from the city in time of famine. If they wished to be selfish, their bishop pointed out, at least they should practice enlightened selfishness: "If so many cultivators are starved and so many farmers die, our corn supply will be ruined for good: we are excluding those who normally supply our daily bread."[32]

Less than two centuries after Ambrose spoke these words, at least one-fifth of agricultural lands had been abandoned by cultivators, exhausted by exorbitant taxes and rents. Sometimes the imperial government would delude itself into believing that full production would be restored by granting landlords tax relief for a number of years. In this way, it was believed, they could be encouraged to spend their profits on farm improvements. However, the chief "improvement" thereupon invested in by the landlords was the re-stocking of their lands with slaves and serfs. Thus the improvement determined upon was the one that entailed the smallest return in terms of productivity. Slaves lacked incentive, and serfs, by the very nature of their status, were burdened with unpayable debts, and thus forever prevented from maintaining their drainage systems, cutting back the encroaching scrub that turned fertile lands into marsh, or undertaking any of the real improvements that would have been needed to restore production and thereby fulfill official hopes.

There was another pressure on rural lands, unwittingly exerted by the urban-based absentee landlord class. This was the increased demand of their lifestyle for timber—timber for their ships, timber for the roofs of their ambitious churches, timber for other buildings. Combined with the immense consumption of wood fuel, mostly in the form of saplings, for the extensive baths of the empire, the new demand for timber contributed enormously to a general deforestation. With the denudation of the forests, the little streams that waxed and waned with the seasons now could become torrents and wash away the soil or cover it with stones and boulders. Reforestation seems to have been rather too sophisticated a concept for the people of the times we speak of— perhaps because at first, of course, from the second to the fifth centuries, ecological damage was not yet extremely serious. It was already becoming a problem, however, and may even have been part of the cause of the peasants' abandonment of their farms.

Finally, the exhaustion of the soil as a result of persistent over-cropping may have been another reason for the abandonment of the lands. Lactantius' reason, however, remains the most important one: fields were deserted and tilled land had reverted to scrub because the resources of the tenants had been exhausted by taxes and rents. In other words, the decline of agriculture must be attributed less to the exhaustion of the soil than to that of the workers of that soil. Weary indeed had they become of a system that made them toil so strenuously for next to naught. The Roman law theory-and-practice of absolute and exclusive ownership of land had been tried now—for more than a millennium—and been found altogether wanting. It was time for some bold, brilliant voices to be heard, to condemn this ideology and propose a more just, more humane alternative.

And those voices were heard. They were the voices of the fathers of the Church, the great Christian philosophers who served their community as dogmatic and moral leaders from A.D. 100 to 750. Now the established ideology would be attacked and a new one proposed. Heard, but not attended to, in their own day, these voices deserve a re-hearing, and attention, today.

Chapter 3

Clement of Alexandria:
The Koinonic Goal

Not a great deal is known of the life of Clement of Alexandria.
He was born at Athens around A.D. 150. After his conversion to
Christianity he travelled to Italy, Syria, and Palestine. In Alexandria, in Egypt, however, with Pantaenus, the head of the Catechetical School of that city, his wanderings ceased. From being an
ordinary disciple, Clement soon became a teacher in the School.
His teaching career came to an end in 202–203, at the beginning of
the persecution under Septimius Severus, which closed the
School. Now Clement took refuge in Cappadocia, in Christian
"Asia," with a former pupil, and there he died, sometime between A.D. 211 and 216.

Clement has been called the pioneer of Christian scholarship.[1]
It was he who brought Christian doctrine face to face for the first
time with other ideas and achievements of the ancient Hellenic
world. His writings are considerable in extent and remarkable in
character. Hardly a page fails to quote from Old or New Testament, but the same pages also make constant reference to the
Greek poets, dramatists, philosophers, and historians.

Clement's purpose in all this was predominantly pastoral, for
above all he was "an educator, a marvelous awakener of souls."[2]
He lived in a time when Alexandria was an active commercial
center in the Mediterranean, with its varied, rich, and busy
market, and a center of intellectual life as well, by reason of its
museum, its library, and especially its scholars, like Ammonius

Saccas and Longinus, and its schools, like that of Philo for the Jews. Toward A.D. 200, through the work of Clement and other scholars, among whom were the Gnostics Valentinus, Carpocrates, and Basilides, Alexandria quickly became the bright new intellectual center of Christianity.[3]

The deeper the new religion penetrated the ancient Hellenic world, the more the need was felt for an orderly, comprehensive, and exact presentation of its tenets. The more numerous its converts in educated circles became, the greater the necessity seemed to be to offer such catechumens an instruction adapted to their environment, and of course to train teachers for that purpose. And so the theological catechetical schools sprang up, the schools of sacred learning. These were first established in the Christian East, and the most famous was that of Alexandria.

The writings of Clement, particularly the *Paidagogos*, are largely the literary record of the instruction and research carried on in the Catechetical School of Alexandria. His other main works, the *Protreptikos* and the *Stromata*, form a trilogy with the *Paidagogos*.[4]

Clement lived at a time when Egypt was host to a strong and rich foreign element. Wealthy Alexandrians, Greek officials, and thousands of business people, scattered all over the country, often owned Egyptian land alongside Alexandrians and their officials.[5] There were also numerous country gentry, nominally soldiers, but certainly landowners. The labor of the natives, in agriculture, industry, and transportation, formed the economic mainstay of the region. The natives had no share in the political administration and were regarded simply as organized labor units: peasants, artisans, sailors, and so on.

The landed gentry did not, as a rule, live in the villages to which their properties were attached. In fact, their estates were widely scattered. Most of them took up actual residence in a metropolis, where it would be easier for them to supervise their scattered parcels of land.

In Alexandria, that rich center whose luxury and vices can be appreciated from Clement's writings themselves—in the *Didaskaleion*, for instance, named for the (Catechetical) "School" that some of these "cultured" and wealthy people attended—and in that Egypt where the highest praise was to be called "happy, rich, and illustrious,'' Clement examined the problem of the relationship between wealth, the social order, and salvation.[6] He focused his attacks on relative wealth, however, and clearly took his distance from those who attacked wealth as such.[7] But he did not share the view that impoverishment was an act of self-liberation that was meritorious in itself.

THE TEXTS

The *Paidagogos*—"The Educator," or "The Tutor"—is an immediate continuation of the *Protreptikos*, or "Exhortation." The *Paidagogos*, consisting of three books, addresses those who have already heard the "exhortation" and have thereupon accepted the Christian faith.

Book 1 of the *Paidagogos* is general in character and discusses the role of the Divine Logos as Instructor. Books 2 and 3 lay out an ethical philosophy for all areas of life, treating of eating, drinking, homes and furniture, music and dancing, recreation and amusements, bathing and anointings, marital life, and wealth.

1. *Autarkeia,* or Self-Sufficiency, As a Purpose of Property

The section of Book 2 where our first text occurs is devoted to a consideration of the luxury of some in social circumstances where other persons are poor. Our author considers luxury an injustice in these circumstances and adduces "farcical and downright ridiculous" examples of rich people "bringing out urinals of silver and chamber pots of transparent alabaster." And he continues:

Those concerned for their salvation should take this as their first principle, that all property is ours to use and every possession is for the sake of self-sufficiency, which anyone can acquire by a few things. They who rejoice in the holdings in their storehouses are foolish in their greed. "He that hath earned wages," Scripture reminds us, "puts them into a bag with holes" (Haggai 1:6). Such is the man who gathers and stores up his harvests, for by not sharing his wealth with anyone, he becomes worse off.[8]

Clement is addressing "those concerned for their salvation." This is not a matter of "supererogation," then. It is a matter of facing objective fact, the demands of reality, and thus keeping in mind the first principle with regard to property. *Chrē proeilephē-nai* literally means "should anticipate," or "prejudge." What is denoted is the assumption of an *attitude*—in this case, the proper attitude toward wealth.

Our author contrasts "use" with "holding." Property, he says, is for use—not for holding or keeping. Holding is not the end of property, but a means: property is "for the sake of self-sufficiency (*autarkeia*), which anyone can acquire by a few things."

Autarkeia is from the verb *autarkein*, which means "to be sufficient [in itself] for. . . . " Hence it connotes contentedness, independence. To the Stoics, *autarkeia* meant self-reliance, a self-determination which would keep the individual from being a burden to others—keep him or her independent in his or her moral self-assurance regarding externals, and hence free for service to others.[9]

Scholars who have researched the Stoic influence in Clement's writings point out that the *Paidagogos* was much influenced by a treatise of the Stoic Musonius, teacher of Epictetus.[10]

To be very precise about the meaning of *autarkeia*, however, is difficult in the concrete, because it is essentially a relative term. Generally it denotes a standard of living enabling one to lead a life consonant with human dignity. To Clement, *autarkeia* is a goal, and ownership, or holding, of property merely a means to that goal. Those who rejoice in holding property as if this were a goal in itself are "foolish."

"Foolish," *atopos*, in Stoic language, was used to describe any deviation from morality as concretely epitomized in "the truly wise person," *ho alēthōs sophos*. After all, a morally good act was "a well-reasoned act that is suited to one's rational nature." Thus Clement calls the greedy "foolish" because they treat as an end what should only be a means. They refuse to face the fact that all property—*pasa ktēsis*—is "for the sake of" (*charin*) self-sufficiency: *autarkeias de charin hē ktēsis:* a means. This is even more evident in another line of the same paragraph: "Expensiveness should not be the *goal* in objects whose *purpose* is usefulness.

Why? Tell me, does a table knife refuse to cut if it be not studded with silver or have a handle of ivory?''[11]

2. *Koinonia* As a Purpose of Property

Chapter 12 of Book 2 of the *Paidagogos* opens with a satire on the luxury of the rich—especially their fondness for stones, pearls, and the like. Clement attacks their false standard of values, and proposes to them the Divine Logos instead, who, he says, is called a pearl in Scripture (Matthew 13:46). Then he takes up an objection. Rich people, after all, say:

A. "Why may we not make use of what God has manifested? I already possess them, so why may I not enjoy
them? For whom have they been made if not for us?" Such
words can come only from those who are completely ignorant of the will of God. He supplies us, first of all, with
the necessities such as water and the open air, but other
things that are not necessary He has hidden in the earth and
the sea (such as gold and pearls).[12]

B. It is God himself who has brought our race to a *koinonia,*
by sharing Himself, first of all, and by sending His Word
(Logos) to all alike, and by making all things for all. Therefore everything is common, and the rich should not grasp a
greater share. The expression, then, "I own something and I
have more than enough; why should I not enjoy it?" is not
worthy of a human nor does it indicate any community feeling. The other expression does, however: "I have something, why should I not share it with those in need?" Such a
one is perfect, and fulfills the command: "Thou shalt love
thy neighbor as thyself."

C. To spend money on foolish desires comes more under the
heading of destruction than of expenditure. God has given
us the authority to use our possessions, I admit, but only to
the extent that it is necessary: He wishes them to be in common. It is absurd that one man live in luxury when there are
so many who labor in poverty.[13]

The absolutist conception of ownership, which Clement questions in these passages, was, as we have seen, the "legitimate" and accepted one for Roman law, just as it is in most modern Western legal systems today. According to this idea of property, to own meant to have an unrestricted right of control over a physical thing. Indeed those who possessed something were not bound to show how they came to be in possession of it, as long as no one else proved title to the same thing. And once considered owners of something, they could do whatever they liked with that thing. Ownership was considered absolute both qualitatively—in the sense that the owners could do whatever they liked with their property—and quantitatively—in the sense that capable and clever persons could lay claim to as much property as their capacity and cleverness enabled them to.[14]

Clement points out that ownership of wealth should not mean the right to do with it as one wills. Rather one should do with it as God wills. "Such words can come only from those who are completely ignorant of the will of God," he says, referring to the absolutist attitude. And Clement the biblical theologian refers us to the biblical notion of property.

However, Clement was just as much a Greek classicist, particularly in Stoic categories, as he was a Bible scholar, and so he also seeks to show that, with a little reflection, one can see why God cannot tolerate the attitude or mentality expressed in the saying which is the starting point of this exhortation. First, he observes that God has supplied us with what we need in order to live—"the necessities," *ta anangkaia*. By contrast, pearls, gold, and "other things that are not necessary He has hidden in the earth and sea." In the true Stoic tradition, our author is appealing to natural facts and events in order to make value judgments. A decade or so before, the Stoic Emperor Marcus Aurelius had come to ethical conclusions in the same manner. "Dost thou not see the little plants, the little birds, the ants, the spiders, the bees, working together to put in order their several parts of the universe?" he asked. "And art thou unwilling to do the work of a human being, and dost thou not make haste to do what is according to thy nature?"[15] In the same style, Clement holds that certain things are easy to acquire because they are necessary. This suggests a natural hierarchy of values to be recognized, and the rich must not allow themselves to be blinded by their passion for luxury at the expense of "so many who labor in poverty," as we see in section C of our text.

The second circumstance alluded to by Clement in his argument for a just and reasonable ethic of property is the fact of human solidarity. We are one race, whom God has brought to a fellowship, or community, a *koinōnia*.

Koinōnia is the abstractive noun from *koinōnein*. The verb means to participate, or share; the noun therefore denotes participation or sharing. *Koinōnos*, "fellow," "participant," implies true partnership with someone in something. The root is especially well adapted to express an interior relationship—by contrast with *hetairos*, the word for a mere companion, one who shares a common enterprise; *sunergos*, a fellow worker; or the colorless, general, *metochos*, "sharer," "participant." Further: *koinōnein* need not mean only to "share" what someone else has; it can also mean to "share" with someone else something I have that he or she does not have.

Koinōnia, then, denotes fellowship, and connotes an interior bond. It implies a mutual relationship of giving and receiving, in either the giving or the receiving term of that relationship. Hence, for example, it can be used to characterize the marital relationship, or even deep friendship, which, in the Greek world, was also considered a supreme expression of fellowship.[16]

If we examine the particular way in which Clement uses *koinōnia*, we observe that he uses it in a sense similar to that of the Stoics. For the Stoic, who regarded the universe as a dynamic and integrated totality, *koinōnia* can obtain not only among human beings, but between God, or the higher universe, and human beings, as well. The Stoic appreciated that to be human is to be a social being—that even in order to seek oneself one must seek others, since there is only one Logos, which adapts Itself to each human being as his or her Reasonable Element.

For the Stoic, the law of nature rested essentially upon the notion of this Universal Reason—the *Koinos Logos*. All human beings are interrelated, all have the same origin and destiny, all stand under the same law and are citizens of one state, for all share in the same Logos. Consequently, all should act in accordance with that *Koinos Logos*—that is, in *koinōnia*. The world itself is a *koinōnia*, of human beings and all other beings, and the necessity of unconditional submission to the laws and requirements of this *koinōnia* must be respected.

To return to our text, however, we find that Clement's ethical reflection betrays a biblical influence even greater than that of the Stoics. Paul had used *koinōnia* in the New Testament, for the religious fellowship ("participation") of the believer in Christ and his blessings, and for the mutual fellowship of believers (1 Corinthians 1:9, 12:12–31; Hebrews 2:14; cf. 2 Peter 1:4). Clement embraces the same concept when he says that "God Himself has brought our race to a *koinōnia* by sharing Himself . . . sending His Word to all alike . . . making all things for all."

Now, in Paul's mind fellowship with Christ necessarily leads to the mutual fellowship of members of the community. And in his use of the verb *koinōnein* the idea of "having a share" often passes over into the idea of "giving a share" (Philemon, v. 17; Philippians 4:15, Galatians 6:6, 1 Corinthians 9:11)—so that in Romans 15:26 and 2 Corinthians 8:4 the abstract term *koinōnia* has become a collection of money for community members in need!

Clement's conclusion from the fact of *koinōnia* is not different from Paul's. Because the human person exists in *koinōnia* with others, "*therefore*, everything is common, and the rich should not grasp a greater share." The purpose of wealth in general is not only to achieve *autarkeia* but also and equally to foster *koinōnia*—equal fellowship that abolishes the differentiation between the few rich who wallow in luxury and the "so many who labor in poverty."

To the Stoics, God, Reason, Fate, and Nature were one and the same.[17] God is imagined as a force within things—as a "creative fire, proceeding methodically to the production of things," or as "honey seeping through the combs." Stoics addressed God as a providential being and father who rules everything in the world for the benefit of all. "Slave, will you not bear with your own brother who has Zeus for his forefather and is born as a son of the same seed as you are, the same heavenly descent?"[18] Clement's disciple, Origen, would later say: "Although they [the Stoics] say that the providential being is of the same substance as the being that he directs, they nevertheless say that he is perfect and different from that which he directs."[19]

Clement's triadology is a forerunner of the later orthodox Christian doctrine of the Trinity, and his Logos is "the glorious Word through whom human nature is born again and receives a great new value."[20] In our passage B, "it is God Himself who has brought our race to a *koinōnia*, by sharing Himself first of all, *and* by sending His Word to all alike, making all things for all." Clement's double reference includes (1) the inner Trinitarian life of God, which is a *koinōnia* (a sharing himself) and (2) the life of all those whom God has created through his Logos—a life which is and which should become more and more a *koinōnia*—after the model of God's own life.

Applying this vision of reality to the realm of ethics, Clement holds that it is not properly human, *ouk anthrōpinon*, to regard property as something with which one may do as one likes simply because it is one's "own." God has made the human being a social being, to live in necessary *koinōnia* with others. To act in a way that is *anthrōpinon*, or properly human, one must act in a way that is *koinōnikon*, "social," or in a spirit of community. The clear call is to cast aside the prevailing, absolutist, individualistic Roman law legitimation of property and embrace a new rationale of ownership, holding all things in such a way that they may be common for all.

According to Clement, one who takes this attitude and acts in this manner is "perfect"—*teleios*. In Stoic language, one is *teleios* if one has performed a *kathēkon teleion*, or *katorthōma*, a perfect duty or right action by virtue of one's conscious conformity with the Universal Logos.[21] One is perfect, the Christian Clement says further, because one "fulfills the command: 'Thou shalt love thy neighbor as thyself.' "

In passage C, Clement states that the source of *koinōnia*—God, who has absolute dominion over all—"has given us the authority (*exousia*) to use our possessions." This *exousia*, however, is not absolute, but only *mechri tou anankaiou*—to the extent of necessity. *Anankaion* is the contradictory of *peritton*, that which is superfluous or excessive. Human authority to use material wealth has a limit—the purpose of the Absolute Lord, who wishes the use of all things to be common—*tēn krēsin koinēn einai bebouleutai*. Human ownership is essentially a means to foster *koinōnia*.

The contrary of *koinōnia*—a situation which permits a few "to live in luxury when there are so many who labor in poverty''—is considered by Clement to be simply absurd: *atopon*. It is absurd and unnatural because it is a denial of the social nature of the human person. It is absurd because it is "out of order," fixing the right of ownership in the static order of "keeping" or "holding" (*keimai*, "to lie still," "to lie idle") instead of recognizing it as a dynamic reality: a duty of "sharing."

3. Limits of the Use of Wealth

In the seventh and eighth chapters of Book 3 of the *Paidagogos*, Clement deals with a "frugality," which consists in being satisfied with what is adequate for one's sustenance. He attacks the custom of amassing wealth in the form of precious objects, garments, and stores of provisions and household goods, a custom that was one of the causes, as well as a result, of current economic stagnation.

> **A.** Just as the foot is the measure of the sandal, so the physical needs of each are the measure of what one should possess. Whatever is excessive—the things they call adornments, but the trappings of the rich are not adornments—are a burden for the body. . . . Scripture declares that really "his own riches are the redemption of the soul of man" (Prov. 13:8), that is, if a man is rich, he will obtain salvation by sharing his wealth.[22]

> **B.** Frugality is exceedingly rich, for it is a quality that is not at all reluctant to spend money on things it requires and that need to be paid for, for as long a time as the need exists.[23]

In this text Clement once more brings out the "sharing" aspect of the right to use material wealth, as opposed, obviously, to the "holding" or "storing" of excessive wealth. More significantly, he points out that there are natural thresholds or limits beyond which the pursuit and use of wealth does not and cannot make sense. Just as it is absurd to try to use a pair of sandals that are too large for one's feet, since the purpose of a sandal is to fit and be useful for one's foot, so everyone should realize that the limits of essential needs are concrete and clear, and that sharing should be the concern of all. Thus *autarkeia* and *koinōnia*, the twin goals of material wealth, will prevail.

4. All Wealth a Gift to All

Quis Dives Salvetur? or *Tis Ho Sōsomenos Plousios?* is a homily on Mark 10:17–31. It employs the Alexandrian method of allegorical, or spiritual, interpretation.[24] To forestall any charge that he has gone over to the side of the rich, Clement begins this work by stating flatly that anyone who praises the wealthy for their wealth is guilty of something more than mere flattery and servility. Flattery of this kind is especially insidious: to praise the wealthy for their riches will have the effect of plunging them still deeper into their pride.[25] Then he continues:

A. When a man lacks the necessities of life he cannot possibly fail to be broken in spirit and to neglect the higher things, as he strives to procure these necessities by any means and from any source. How much more useful would it be, on the other hand, if a man, possessing sufficient, should be in no distress about his possessions but should come to the aid of those he ought? For what sharing would be left among men if nobody had anything?[26]

B. It is on this condition that He approves their use, and with this stipulation—that He commands them to be shared, to give drink to the thirsty and bread to the hungry, to receive the homeless, to clothe the naked. And if it is not possible to satisfy these needs except with riches, what else would the Lord be doing than exhorting us to share and not to share? But that would be the height of unreason.[27]

C. Possessions were made to be possessed. Goods are called goods because they do good, and they have been provided by God for the good of humanity. Indeed, they lie at hand and are put at our disposal as a sort of material and as instruments to be well used. . . . You can use [wealth] rightly; it ministers to righteousness. But if one uses it wrongly it is found to be a minister of wrong. For its nature is to minister, not to rule.[28]

D. He who holds possessions . . . as gifts of God . . . and knows that he possesses them for his brothers' sake rather than his own . . . is the man who is blessed by the Lord . . . a ready inheritor of the kingdom of heaven.[29]

E. "Make to yourselves friends from the mammon of unrighteousness that when it shall fail, they may receive you into the eternal habitations." (Lk. 16:9) Thus He declares that all possessions are by nature unrighteous, when a man possesses them for personal advantage as being entirely his own, and does not bring them into the common stock for those in need; but that from this unrighteousness it is possible to perform a deed that is righteous and saving, namely, to give relief to one of those who have an eternal habitation with the Father.[30]

In these texts, Clement is arguing, on the one hand, against certain people who went about teaching others that material goods in themselves were evil and impoverishment in itself virtuous—preachers who made absolute renunciation an end in itself.[31] On the other hand, he also attacks the absolutist conception of ownership in his time. Then he presents what he considers to be the proper ethical view of material wealth.

First, Clement says, it is obvious that people need material goods. Denying them these would only result in their striving to procure them "by any means and from any source," and thereby easily "neglecting the higher things." But this would defeat the very purpose of the absolute renunciation preached by the exaggerated ascetics themselves.

Moreover, without something materially concrete to share, we could no longer speak of a *koinōnia*—a sharing in common. It would be "the height of unreason" to be commanded to have the hungry fed, the naked clothed, and the homeless sheltered, while practicing the absolute renunciation of food, clothing, and shelter. The use of material goods is necessary. These have been "provided by God." They are "gifts of God," they come from "God the Giver."

Playing on the words, *chrēmata* (riches, or things that one uses or needs), *chrēsima* ("useful"), and *chrēsis* ("use"), all of which have the same etymology, Clement asserts that "goods are called goods because they do good, and they have been provided by God for the good of all. Indeed, they lie at hand and are put at our disposal as a sort of material and as instruments to be well used." The food, clothing, and shelter-producing resources are there as gifts for all, and their products are to be brought "into the common stock for those in need."

The only Absolute Owner of all these is "God the Giver," and "*it is on this condition that he approves* [or "sanctions"— *epainei*] their use, and with this stipulation, that he commands them to be shared." The true nature of property and all material goods is to "minister" to the needs of all.

SUMMARY

Clement of Alexandria is not what we would today term a social theoretician, nor does he write ex professo as a philosopher of ownership. Even his *Quis Dives Salvetur?* is a homily (though it is certainly a practical treatise as well). However, from the examination we have made of his writings, we can see that Clement did more than merely moralize on wealth and luxury. He discussed the philosophic foundations of an ethic of ownership.

Rejecting both the novelty, in vogue in his time, of absolute renunciation, and the prevailing Roman law philosophy of absolute ownership, Clement soberly proclaims that material goods are gifts of "God the Giver," and not destined for the luxury of a few while the many toil in poverty. Rather, wealth-producing resources are there in common for the use of all.

Autarkeia—personal independence, self-reliance, and self-sufficiency—together with *koinōnia*, or community, are the twin goals of the holding and use of material wealth. This wealth is essentially and only a means to achieving those goals. The right of possessing material goods is intrinsically conditioned by the purpose of that right. This intrinsic teleological limit makes property-holding a *tantum-quantum* affair—a "so much . . . as much . . ." right of control over physical things, a right proportioned to the capacity of those material things to further *autarkeia* and *koinōnia*—in contrast with the Roman law notion of absolute and exclusive right. Moreover, there are natural thresholds, or limits, beyond which the pursuit and use of wealth does not and cannot make sense, cannot be reasonable.

The functions of property—"to be shared," "to minister to" and serve "the welfare of all"; "not for personal advantage as being entirely one's own," but "for those in need"; "to achieve *autarkeia*," and "to foster *koinōnia*"—are not, in Clement's view, incidental or transitory characteristics of property. They constitute its very essence.

Christian individuals and groups who took Clement's doctrine seriously—the "haves," rich or not so rich—increased their alms-giving and their contribution to the common fund and their renewed *koinōnia* of service and goods became the main form of Christian redistribution of wealth to the needy.[32]

Chapter 4

Basil the Great:
Robbery by Any Other Name . . .

Basil was born in Caesarea, in Cappadocia, about A.D. 330. His father, also called Basil, was illustrious in Pontus and Cappadocia for his lands, his stature as a lawyer, his professorship of rhetoric, and a holiness of life unspoiled by his vast property holdings. Basil's mother, Emmelia, was the daughter of a martyr and the mother of three bishops, a nun, and a monk. Three of her children are revered as saints.

Basil received his literary education first in Caesarea, then in Constantinople, and finally during five years in Athens, where he shone as a brilliant student. On his return to Cappadocia he found himself the owner of properties scattered over three provinces, for he had fallen heir to the wealth of his grandmother and father, both of whom had died during his long absence from Pontus.

A chair of rhetoric was now offered Basil in Caesarea, and he accepted. After two years in his father's footsteps, however, he determined upon the monastic life for himself. Distributing all his possessions to the poor, he fled the world. But in 370, when Bishop Eusebius of Caesarea died, Basil was chosen to be his successor. Short of duration, his episcopate was nonetheless most fruitful in pastoral activity. He organized communal institutions, including schools of arts and industries, orphanages, and retreat houses so extensive that they all but formed another town on the outskirts of Caesarea.[1]

Although Basil renounced his property in early youth, a certain

47

portion of it was leased to a foster brother, who helped support Basil from its income.[2] Basil died January 1, 379, not more than fifty years of age. The cognomen "the Great" was attributed to him even by his contemporaries.[3]

Basil possessed a harmonious abundance of the most varied talents. He was both a theoretician, whose clear and precise teaching set the moral tone for an entire Christian generation, and a man of action, who resolutely undertook the means to his ends. He was called "a Roman among the Greeks" because of his concern for the practical moral consequences of his doctrinal tenets.[4]

The Roman Province of Asia Minor in the time of Basil the Great was a rich and prosperous region.[5] Agriculture, accordingly, was the economic mainstay. Many types of land tenure were in vogue. The first was the system of ownership which prevailed in the territories of the Greek cities and was recognized by the Romans. Land owned in this way was cultivated by either the owner or by slaves and tenants.

Besides these lands, which were cultivated by enfranchised citizens, many ancient Greek cities possessed extensive tracts which were cultivated and inhabited by the native lower classes. There might be whole villages inhabited by these "by-dwellers," who did not have the full rights of municipal citizenship. Roman law considered these villages "attached" to the city. But other tracts of land were outside the territory of any city, and were owned by wealthy or noble families. The peasants who cultivated the soil as tenant-serfs of these families lived in villages far removed from the cities and wholly alien from them in life and civilization. These tenants were, as we saw in Chapter 2, gradually replacing the slaves on these estates.

The Latin word for "tenant" was *colonus*. In works on private law, *colonus* simply denotes a free person who enters into a free contract of *locatio-conductio*, or lease, with the owners of the land.[6] In fact, however, tenants were in a very dependent position, very often subject to compulsory labor for their landlord or for the state, and not seldom in arrears with their rent.

As taxation became more oppressive and the farming population decreased, a great deal of land fell out of cultivation, as we saw in chapter 2, and ceased to provide revenue to the state. To remedy this, the government began to force landowners to take over additional land and become responsible for its taxes. At the same time it assigned them power over the cultivators of this new land. Soon there was less supervision of the landowners and large leaseholders with respect to their treatment of the small tenants: as long as taxes were paid, the government closed its eyes to oppression.

In the fourth century, with all the development of large and prosperous cities elsewhere in the Empire, Cappadocia, like the rest of Asia Minor, remained a land of peasants and villages. To be wealthy meant, more often than not, to be a landlord or large leaseholder.

It was in this socioeconomic context that Basil the Great, as Bishop of Caesarea, delivered his sermons to the rich, in which he set forth his ethics of property.

THE TEXTS

1. The Rich Are Thieves

In our first passage, we find part of what Basil has to say on Luke 12:18, "I will pull down my grain bins and build larger ones. All my grain and my goods will go there." Passages B and C are from a sermon to the rich about the morality of ownership and wealth.

A. "Whom do I injure," [the rich person] says, "when I retain and conserve my own?" Which things, tell me, are yours? Whence have you brought them into being? You are like one occupying a place in a theatre, who should prohibit others from entering, treating that as one's own which was designed for the common use of all.

Such are the rich. Because they were first to occupy common goods, they take these goods as their own. If each one would take that which is sufficient for one's needs, leaving what is in excess to those in distress, no one would be rich, no one poor.

Did you not come naked from the womb? Will you not return naked into the earth? (Job 1:21). Whence then did you have your present possessions? If you say, "By chance,'' you are godless, because you do not acknowledge the Creator, nor give thanks to the Giver. If you admit they are from God, tell us why you have received them.

Is God unjust to distribute the necessaries of life to us unequally? Why are you rich, why is that one poor? Is it not that you may receive the reward of beneficence and faithful distribution . . . ?[7]

B. Do you think that you who have taken everything into the unlimited compass of your avarice, thereby depriving so many others, have done injury to no one? Who is avaricious? One who is not content with those things which are sufficient [*autarkeia*]. Who is a robber? One who takes the goods of another.

Are you not avaricious? Are you not a robber? You who make your own the things which you have received to distribute? Will not one be called a thief who steals the garment of one already clothed, and is one deserving of any other title who will not clothe the naked if he is able to do so?

That bread which you keep, belongs to the hungry; that coat which you preserve in your wardrobe, to the naked; those shoes which are rotting in your possession, to the shoeless; that gold which you have hidden in the ground, to the needy. Wherefore, as often as you were able to help others, and refused, so often did you do them wrong.[8]

C. If that were true which you have affirmed, that you have obeyed the commandment of love from youth (Mark 10:20), and have given to everyone as much as to yourself, whence, I ask, have you all this wealth? For the care of the poor consumes wealth, when each one receives a little for one's needs, and all owners distribute their means simultaneously for the care of the needy. Hence, whoever loves the neighbor as oneself, will possess no more than one's neighbor.

Yet it is plain that you have very many lands. Whence all these? Undoubtedly you have subordinated the relief and comfort of many to your convenience. Therefore, the more you abound in riches, the more you have been wanting in charity.[9]

D. God has poured the rains on a land tilled by avaricious hands; He has given the sun to keep the seeds warm, and to multiply the fruits through his productivity.

Things of this kind are from God: the fertile land, moderate winds, abundance of seeds, the work of the oxen, and other things by which a farm is brought to productivity and abundance. . . . But the avaricious one has not remembered our common nature, has not thought of distribution. . . .[10]

This is one of the texts analyzed by John A. Ryan many years ago. Ryan's book, as we have seen, seems to be primarily an apologia for private property.[11] It proceeds on the a priori that the fathers of the Church could never have denied the right of private property, and tends to downplay evidence to the contrary.[12] A priori reasoning to the effect that the teaching of the early Christian philosophers must be interpreted in a way consistent with their actual conduct (such as Basil's retention, through another person, of a small portion of his huge properties) is not very felicitous, since a writer can have been propounding a view of property which was not yet practicable in toto and yet propounding it indeed, just as later centuries saw the growth of a utopian literature (Thomas More, Fénelon) which propounded a strictly koinonistic society—much more strictly so than we see in today's so-called communist societies—but whose lives were of themselves inadequate testimony to the koinonistic doctrine found in their writings. One must, then, analyze these texts of Basil all over again and follow him faithfully in his own points of emphasis.

It will be useful to acknowledge at the outset that Basil was a consummate orator and surely made use of figures of rhetoric in denouncing the gap between rich and poor. But, just as surely, certain commentators have been too quick to call some of Basil's writing "rhetorical" simply because to them this writing appeared to be too radical.

Now to our text. First, we note, in passage A Basil is dealing not so much with the prevalent absolutist conception of ownership, but with the very right to own at all. The rich person is asking not what he or she may do with property, but whether he or she may have property at all: "Whom do I injure when I retain and conserve my own?"

Second, Basil seems quite unconcerned with any of the proximate titles the rich may have to their property. He is mainly concerned with the ultimate, philosophic justification of property. His reflections center around the origin of property and wealth: "Did you not come naked from the womb? Will you not return naked into the earth? Whence then did you have your present possessions?" One would truly own only what one had brought into this life from elsewhere. And he cites the book of Job to the effect that there are no such things.

Now Basil places the rich before a perfect disjunction. One must view property either from a theistic, or an atheistic, position. If you say you have your property "by chance," *apo tautomatou*, you are godless, an atheist: *atheos ei*. "You do not acknowledge the Creator nor give thanks to the Giver." And the other horn of the disjunction is, "If you admit they are from God, tell us *why* you have received them."

Atheos here denotes the practical atheist, the "godless" one who may not deny God speculatively, but leaves God out of his or her practical considerations and behavior. The word may be used of anyone who "disdains God or the gods and their laws."[13]

But if God is the source of one's possessions, the next question is for what purpose—*dia ti*—God has given them. Basil's ethical investigation now progresses: "Is God unjust to distribute the necessaries of life to us unequally? Why are you rich, why is that one poor?" If all have the right to life equally, how comes it that you have more than enough—*peritton*—and others have less than sufficient to lead a decent human life?[14] Basil's pointed question centers on whether the goods of the earth are destined only for a few, or whether they have been designed for the common use of all. His answers are in conformity with his Christian conviction of the paternal providence for all of God the Creator. No, God is not unjust. Hence, since an unjust differentiation between the few rich and the many poor cannot be denied, it must be the few rich who are the unjust cause of the poverty of the many. The poor seek to satisfy their essential needs, while a few possess more than they need for *autarkeia*—and so the many remain needy.

The acknowledgement that the goods of earth ultimately come from the Creator should have led to the corollary acknowledgement that they have been received for the purpose of "faithful distribution.'' The Author of nature and Provider of all things exercises his absolute dominion by continually giving us all the riches of the earth—hence, Basil concludes, the subordinate human owner must consider the function of ''faithful distribution'' to be the purpose of wealth.

From the foregoing it is clear that Basil is discussing wealth in general. At the same time, he is discussing land in particular. In the Cappadocia of Basil's time, the rich were usually landowners, lords both of tracts of lands and of the peasants who lived on them. Property was essentially landed property. The simile Basil uses of ''one occupying a place in a theatre'' helps to suggest that he is thinking not only of wealth in general but of land and its products in particular. This is made explicit in passage C, when he says, ''it is plain that you have very many lands.'' Finally, the description of property in passage D is unmistakably a reference to landed property and its rich revenue.

In passage C, speaking of the distribution of wealth, riches or money, Basil uses the words *ktēmata* and *chrēmata*, and he uses them interchangeably. But *ktēma* is strictly ''landed property, field, piece of ground.''[15]

Basil's view is that, basically, all persons have an equal right to the land, just as they all have an equal right to the air they breathe—a right deriving from, and hence proclaimed by, the fact of their very existence, or creation.

Land, and the whole ''theatre'' of air, rain, the sun, the winds, and the other things to which no one can lay claim of merit or origination, are termed *koina* by Basil. They are just there—not in any way due to anyone's merit or labor, but to nature's bounty—or more precisely, to the direct bounty of nature's God, to his never-ceasing personal care: ''He has poured the rains . . . given the sun . . . winds . . . .''

Ta koina (''common goods'') are contrasted by Basil with *ta idia* (one's ''own things''). Our rhetorician's irony implies a clear distinction between things that are communal or public, by nature, and those that are ''private'' by reason of their being the product of human beings' own exertions—or, in his words, because ''you have brought them into being.'' Basil criticizes those who make *idia*, or private, what should actually be *koina*, or public—''designed for the common use of all.'' Morally speaking, no one can own things (like limitless or huge tracts of land, or other such wealth-producing resources) that are just "there," even though, physically and by current legitimation, one may be able to do so indeed.

The phrase, "they were first to occupy [literally, "preoccupy," *prokataschontes*] common goods," or the phrase, "they take these goods as their own" ("by anticipation," the original adds here—*dia tēn prolēpsin*—that is, they preempt them) show that Basil condemned the position legitimating ownership of tracts of land by sheer title of first occupancy. Quite probably, many of the wealthy landowners whom Basil is addressing in this sermon have obtained their wealth, in the form of landed property—like Basil himself, indeed—by inheritance. In the case of many of them, perhaps, land titles went back many generations, to a so-called "original" title resting on force rather than on right.

Whether the title rests on first occupancy or force of conquest, however, Basil declares that goods created as *koina* may not be treated as *idia* except to the extent necessary for achieving *autarkeia*. And even in the case of *koina* which have been appropriated in order to be made productive, their character as *koina* is to be maintained withal—through "faithful distribution" of the product.

By tilling the land, people invest labor in it, for which they may of course have what is their due. Nevertheless, according to Basil, the exertion of one's labor is only a minor factor. Most of the merit for the productivity of the earth must be attributed to nature's bounty—or rather, to the God who personally and directly conserves all things in being and makes the earth productive for the sustenance of all living things. Basil finds it unthinkable that God's providence has been solely for the sake of a few, and so he asks, "Is God unjust to distribute the *necessaries* of life to us unequally?" No, the inequity must be of human procurement.

Now, among the "necessaries of life" of Basil's time was, certainly, land. Land was, as it still is, the habitation of people and the storehouse upon which they must draw for all their needs, the material to which their labor must be applied in order to obtain all the rest of their "necessaries"—"for even the products of the sea cannot be taken, the light of the sun enjoyed, or any of the forces of nature utilized, without the use of land or its products. On the land we are born, from it we live, to it we return."[16] Using the same illustration, of a first-comer monopolizing all the seats in a theater, to show how far the principle of private property tends to be carried, some modern social theoreticians, too, have argued that private property in land by title of first occupancy is morally wrong.[17]

Basil's practical application is simple. "If each one would take that which is sufficient for one's needs, leaving what is in excess to those in distress, no one would be rich, no one poor." Then he carries his moral argument further, condemning the concentration of wealth in the hands of a few. "Do you think that you . . . have done injury to no one?" he asks. Of course, one could always argue that Basil is using rhetorical hyperbole when he says that anyone who refuses to share his or her wealth is as guilty as one who forcibly deprives someone of the same. After all, it may be argued he is surely speaking figuratively when he says that the rich have taken everything into the unlimited (incapable of being satisfied) "bosoms" (*kolpois*—"compass," in our translation by Ryan) of their avarice. Hence, "Are you not avaricious? Are you not a robber?" would likewise be exaggeration for effect. Is there no distinction, after all, between sins of omission and sins of commission—here, between refusing to give and forcibly taking away?

Basil leaves no room for this specious objection. He clearly states that refusal to cooperate in the distribution of wealth is robbery. The private appropriation of the *koina*, such as land, is robbery. Hence, continued landownership is but fresh and continued theft. Indeed, the hoarding of other things, too, which one does not need, but which others do need, is itself a form of theft: "That bread which you keep, belongs to the hungry; that coat which you preserve in your wardrobe, to the naked."

A robber is one who takes the goods of another by force. A thief is one who takes the goods of another by stealth. And so, if you make your own the things that are *koina* by right, the things that are there for everyone who needs them, then it is clear that you are one or the other. In Basil's view, the rich and the poor share a single, common nature (*koinēs phuseōs*), and nature's bounty is the source of so much of the wealth of the few who are rich. Therefore a great deal of this same wealth is owed the community, for the use of those in need.

2. The Injustice of Usury

Commenting on Psalm 14, a lament upon widespread corruption, Basil opens with a description of the practices of usurers of his time, excoriating them for their exploitation of the poor. Then he goes on:

> It was your duty to relieve the destitution of the man, but you, seeking to drain the desert dry, increased his need. Just as if some physician, visiting the sick, instead of restoring health to them would take away even their little remnant of bodily strength, so you also would make the misfortunes of the wretched an opportunity of revenue.
>
> And just as farmers pray for rains for the increase of their crops, so you also ask for poverty and want among people in order that your money may be productive for you.
>
> Do you not know that you are making an addition to your sins greater than the increase in your wealth which you are planning from the interest?[18]

The lines immediately preceding this in Basil's homily picture a rich man fawning upon and enticing someone with such words that he finally succeeds in binding his victim by contract. Taking advantage of the latter's poverty, the usurer has managed to persuade the borrower to undertake to pay an interest whose term amount is not revealed, and which is so great as actually to be impossible to pay, so that in effect the borrower is contracting a voluntary servitude for life. This unjust practice is the subject of the homily. Basil tells the perpetrators of this crime bluntly, "You are increasing your sins more than you are increasing your wealth." Such usury is unjust and immoral.

3. The Injustice of Luxury in the Midst of Poverty

In the following passage, Basil is preaching another sermon on the urgency of the redistribution of wealth among the needy. In particular, he questions the morality of luxurious living amidst poverty—even granting that one is the "legitimate" proprietor of one's wealth.

> Do you gird yourself with costly vestments? Is a tunic of two cubits not enough for you, and does one covering not satisfy all the need for clothing? Do you use your riches for more sumptuous living? And yet one loaf of bread is sufficient to satisfy your stomach. . . . Those who treat their property correctly and according to right reason, and are stewards of the goods given by God, and do not store them up for their own enjoyment, are worthy to be honored and loved for their fraternal, social ways.[19]

In this text, one can see a clear Stoic influence in Basil's ethical thought. "Those who treat their property . . . *according to right reason* [*kata ton orthon logon*]" is an expression of a Stoic category. The Stoics were concerned primarily with the problem of morality and used moral principles of reason against the degradation and injustice of society. They emphasized virtue guided by reason and rejected hedonism. The goal of life, they proclaimed, is to live in conformity with nature, or "according to right reason." Applying this philosophy of daily conduct and social institutions, Stoics believed that luxury is wrong, something to be shunned, and they upheld an ideal of simplicity and frugality.

In this passage, Basil reiterates his view: luxury on the part of a few frustrates the purpose of property and wealth when many others are needy. If one wishes to behave "according to right reason" with respect to wealth, one must first of all recognize that all wealth is "given by God" for all humanity, who are brothers and sisters. As owners of material goods, and being what God has made them—social beings—the rich must develop their conduct along "fraternal, social" lines and resist the prevalent view that their wealth is for themselves alone to do with as they please.

SUMMARY

Basil the Great was most sensitive to the grave social injustice of his time. He saw that the needy majority were poor, dependent, and powerless, and consequently insufficiently fed, clothed, and sheltered. He saw that a privileged few were exceedingly rich, ostentatious, and powerful, inasmuch as wealth, particularly the wealth-producing resource, land, was concentrated in the hands of a few. He did *not* see the wealthy few and the destitute majority existing side by side fortuitously, without a relationship of causality between their two states. He saw that one state caused the other. The enormous wealth and sumptuous living of the few caused the impoverishment and misery of the many. An unjust relationship existed on a massive scale, in Basil's view. Pious and wise, he could not accept this state of affairs as one willed by God.

It is not for nothing that Basil was called a Roman among the Greeks. He was the practitioner among theoreticians, the pastor among theologians. If the status quo was unjust and wrong, he denounced it. An appeal to the status quo as a principle of moral legitimation was, in Basil's view, irrational and exasperating. He rejected the prevailing, sacrosanct notion of ownership, which was absolutist and individualistic and which created a yawning chasm between the few haves and the many have-nots. He excoriated the exploiting classes, calling them rich robbers and thieves. But above all, he tried to reason with them and show them how the wealth they had was ill-gotten and the result of theft, with a view to moving them to restore it by redistribution.

Our rhetorician lacked neither courage nor penetration. And yet he demonstrated a certain gentleness. Not only was he brave enough to point out concretely that prevalent practices were morally wrong and wise enough to be able to show just why they were wrong, but he proposed alternatives. He proposed an ethical notion of property that *was* just, in that it led to a more rational, more caring dispensation. He taught a new philosophy of ownership, based on the view that God was Father and Giver and Provider for all, and that therefore a few must cease stealing the food-producing resources that God had destined for the use of all. Then the many, everyone, could celebrate their effective participation in the same common nature—in the one human family, to which they all belonged.

Chapter 5

Ambrose:
Born Naked

Ambrose was born most likely in A.D. 333, probably at Treves, a frontier garrison town, where Roman legions had been stationed to keep the Germans at bay. His father, a Christian, was *Prefectus Praetorius Galliarum*, and thus one of the most highly-placed officers of the Empire.[1] After his father's early death, Ambrose was taken to Rome by his mother, along with his brother and sister, so that the three might finish their education there. He received a rhetorical and legal training, practiced law for some time, and while he was still young, about the year 370, entered upon an administrative career, in which he was sponsored by a powerful patron, the Praetorian Prefect of Italy. He became Governor of Milan—*Consularis Liguriae et Aemiliae*—with his official residence in the city of Milan.[2]

Ambrose had been governor of Milan for a year when the Arian Bishop, Auxentius, died, and the people clamored for Ambrose to be made bishop. Ambrose accepted, and his first care on taking possession of his episcopal see was to divest himself of his great wealth and distribute it to the poor, both directly and through the stewardship of others, whom he commissioned to manage his investments for the benefit of the community.

Ambrose was a bishop in the service of all, without distinction of class. Anyone could approach him, says Augustine,[3] except when the crowd of the poor and miserable became so great that no one could pass. His political activity was most extensive. He was the confidant of the Emperor Gratian, who abandoned Trèves in favor of Milan. He won respect even from the Emperor Theodosius, whom he made to submit to public penance for the massacre of seven thousand people at Thessalonica.

Ambrose was an authentically Roman, practical personality. Still, despite his extensive pastoral and teaching activity, he found time to write a great deal. A pastoral and moral interest, however, predominated even in his writings.

Italy in the time of Ambrose was no longer one of the best cultivated regions of the Empire. The process of concentration of landed property in the hands of wealthy landowners[4] was assuming larger proportions than ever and went on at the expense not only of the peasants, but also of city dwellers. The ancient aristocracy of Rome had disappeared. The land held by this aristocracy in the provinces had mostly become the property of the Emperor. Those who fulfilled important offices in the administration of the Empire increased their fortune at the Emperor's hands.

Even legally honest governors not only had large salaries, but also various other opportunities of enriching themselves without overstepping the limits of legality. Rarely did a landlord live on his estates, as he was sure to be busy in the city. He worked in such a way as to have as little trouble as possible, and the safest way to receive a good income from the land was not to cultivate it himself—which involved a great deal of personal attention—but to rent it to others to cultivate.

However, the numbers of people willing to rent the land of the large estates was decreasing relatively to the growing demand. Tenants still formed the majority of the population in Italy. They still lived in their *vici* and *pagi*. But they were no longer the landowners. The plots they cultivated were the property of an absentee landlord. Although, politically, there was no distinction among them, since all free residents of Italy were Roman citizens, yet socially and economically the rural population formed a lower class than that of the landlords, who usually resided in Rome, Milan, or other Italian cities.

These are the circumstances one must bear in mind when reading the moral pronouncements of Ambrose on property and wealth. Ambrose was well versed in Roman law. He was also a bishop. After Christianity had become the religion of the Empire, better protection could be obtained by the poorer classes from the bishops, who not only had the weapon of excommunication at their disposal, but who saw their temporal power constantly increasing as well.

Throughout his works, with an earnestness and power like that of a Hebrew prophet, Ambrose cries out against the great evil of his time: the heinous gap between the status of the few rich and the many poor. He shows a clear and profound understanding of the social problem, bravely questioning and reevaluating the very meaning of ownership and property. His approach is not so much from the legal side—he is not speaking as a legislator, or even as an imperial administrative official. Rather he investigates the moral and philosophical motive of ownership. He is speaking not as a senator or governor would, but as Bishop of Milan.

THE TEXTS

Ambrose wrote the *De Nabuthe Jezraelita* to combat the inveterate social evil of the Roman Empire: the avarice and luxury of the rich and their oppression of the defenseless poor, which were especially notorious in the fourth century. The date of the composition of the *De Nabuthe* cannot be fixed definitely, but it probably falls within the years 386–389.[5]

The sources of the *De Nabuthe* can be classified chiefly under three heads: the Bible, Basil the Great, and the classical authors. The extensive indebtedness of Ambrose to Basil has been noted by a number of scholars.[6]

Migne suggests that the *De Nabuthe* was originally a pair of sermons, delivered by Ambrose to rich persons who were not necessarily the most notorious for their exploitation of the *humiliores*, the poor masses of Italy. In its present form it consists of seventeen short chapters, constituting a running commentary on chapter 21 of the First Book of Kings.

1. The Natural Equality of All in Womb and Tomb

Our first text is a sort of introduction to the whole treatise. The avarice of the rich and their heartless oppression of the poor is taken for granted as common knowledge. That Ambrose clearly presupposes its wide prevalence in the Roman Empire at this time is shown by the style he employs. The interrogatory ''Who of the rich . . . Who of the wealthy . . . Who is content . . . What rich man's heart . . . ?'' suggests the rhetorical no-exceptions-to-this-rule tone.

A. The story of Naboth is old in time but daily in practice. For who of the rich does not daily covet the goods of others? Who of the wealthy does not strive to drive off the poor man from his little acre and turn out the needy from the boundaries of his ancestral fields? Who is content with his own? What rich man's heart is not set on fire by a neighbor's possessions?[7]

B. How far, O ye rich, do you push your mad desires? ''Shall ye alone dwell upon the earth?'' (Is. 5:8) Why do you cast out the fellow sharers of nature, and claim it all for yourselves? The earth was made in common for all. . . . Why do you arrogate to yourselves, ye rich, exclusive right to the soil? Nature, which begets all poor, does not know the rich. For we are neither born with raiment nor are we begotten with gold and silver. Naked it brings people into the light, wanting food, clothing, and drink; naked the earth receives whom it has brought forth; it knows not how to include the boundaries of an estate in the tomb. . . . Nature, therefore, knows not how to discriminate when we are born, it knows not how when we die.[8]

Here Ambrose first of all describes how landed property was being concentrated in the hands of large investors and landlords, who were extending their *latifundia* at the expense of eviction from the land for the peasant masses. The Latin word, *possessio*, which he uses here, is taken in the sense of ''estate.'' In classical Latin the plural form had been the usual word for ''possessions.''

For those who have taken the route of individualistic wealth-accumulation, Ambrose says, there is no end to expansion. Objectively, accumulated wealth must grow or cease to be. Subjectively, then, in the individuals who have taken this route, limitless greed is born and daily nourished till oligopoly or monopoly is achieved. Ambrose, the ethical philosopher, finds in this phenomenon of the avaricious rich a basic ignorance or misunderstanding of the true meaning of ownership. And to him, the contemporary social order merely manifested in the concrete the error and injustice of the accepted ownership concept.

The starting point for passage B is in Isaiah 5:8: "Woe to you who join house to house, who connect field with field, till no room remains and you are left to dwell alone in the midst of the land!" And indeed Ambrose is critically viewing *landed* property here, the primary form of wealth in his time.

At once our Stoic categories reappear, as they appeared in our texts from Basil in the chapter we have just concluded. The Stoics, it must be remembered, wielded great influence over the thought of nascent Christianity, through such authors as Seneca and Epictetus, or Roman eclectics like Cicero and Varro. So intimate, indeed, was the contact between Stoicism and Christianity that legends sprang up concerning a supposed correspondence between Seneca and Paul.[9] Thus in our text as well, after quoting the last part of the verse from Isaiah we have cited, Ambrose asks: "Cur ejicitis consortem naturae?—Why do you cast out the fellow sharers of nature and claim it all for yourselves?" For, according to the Stoics, all persons share a single human nature, since they all share in the Universal Reason (*ho koinos logos*)—and therefore all possess in common the rest of nature as well, which is subordinated to the *koinos logos*. All are like one another, all possess the same rights and laws. Everyone, as *consors naturae*, is a cosmopolite. One's native land is the whole world.[10]

Ambrose elaborates on this idea when he writes: "Nature, which begets all poor, does not know the rich. . . . Naked it brings people into the light, wanting food, clothing, and drink. . . . Nature, therefore, knows not how to discriminate when we are born, it knows not how when we die." The conclusion he draws is that we all have the same and equal claim to the goods of nature: "Why do you arrogate to yourselves, ye rich, exclusive right to the soil?" And: "The earth was made in common for all." When some seek to acquire house after house, field after neighboring field, then of course all the world goes wanting, and the rich are "left to dwell alone in the midst of the land." The poverty of the many is caused by the accumulated wealth, the ever expanding wealth, of a few.

Ambrose underscores our natural poverty at birth and death because, in Stoic categories, he seeks to know what was "in conformity to nature" or "according to right reason" regarding ownership of property. "Naked birth" levels the claim of every *consors naturae* to nature's bounty. Hence it is not in accordance with nature, and therefore, in Ambrose's phrase, it is "mad," to arrogate to oneself unlimited or huge tracts of land and thus to exclude one's "fellow sharers of nature" from this land.[11]

To Ambrose it is not a question of being able to, but of being permitted to, claim for oneself alone what others have a right to share in as *consortes naturae*. Moreover, Ambrose finds it pointless—that is, lacking in the Stoic idea of finality and purposiveness—to be owner of so much, when nature "knows not how to include the boundaries of possessions in the tomb." Or, as he says elsewhere in the same chapter, "Redoperi terram, et si potes, divitem deprehende. Eruderato paulo post tumulum, et si cognoscis egentem, argue; nisi forte hoc solo quod cum divite plura pereunt." That is, "Open the earth, and pick out a rich person, if you can. Then dig for a poor one, and show us how you know the difference—unless perchance because so many things perish with the rich."

Ambrose wishes all to understand that nature's bounty is basically common—land, sunshine, air, and all nature's gifts. To arrogate to oneself "exclusive right" to these (the Roman law phrase for the ownership right, with which Ambrose the lawyer was so familiar), is wrong, and "mad." One simply does not have this right, because other people are sharers in human nature—an ontological fact—and therefore may not be prevented from exercising their right to share in the rest of nature's bounty—an ethical demand following from the ontological fact. As Ambrose will say in another work, "Lex quaedam naturae est tantum quaerere quantum sufficit ad vitum . . .": "it is a law of nature that we must seek only so much as is required for living."[12]

2. The Wealthy Few Cause the Many to Groan in Misery

A. The whole people groan, and you alone, O rich man, are not moved. . . . But perhaps you may return home and talk with your wife. She may urge you to redeem the one sold. Nay, rather will she urge you to purchase female ornaments and finery with what you can free a poor man even at a small cost. She will impose upon you the necessity of expenditures that she may drink from a goblet set with stones, sleep on a purple couch, recline on a silver sofa, and load her hands with gold and her neck with strings of gems.[13]

B. Or do spacious halls exalt you, which should rather sting you with remorse, because, while they hold crowds they exclude the cry of the poor—although it would be of no avail that this cry be heard, which even when heard gains nothing. Furthermore, your very palace itself does not remind you of your shame, who in building wish to surpass your riches and yet do not vanquish them. You cover your walls, you strip men naked. The naked man cries before your house, and you neglect him. He cries, and you are solicitous as to what marbles you will use to cover your floors.

C. The poor man seeks money and has it not; a man asks for bread, and your horse champs gold under his teeth. And precious ornaments delight you, although others do not have grain. . . . The people are starving, and you close your barns; the people weep bitterly, and you toy with your jewelled ring. . . . The jewel in your ring could preserve the lives of the whole people.[14]

These passages concretize social conditions in the fourth century, when the line between rich and poor was more sharply drawn than ever before.[15] Enormous sums were spent by the rich for luxury, as in the construction of floors, the mosaic work of which in many instances remains unrivaled today.[16] So formidable had the passion for building become in the times of Ambrose that severe penalties were fixed by law to curb public officials, at least, from erecting unnecessary buildings at public expense.

Ambrose denounces these practices as immoral. He excoriates the rich for being so proud of their property, when by rights they should be stung with remorse. Their clinging to wealth causes the continued poverty of others. They are stripping others naked when they cover their walls, because what should have been spent to clothe the naked is spent foolishly to beautify the walls. "Precious ornaments delight you, although others do not have grain. . . . The jewel in your ring could preserve the lives of the whole people."

There is no doubt in Ambrose's mind about the causal relation-

ship between the wealth of the few and the continued misery of
the many. The wanton and luxurious living of the wealthy is only
so much insult added to the prior and continuing injury and deprivation of the poor. The Roman law concept of property that has
caused this scandal, and allowed it to continue, is in Ambrose's
view a distortion of the true ethical essence of ownership. In fact,
as he makes clear in a related passage of the same work, Ambrose
considers it diametrically opposed to the true meaning of ownership if one desires "not so much . . . to possess, as it were, something useful but . . . to exclude others."[17] There is a limit to the
essentially useful things one may rightfully possess. However,
there is no limit to the wealth one can and will seek to accumulate
if the "legitimate" view of the ownership right (as Roman law
had it) essentially means the right to "exclude others."

For Ambrose, then, it is a perversion of the human right to the
wealth of the world when human owners can exercise that right as
if they were not part of the whole of humankind. Such a "right"
legitimates unlimited greed, in place of communal responsibility.
Things are given more attention than persons, and the *human*
right to wealth becomes a caricature and loses its ethical authen-
ticity.

3. The Earth Belongs to All:
The Wealthy Few Have a Duty of Restitution

A. Why do the injuries to nature delight you? For all has the
world been created, which you few rich are trying to keep
for yourselves. For not merely the possession of the earth,
but the very sky, the air, and the sea are claimed for the use
of the rich few. How many people can this air feed which
you include within your widepread estate?[18]

B. Not from your own do you bestow upon the poor man,
but you make return from what is his. For what has been
given as common for the use of all, you appropriate to yourself alone. The earth belongs to all, not to the rich; but fewer
are they who do not use what belongs to all than those who
do. Therefore you are paying a debt, you are not bestowing
what is not due. Hence Scripture says to you: "If a poor
man speak to thee, lend him thy ear without grudging; give

him his due, and let him have patient and friendly answer"
(Ecclus. 4:8).[19]

C. You who bury gold in the earth are the custodian, not the
master of your wealth; surely you are its servant and not its
lord. But: "Where thy treasure is, there is thy heart also."
Hence with that gold you have buried your heart in the
earth. . . .

"If thou wilt be perfect," he says, sell what thou hast and
give to the poor, and thou shalt have treasure in heaven."
(Matt. 19:21) And do not become sad when you hear these
words lest it be said to you also: "How hardly shall they that
have riches enter into the kingdom of God." Rather when
you read this, consider that death can snatch those things
from you. . . .[20]

D. A possession ought to belong to the possessor, not the
possessor to the possession. Whosoever, therefore, does not
use his patrimony as a possession, who does not know how
to give and distribute to the poor, he is the servant of his
wealth, not its master; because like a servant he watches
over the wealth of another and not like a master does he use
it of his own. Hence, in a disposition of this kind we say that
the man belongs to his riches, not the riches to the man.[21]

"Why do the injuries done to nature delight you?" One of the
noblest fruits of Stoic ethics is the concept of the natural law and
the ideal of humanitarianism associated with it. The Stoics were
of the opinion that the law of nature is evident. It is present with
reason as such and is discovered by right reason.

What are the "injuries done to nature" of which Ambrose
speaks? A few rich are trying to keep the earth for themselves, he
says, so that, in consequence, "fewer are they who do not use
what belongs to all than those who do." Here, true to his Stoic
influences, Ambrose feels he is pointing out a fact which is in
itself altogether evident, but which is often lost sight of due to
blindness caused by individual ownership's drive for ever greater
wealth: the sky, the air, the sea, and the land have been "given as
common for the use of all."

"The earth belongs to all, not to the rich," Ambrose insists, and he deplores the fact that "fewer are they who do not use what belongs to all than those who do." And he belabors the point: "How many people can this air feed which you include within your widespread estate?"

From the foregoing considerations, what conclusions does Ambrose draw? He holds that it is only just that a redistribution of wealth take place: "Not from your own do you bestow . . . you are paying a debt." *Redistributing wealth is simply an act of restitution*, for the concentration of wealth in the hands of a few has deprived the poor majority of their birth right.

In the time of Ambrose, as we have seen, "wealthy" generally meant wealthy landowners. Conversely, the "poor" were in general the *coloni*, or tenants, who formed the majority of the population in Italy and who, although politically Roman citizens, formed a socially and economically lower class than that of the landlords. They were the masses, who groaned behind their primitive plows on the *latifundia,* but whose toil and pain were not for themselves.

In this light it is easy to understand why Ambrose, developing an insight which he, like Basil, has into human equality in nature and human beings' consequent *equality of claim* to nature's bounty, insists that it is only a "debitum" (something due) for the rich (landlord) to give to the poor (*coloni*), since much of the wealth of the former is due to nature's bounty, not to mention the toil of the *coloni*/tenants.

Ambrose, lawyer and moralist, casts aside the prevalent notion of the right to own as an absolute and exclusive right. He then lays bare the paramount aspect of the human right to the goods of earth: namely, the originally communal purpose of property, whereby material goods are essentially ordained for the requirements of the human race—so that, under whatever arrangements of ownership, the primary communal purpose of material goods ought to be safeguarded.

In the following passages (C and D), Ambrose the rhetorician employs a different style of address. The content, however, remains the same. To the individual owner attached to the idea of property, he says in effect: If ownership is what you seek, then be a *real* owner, a real *dominus*, and not merely a custodian or servant of property. In their attachment to property, Ambrose complains, owners are possessed by wealth instead of possessing it.

They are made powerless by property, having no power to part with it. The rich youth in the Gospel parable had lost the capacity to part with his possessions because he was enslaved by them. Instead of possessing property, he was possessed by property.

The challenge to a real owner, a true *dominus*, is to exercise the power to give and to facilitate the sharing of wealth.

4. Helping Others Places God in Our Debt

The following passages are an exegesis of Luke 12:16-21. The last lines of passage A are a paraphrase of Job 29:15-16.

A. "Thou hast," he says, "much goods." The miser does not know how to mention goods, except which are lucrative. But I agree with him that those things which are pecuniary may be called goods. Why, therefore, do you make evil from goods, since you should rather make good from evils? For it is written: "Make unto yourself friends of the Mammon of iniquity." For him, then, who knows to use them, they are goods; for him who does not, they are rightly evils. . . . They are goods if they bestow them to the poor, wherein you make God your debtor by a kind of pious usury. They are goods if you open the barns of your justice so that you may be the bread of the poor, the life of the needy, the eye of the blind, and the father of the orphan children.[22]

B. "Thou hast much goods laid up for many years." You can abound both for yourself and for others, and then you have plenty for all: why do you pull down your barns? I will show you where you may better preserve your grain, where you may enclose it well, so that thieves cannot take it from you. Store it in the hearts of the poor. . . . Now God gives abundance to you that it may either overcome or condemn your avarice; wherefore you cannot have an excuse. Yet you reserve for yourself alone what he has wished to be grown through you for many; nay you even deprive yourself of it, for rather would you be laying up for yourself if you were distributing to others. . . . If the earth returns to you more abundant fruits than it has received, how much more will the remuneration of mercy return to you many times what you have given?[23]

In passage 4A, Ambrose says that property and wealth are good or bad depending on how one uses them—depending on whether they attain their reason for being. "For him then who knows how to use them, they are goods, for him who does not, they are rightly evils."

In Ambrose's view, the ethical nature of the right to wealth is essentially defined by its function. The right to wealth is a means to an end. Ambrose is unconcerned, in these passages, how one has come to possess the goods that are one's property. Rather he endeavors to clarify, for those who are in fact owners, the ethical essence of their right to property, and how best to take advantage of it as Christians.

Employing an arresting figure in order to emphasize his condemnation of the exploitative practices of his time, such as the practice of usury, Ambrose urges the rich to be wise and practice a kind of "pious usury," making God their "debtor."

5. The Most Excellent Christian Quality

Ambrose further develops the idea of God as our debtor in another work, *De Officiis Ministrorum.*[24] It was a key principle of Stoic ethics that only a person who does good because he or she thinks it should be done—because it is one's duty to do it—can be said to be perfect. Seneca, for instance, can demand, "You must live for another, if you want to live for yourself" (Epistle 48:2); or Epictetus, "I hold it to be better to do as God wills and not as I will."[25] Ambrose baptizes these categories of Stoic ethics.

Nothing so recommends [a Christian] . . . as mercy: in the first place, [mercy] toward the poor, namely that you consider them common partakers [lit., "children"] of nature, which produces fruits of the earth for the use of all; that of what you have you bestow liberally on the poor; that you help . . . your neighbor. . . . If you clothe the naked, you are clothing yourself with justice. If you receive a stranger into your house, if you support the needy one, he or she acquires for you friendship with the saints and an eternal abode. . . . Happy those who understand the need of the poor and the infirm and the hardships of the indigent. In the day of judgment, they shall obtain salvation from the Lord, whom they shall have as a debtor of their mercy.[26]

Ambrose, like Basil, has a talent for synthesizing Stoic and Christian ethics. Ambrose the Stoic begins with the fact of a single human family. There is no one who is not our *consors* and *conformis*, by the mere fact of being human. We are all sharers in the same nature and are consequently equally entitled to the use and enjoyment of nature's bounty. Ownership therefore is not intended as a means to deprive our *consortes* of their birthright, but a means to help them enjoy this right.

But then, for Ambrose the Christian, there is the fact of the Incarnation. Everything we do to others is done to God (cf. Matthew 25:31–46). Those who are in the habit of exploiting others through usury, then, Ambrose urges in a powerful burst of rhetoric, may as well avail themselves of the opportunity, so ready at hand, of binding God himself in their debt by bestowing their wealth on him in others. By bringing their wealth to the common store, they will make God their debtor. "Right action" consists not in keeping wealth, but in sharing it. "Bona . . . misericordia, quae et ipsa perfectos facit, quia imitatur perfectum Patrem." Mercy is good because it makes people perfect. It imitates the perfect Father.

6. We Lose Things That Are Common When We Claim Things As Our Own

The first and second passages of our next reading are from one of Ambrose's masterpieces, the *Hexaemeron*, a study of the work of the six days of creation. In this work Ambrose draws a moral lesson from nearly every verse of the creation accounts in Genesis. Passage C is a related text, but from a commentary of Ambrose on the Gospel of Saint Luke, another of his major works.

A. Fish know their own confines, which are not bounded by city walls, by gates, or by buildings; neither are they marked as in the boundaries of the fields. But each has a terminal limit of space in accordance with its need, so that only so much is given to each as to satisfy completely its wants—not so much as its unregulated greed can claim for itself. There is, if I may say so, a law of nature that one can seek only what suffices for nourishment and that the allotment "which thy fathers have set" (Prov. 22:28) should be in proportion to the need for food.[27]

B. The elements have been granted to all for their use. Rich and poor alike enjoy the splendid ornaments of the universe. . . . Hence it was said of those who join house to house and estate to estate: "Shall you alone dwell in the midst of the earth?" (Is. 5:8) The house of God is common to rich and poor.[28]

C. Look at the birds of the air (cf. Matthew 6:26). . . . If there is enough produce from the abundance of harvest for the birds of the air who do not sow, yet nevertheless Divine Providence gives them unfailing nourishment, then indeed avarice must be the cause of our need. . . . We lose the things that are common when we claim things as our own. . . . Why do you esteem your riches when God has willed your food to be common with others? The birds of the air appropriate nothing special for themselves, and hence they do not know to be in need of food because they do not know to be envious of others.[29]

The patristic concept of natural law is mainly of Stoic origin. The natural law is the unwritten, eternal law. It serves as the norm for all positive law, and is identical with cosmic reason. According to this law, every being must do or become what is demanded of it by its nature.[30] We have seen how the Stoic emperor, Marcus Aurelius, exhorted his fellow human beings to emulate "the little plants, the little birds, the ants, the spiders, the bees," and to do "the work of a human being" by acting in accordance with human nature.[31] In the same fashion, in text 6A, by observing the law that naturally governs the mode of "ownership" among existents other than human beings, Ambrose concludes to a precept of the natural law that individual human ownership of property, as well, should be regarded as essentially limited by its common purpose.

Our true needs determine the limits of ownership. To legitimize unlimited accumulation, and thus promote avarice, causes poverty. Fish and birds know their own limits, and thus are given "unfailing nourishment." "Avarice, then," Ambrose concludes, "must be the cause of our need."

Ambrose the Christian, however, speaks of "Divine Providence," or "the house of God," rather than of "nature." We are not only *consortes naturae*. We are brothers and sisters, children of one Father. Consequently, the universe, which is the "house of God" (the reference is probably to Baruch 3:24–25), belongs naturally to all of us. This, according to Ambrose, is the basic consideration where material goods are concerned. One's personal right to them is a minor and subordinate question. "Why do you [the owner] esteem your riches [property] when God has willed your food to be common with others?"

The value of community is easily lost sight of in human arrangements of private ownership. "We lose things that are common when we claim things as our own."

7. Nature Is the Mother of Common Right, Usurpation of Private Right

The first part of Text 7 is a passage from one of Ambrose's sermons on the Psalms. The second part is taken from the *De Officiis*, which in turn is modeled on a book by the Stoic Panaetius (died 110 B.C.). In the *De Officiis*, Ambrose retains the general outline sketched by Cicero and adopts several notions of Stoicism, like the sovereign good, the distinction between reason and the passions and relative and perfect duties, and the classification of the four moral virtues (prudence, justice, fortitude, and temperance). But he cites the authority of Scripture far more than that of the philosophers, as a glance at any page of the work will show.

A. Mercy is indeed a part of justice, so that if you wish to give to the poor, this mercy is justice, according to that saying, "He has spent largely, and given to the poor; his justice lives forever" (Ps. 112:9). Since therefore he is your equal, it is unjust that he is not assisted by his fellow men; especially since the Lord our God has willed this earth to be the common possession of all and its fruit to support all. Avarice, however, has made distribution of property rights. It is just, therefore, that if you claim as your own anything of that which was given to the human race, indeed even to all living beings, in common, you should distribute at least a part among the poor, in order that you may not deny sustenance to those who ought to be fellow sharers of your possessions.[32]

B. Justice has a relationship to the society of humankind and to the community. . . . But what the philosophers consider to be the very first function of justice is, in our opinion, to be excluded. For they say that the first duty of justice is not to harm anyone unless provoked by injury; but this is voided by the authority of the Gospel (cf. Luke 9:55). . . . Next, they deem it a duty of justice to consider the things that are common, that is, those that are public property, as public property indeed, and those that are private as private. But the latter term is not according to nature, for nature has brought forth all things for all in common. Thus God has created everything in such a way that all things be possessed in common. Nature therefore is the mother of common right, usurpation of private right.[33]

It was customary, among Christian theorists of Ambrose's time, to distinguish duties either (1) as demanded by (*a*) civil law, (*b*) natural ethics, or (*c*) Christian charity; or, more commonly, (2) as demanded by (*a*) justice, or (*b*) charity or mercy. In the first passage above, reflecting on the nature of ownership, Ambrose maintains instead that "mercy is . . . a part of justice." As in our text 3B, so also here, he maintains it is only just for rich owners to part with their property and have it redistributed among the poor.

The notion of "original common ownership of goods," which Ambrose has developed in Text 3, is also treated here. The same emphasis on equality of nature is here. But now the theistic element is explicitly introduced: "The Lord our God has willed this earth to be the common possession of all. . . ." God's intention and our social nature constitute the two basic reasons for the "original common ownership of goods," which must not be lost sight of in human arrangements of ownership.

This is why Ambrose says, "It is just, therefore, that if you claim as yours," in virtue of a positive legal title, "anything of that which was given to the human race . . . in common"—the air, the sunshine, the land and the fruits of the land—then "you should distribute at least a part among the poor, in order that you may not deny sustenance to those who ought to be fellow sharers of your possessions"—that is, in order that property and wealth may not be frustrated in their essential role as a means to the use and enjoyment of sub-rational nature by all the *consortes naturae*: all the sharers of rational, human nature.

In the same passage (text 7A) Ambrose asserts: "Avarice, however, has made a distribution of property rights"—*avaritia possessionum iura distribuit*—that is, the rich owners' insatiable drive to "join house to house" and "connect field with field," protected by civil law, had effectuated a maldistribution of property.

In 6A, as we have seen, Ambrose maintains that mercy is a part of justice. The same assertion is found in 6B, in even more explicit language: private possession "is not according to nature, for nature has brought forth all things for all in common."

Thus Ambrose has taken up the Stoic notion of justice, as he himself has begun to develop it in the *De Officiis*, and improved upon it. The Stoics conceived justice to be the proper bearing of all members of a community toward one another, and the first duty of justice to be not to injure anyone "unless provoked by injury." Ambrose now recasts this duty positively and introduces the teaching of the Christian Scriptures. Justice, then, for Ambrose, is a synthesis of the Stoic concept and the biblical one. What is just with regard to property depends entirely on (1) God's intention and (2) nature's disposition. Hence there is no reason why the duty of justice should be a negative one. For what positive purpose has God created all things, for what purpose does nature bear its fruits? Is it not for all, since we are all children of God and sharers of the same nature? Hence the first duty of justice is to share our goods.

Private possession, we read in 7B, "is not according to nature." Nature has made no distribution to individuals or given anyone a title deed to a particular portion of the earth. The distribution of property is of human fabrication. It may be just, or it may be unjust, and if it is unjust, it should be changed.

"Nature is the mother of common right (*natura . . . jus commune generavit*), usurpation of private right (*usurpatio jus fecit privatum*). *Usurpatio*, by Ambrose's time, had acquired its modern meaning of "usurpation." And yet its original classical meaning, "acquisition," "appropriation," was not far out of mind; and Cicero, the author of the work which Ambrose is discussing in this passage, derived it from *usus* and *rapio*, so that its etymological meaning would merely be to "seize for use"—not necessarily injuriously or unjustly.[34] Here, in context, evidently both shades are present—that of a private appropriation of land that would be, on the face of it, morally neutral, but which in reality (in view of God's intention and nature's disposition) is indeed "usurpation" in the latter sense of the word.

For, while humankind has received from nature the right to subsist from nature's bounty—a right common to all—human society takes the common right and transforms it into individual rights. But when this occurs, either a few suddenly have a way to deprive others of their common right, or, ideally, these same few acquire a means to achieve the original purpose of the God of nature in bestowing this (common) right to humankind: "God has created everything in such a way that all things be possessed in common."[35] That is, those who enjoy a private "right" to the goods of nature now have the opportunity to redistribute these goods—to place them at the common disposal.

8. His Sun Rises for All, His Rain Falls on All, and He Has Given the Earth to All

The following passages, from Ambrose's *Commentary on the Second Epistle of Paul to the Corinthians*, confirm what we have just seen.

A. As it is written: "He scattered abroad and gave to the poor, his justice endures forever" (2 Corinthians 9:9, citing Psalm 112:9). . . . This mercy, therefore, is called justice because the giver knows that God has given all things to all in common—that his sun rises for all, his rain falls on all, and he has given the earth to all. On that account the giver shares with those who do not have the abundance of the earth. . . . They are just, therefore, who do not retain anything for themselves alone, knowing that everything has been given to all. And such are just not only in time, but forever, because they shall have this justice secure in the world to come.[36]

B. "He who supplies seed for the sower and bread for the eater will provide in abundance; he will multiply the seed you sow and increase your generous yield" (2 Corinthians 9:10–11). Everything belongs to God—both the seeds and the seedlings that grow at his nod, and are multiplied for the use of humankind. It is God, therefore, who gives these things, and he himself who orders them to be shared with those who need them. . . . This is justice: that one restore to the needy, because it is God who gives.[37]

Thus in text 8 we again find Ambrose insisting on the duty of the rich to effectuate a redistribution of wealth. He calls this a matter of justice. If the rich recognize that everything has been given to all, then it is only a matter of justice that they not retain anything for themselves alone. If one proprietor happens to own a great deal, while others have barely enough to live—regardless of the manner in which that one may have attained his or her property—Ambrose sees in that ownership right only a duty in justice to restore (*retribuere*, to give one back one's due) to those in need "because it is God who gives."[38]

Mention is made again in this text of the things that are "common": the rain, the sun, the land. It is God who is the Creator and Supreme Lord of all things. Our right of ownership is subordinate to his absolute dominion. The human right to own is not absolute, but relative to God's will with regard to the things he has made and owns: "He himself . . . orders them to be shared with those who need them."

9. It Is Idolatrous of the Rich to Usurp God's Absolute Dominion

Ambrose writes:

> Just as idolatry endeavors to deprive the one God of his glory, so also avarice extends itself into the things of God, so that, were it possible, it would lay claim to his creatures as exclusively its own—the creatures which he has made common for all. Hence God says through the Prophet: "Mine is the silver and mine the gold" (Haggai 2:8). Both are inimical to God, for both deny God the things that are his.[39]

This passage is the clearest expression in Ambrose's writings of the theistic element in his ethics of ownership. A recognition of God's absolute dominion must be the first premise for the Christian in an ethical consideration of property. Unlimited accumulation, or avarice, is tantamount to idolatry. Whatever civil laws or other merely human considerations may permit, human ownership in its ethical essence remains limited and relative, as the means is related to the end, and as therefore all human rights are subordinate to God's rights and purposes.

But the Stoics, too, were emphatic in their condemnation of avarice and unlimited accumulation. Greed was one of the four things that must be shunned at all costs—the other three being fear, grief, and "excitement." If avarice was so detestable for the Stoics, it held a still deeper revulsion for the Christian Ambrose, for his specifically Christian theistic reasons.

SUMMARY

Predominant in the Ambrosian property ethics is what one might term its *theistic element*. Ambrose always begins his argumentation from a point of departure in the existence of a personal God who has supreme dominion over all things, and who extends a fatherly providence to all men and women. Therefore the right to own is the outgrowth, not of the law of the jungle, of the survival of the fittest, but of God's absolute dominion and will. The limit of the right of ownership is fixed by God's intention. The ownership right cannot be absolute: it cannot be the same as God's absolute right, otherwise it would involve idolatry.

But the other important premise in the Ambrosian philosophy of ownership is the great Stoic premise, the fact of *our common nature* with one another, and the social character of human nature. We are humans all, even the lowliest and the poorest. In virtue of our common nature, we all have basically the same and equal claim to the wealth-producing resources of nature. All of us are *consortes* in human nature and *conformes* with one another—equally human, with the same, primary right to life and sustenance.

Nature begets all poor and needy. It is clear, therefore, that *the earth was made to be common to all*. The wealth of earth belongs to all the children of the human family, and not only to a rich few. Nature has made no distribution, nor given any one a title deed to a particular portion of the earth. The right to subsist on nature's bounty is a right common to all.

The most basic title to property is the title of need. To this title all other titles are subordinate, and by this title the right of ownership is limited. Any individual right of ownership is limited by the equal rights of others.

The only valid, legitimate, ethical view of property, then, is one that considers its purpose. The right which human arrangements may accord individuals to own material goods cannot be anything but a *means to achieve the end* of these material goods, namely, the sustenance of all. It would be a frustration of the goals of wealth if one desired "not so much . . . to possess, as it were, something useful, but . . . to exclude others." It would be an "injury done to nature" if the rich, no matter how "legally," sought to keep for themselves alone what had been created for all.

Therefore, according to Ambrose, for the rich to share their wealth only constitutes an act of restitution, because they have accumulated so much (no matter how they have accumulated it) that the poor have been deprived of their birthright.

The differentiation between rich and poor prevailing in Ambrose's time was, for the Bishop of Milan, without sense and contrary to the will of God. It was the sheer product of exploitative human arrangements, and, as such, was something to be changed.

Chapter 6

John Chrysostom:
You Are Possessed by Possessions

The exact date of birth of John Chrysostom at Antioch cannot be determined, but it must have been between A.D. 344 and 347. He received his early education from his mother, Anthusa, who had been widowed when she was only twenty years of age and John was still an infant.

As happened so frequently in his time, John's baptism was postponed to young adulthood. But once formally a Christian, at twenty, he took up a life of rigorous asceticism, was ordained a priest, and was appointed preacher in the principal church of the city of Antioch. For twelve years he acquitted himself of this special duty with a talent and power that earned him his surname, "Chrysostom," or "Mouth of Gold."

Chosen Bishop of Constantinople at the close of the fourth century, John immediately applied himself to what he saw as a much needed task of reform, suppressing all the luxury of the bishop's palace and using his rich new revenues to establish hospitals and otherwise to succor the poor. He also prohibited the clergy from taking advantage of the selective generosity of the wealthy to the neglect of the poor. Finally, he reorganized the administration of diocesan property in such a way as to be able to foster projects of direct benefit to the poor.

John Chrysostom was unsparing in his protests against the abuses and injustices of his time. The historian J. B. Bury described him as a preacher "who actually held theories of social-

81

ism . . . which might have been very dangerous to the established order of things if he had carried them to any length." And Bury goes on:

> He rejected not political but social inequality, in fact he held a sort of socialism. It might seem that such a theory, if it gained ground, would necessarily lead to a political revolution, an overthrow of the Empire; but there was no danger of such a catastrophe. The idea of the Empire was almost a necessity of thought to the Romans of that time; it would not have been possible for them to conceive the world without the Empire; the end of the Empire would have seemed to them the Deluge. But Chrysostom's spirit attracted the lower classes, and his tirades against the rich delighted the poor.[1]

Chrysostom's campaign against luxury in the midst of poverty and the causal relationship between the two was scarcely popular with the Empress Eudoxia and her advisors, the aristocratic ladies Marsa and Eugraphia. Their hatred for John Chrysostom has been likened to that of Herodias for John the Baptist.

The climax came when Chrysostom openly called Eudoxia a "Jezebel" who had robbed poor people of their lands as Ahab had robbed Naboth. Eudoxia now consorted with Chrysostom's enemies within the Church, who were in the same position as she where vulnerability to the allegation of luxurious living amidst the poverty of others was concerned, and organized a united front against this outspoken "socialist." John was declared deposed as Bishop of Constantinople at the Synod of the Oak, which he did not attend, and then exiled by order of the Imperial Court. He was subsequently recalled, thanks to his popularity among the common folk, but he seemed not to have learned his lesson, continued to favor the poor against the rich, and was exiled again. He died on September 14, 407, at Camana, in Pontus, once more an exile.

Antioch, the capital of the Roman province of Syria, where John Chrysostom spent most of his life, was one of the largest and most beautiful cities of the Empire. In the fourth century the greater part of the municipal land there was in the hands of a few rich landowners—the proprietors of the fine villas described by Chrysostom in his works. The well-preserved ruins of these villas show them to have been large and solidly built, with stables and slave quarters on the ground floor and luxurious apartments for the owners and managers above. The wealthy owners represented only about one-tenth of the population. Living in the city, they had succeeded in concentrating in their few hands most of the agricultural lands of the countryside.

Free tenants and hired laborers worked these lands. Exploited by the city landlords, the peasants lived in extreme poverty. They had no share in the life of the city and could not even dream of ever becoming citizens.

In such a society where the rights of private property gave rise to numerous abuses and instances of social exploitation, unaccompanied by any discussion of principles, John Chrysostom vehemently responded for the poor—so that on the occasion of some of his sermons he was accused of attacking the rich "without reason." He was surely to pay a high price for courageously treading the ground of social justice.

THE TEXTS

1. Not to Share One's Resources Is Robbery

Most of Chrysostom's writings, like the first text we are about to analyze, are exegetical homilies on the books of the Old and New Testaments. Most of these sermons were delivered at Antioch between 386 and 397. The following passages are from a commentary on Luke 16, the parable of the Rich Person and Lazarus.

A. This is robbery: not to share one's resources. Perhaps what I am saying astonishes you. Yet be not astonished. For I shall offer you the testimony of the Sacred Scriptures, which say that not only to rob others' property, but also not to share your own with others, is robbery and greediness and theft. . . . "Bring the whole tithe into the storehouse, that there may be food in my house" (Malachi 3:10—John reads, "for the robbery of the poor is in your houses," for the last clause). Because you have not made the accustomed offerings, the prophet says, therefore have you robbed the things that belong to the poor. This he says by way of showing the rich that they are in possession of the property of the poor, even if it is a patrimony they have received, even if they have gathered their money elsewhere.[2]

B. And again we read, "My son, rob not the poor man of his livelihood" (Ecclus. 4:1). The one who despoils takes the property of another. For it is called spoliation when we retain others' property. On this account let us learn that as often as we have not given alms, we shall be punished like those who have plundered. . . . God has given you many things to possess, not in order that you may use them up for fornication, drunkenness, gluttony, costly clothes, and other forms of soft living, but in order that you may distribute to the needy. Therefore . . . those who have something more than necessity demands and spend it on themselves instead of distributing it to their needy fellow servants, they will be meted out terrible punishments. For what they possess is not personal property; it belongs to their fellow-servants.[3]

Chrysostom makes it clear enough in our first lines here that he is speaking literally when he says, "This is robbery: not to share one's resources." Not only to take what belongs to others, but also to refuse the needy a share in one's property, is theft in the strict sense. He uses three synonyms, *harpagē, pleonexia,* and *aposterēsis,* to emphasize that he is speaking literally. He adds expressly that it does not matter how the rich owner has actually come into the possession of property—whether by inheriting it from parents or by some other means. If one does not share with the needy, one is a robber.

What is the reason for John's "astonishing" assertion? Passage 1A appeals to the authority of the Bible. All that we have, no matter how we have come to possess it, essentially belongs to God. God is the Supreme Lord and we are all fellow-servants: *sundouloi.* The poor and the needy are therefore just as much under God's care and entitled to God's providence as the rest, for all, even the rich, have received whatever they have from God.

If the poor do not receive what is needed for their sustenance, it is because the rich have robbed them of what is due them from the material goods that essentially belong to God. The purpose of property is "not in order that you may use it up for fornication, drunkenness, gluttony . . . but in order that you may share it with the needy."

We are all alike—we are all fellow-servants—so that we have essentially the same right to the goods of earth, which never cease to belong primarily to the Supreme Lord. Those therefore who do not share with the needy as God shares with them are nothing more than robbers. Chrysostom uses the same word for "sharing" which Clement of Alexandria used: *metadidonai*. Unlike Clement, however, John was not a great friend of pagan philosophy and preferred to work as a biblical exegete.[4]

2. The Meaning of "Mine" and "Not Mine"

The following group of passages are all directly concerned with the meaning of the concepts "mine" and "thine." Passage A is part of an address John delivered at Antioch while he was still a deacon. The topic is virginity. In this section of his sermon he speaks of calm and tranquillity as characteristics of virginity. Avarice, he says, and a misunderstanding of the real meaning of ownership, cause the loss of tranquillity, and anxiety.

A. But what is the meaning of "mine" and "not mine"? For, truly, the more accurately I weigh these words, the more they seem to me to be but words. . . . And not only in silver and gold, but also in bathing places, gardens, buildings, "mine" and "not mine" you will perceive to be but meaningless words. For use is common to all. Those who seem to be owners have only more care of these things than those who are not. The former, after so much effort, obtain but just as much as those who have expended no effort.[5]

B. God generously gives all things that are much more necessary than money, such as air, water, fire, the sun—all such things. It is surely not true to say that the rich person enjoys the sun's rays more than the poor person does. It is not correct to say that the rich person takes in a more abundant supply of air than the poor person does. No, all [these] things lie at the equal and common disposition of all. . . . That we may live securely, the causes of virtue are given to us in common: . . . again, that we may have an occasion for growth and merits, money is not made common, so that, hating avarice and following justice, and sharing with the needy, we may seize through this means some remedy for our sins.[6]

C. For "mine" and "thine"—those chilly words which introduce innumerable wars into the world—should be eliminated from that holy Church. . . . The poor would not envy the rich, because there would be no rich. Neither would the poor be despised by the rich, for there would be no poor. All things would be in common.[7]

Setting aside the prevalent Roman legal point of view and meditating from a purely Christian position, John says that the more he delves into the inner meaning of ownership, by which one can call a thing "mine" or "not mine," the more he is convinced that those words have no realistic content. The use of material goods should be common to all. No one can have a claim to the exclusive use of material goods. Therefore the legal proprietors of worldly goods, "who *seem* to be owners," or "masters"—*"hoi dokountes auton einai kurioi"*—differ from those who are not even legally owners only by the fact that they have a greater responsibility to society. The difference, ethically, does not imply the owners' right to do what they wish with "their" property, or to use it exclusively for themselves—"for use is common to all."

In Passage B, Chrysostom states the reason why the use of property is common to all and not an exclusive right of owners: all things, not excluding those that are "owned," essentially belong to God. It is God who "generously gives all things."

Having stated this general principle, Chrysostom proceeds to distinguish between (1) *anankaiotera*—"the things which are more necessary," or the "causes of life"—and (2) *chrēmata*—"money," "fortune." Under the former category he lists "air, water, fire, the sun—all such things."

In which of the two categories will land be included? Surely in the former. Land, too, is a free gift of nature, which everyone can find to be simply *there* and of which therefore no one can claim merit or origination. Chrysostom says that all such things have been intended by God for all equally and in common—precisely because they are absolutely necessary, because they are the "causes of life."

Other things which some possess in greater measure than others, but which are not strictly necessary, are not made common. Those who have these—"money," or "fortune," that is, luxuries—must share them with those who may still lack the necessities.

In Passage C, Chrysostom elucidates for Christians of his time what it means to be in "that holy Church"—a reference to Acts 4:32, on which the whole passage is a commentary. The differentiation between rich and poor must be abolished. The "chilly words" "mine" and "not mine" are to be banished. Envy, contempt for others, and wars would all no longer exist where exclusive individual ownership ceased and where there were no more "mine" and "thine" but only "ours."

Property should be a matter of social ownership. In Chrysostom's view, in light of the message of Acts 4:32, or what has been called the socialist thought and practice of the first Christians, to be a Christian implies subscribing to this idea and spelling it out in practicable arrangements.

3. To Possess and Not Be Possessed by One's Possessions

John Chrysostom was accused of attacking the rich "without reason." And he defends himself:

A. I do not say these things simply to accuse the rich or praise the poor. For it is not wealth that is evil, but the evil use of wealth. Nor is poverty good, but the use of poverty. That rich person who lived at the time of Lazarus was punished not because he was rich, but because he was cruel and inhuman.[8]

B. It is not wealth, therefore, that is evil, but the illegitimate use of it. . . . Every creature of God is good, . . . so now

I am not accusing the rich, nor do I begrudge them their wealth. . . . Money is called *chrēmata* so that we may use it (*chrēsōmetha*), and not that it may use us. Therefore possessions are so called that we may possess them, not they possess us. Why do you regard the master as a slave? Why do you invert the order?[9]

Like Clement of Alexandria before him, Chrysostom asserts the goodness of all creation. Wealth or material goods are not evil; rather, in themselves they are good. "Every creature of God is good." It is not wealth itself, but the evil or illegitimate use of wealth which is morally bad.

There is, then, according to Chrysostom, a law regulating the use of wealth. If one owns wealth, one should act as a real "owner" or "master," as one possessing the property rather than one possessed by it. Otherwise one would be a mere *doulos*, or slave. The word *doulos* connotes the classic picture of bondage and limitation, and to call anyone by this name was one of the worst insults one person could hurl at another.[10]

The etymological root of the Greek word for "money" (*chrēmata*) meant "use." The rich, however, as Chrysostom observed, were so attached to this material called money, which should have been for use rather than for hoarding, that they put their whole hearts and minds to pursuing money endlessly—not for common use, but simply for unlimited private accumulation. John endorsed the goodness of all creation, including wealth or material goods. But he condemned the drive for what seemed like unlimited private accumulation.

4. The Many Poor Are Not Slothful: The Huge Inheritance of a Few Is Unjust

The following passages are from sermons John delivered at Antioch before he became bishop. The first is part of one of his thirty-two homilies on the Epistle to the Romans. The other two are from a sermon he preached one winter season on the subject of the beggars and other poor people who he saw had come to the principal church of the city. All our passages are in some fashion concerned with possession by inheritance and with toil.

A. If you wish to leave much wealth to your children, leave them in God's care. For he who, without your having done anything, gave you a soul, and formed you a body, and granted you the gift of life, when he sees you displaying such munificence, and distributing your goods, must surely open to them all kinds of riches. . . . Do not leave them riches, but virtue and skill. For if they have the confidence of riches, they will not mind anything besides, for they shall have the means of screening the wickedness of their ways in their abundant riches.[11]

B. "Anyone who would not work should not eat" (2 Thessalonians 3:10). . . . But the laws of Saint Paul are not merely for the poor. They are for the rich as well. . . . We accuse the poor of laziness. This laziness is often excusable. We ourselves are often guilty of worse idleness. But you say, "I have my paternal inheritance!" Tell me, just because he is poor and was born of a poor family possessing no great wealth, is he thereby worthy to die?[12]

C. You are often idling at the theatres all day, or in the council-chambers, or in useless conversation. You blame many—but you fail to consider yourself as ever doing anything evil or idle. And do you condemn this poor and miserable person who lives the whole day in entreaties, tears, and a thousand difficulties? Do you dare bring him or her to court and demand an accounting? Tell me, how can you call these things human?[13]

First, Chrysostom calls into question the practice of amassing wealth and leaving it to one's children. Given the fact of God's providence, he argues, such an idea is not logically tenable. The God who has given us all that we are and have will also grant those who come after us the things that they need. To accumulate possessions for the sake of future security and to neglect the present demands of social justice is diametrically opposed to faith in Providence. Instead of providing for the future good of their children, the rich who accumulate wealth on that pretext are actually depriving their children of effective incentives to work and leaving them with so much "confidence in riches, they will not mind anything besides, for they shall have the means of screening the wickedness of their ways in their abundant riches." The important thing to give one's children is not an accumulation of wealth, but *arete*—virtue, both in the general sense of "skill" and in the specific sense of morally good habits.

In passages B and C, John shows that he holds that one may be required to work for a living by citing Paul to this effect. But he questions whether this principle is correctly invoked by those who hurl the general accusation of indolence at the many poor, the accusers themselves belonging to the few rich. As he observes the concrete historical situation of wealth and poverty, Chrysostom sees the alleged idleness of the poor as much more easily excusable than that of the wealthy owners, who have gained so much of their property by "right" of succession. He considers a situation unjust where the descendants of a rich family can enjoy ever greater wealth in relative idleness, wasting their days in idle prattle, while those of a destitute family should sink into ever deeper misery despite honest efforts to overcome their poverty.

> **D.** "Why does he not work?" you say. "And why is he to be maintained in idleness?" But tell me, is it by working that you have what you have? Have you not received it as an inheritance from your father? Or, even if you do work, is this a reason why you should reproach another? Do you not hear what Paul says? For after saying, "Anyone who would not work should not eat," he says, "You must never grow weary of doing what is right" (2 Thessalonians 3:13).[14]

> **E.** "But," you say, "he is an impostor." What are you talking about? Do you call him an impostor for the sake of a single loaf or garment? "But," you say, "he will sell it immediately." And do you manage all of your own affairs well? But what? Are all the poor poor through idleness? None from being robbed? None from catastrophe? None from illness? None from any other difficulties?[15]

John Chrysostom cannot emphasize enough the fact which he seems to think really ought to be self-evident, that not all the poor are poor because they refuse to work. As wealth begets more wealth even among idle heirs, so poverty breeds "a thousand difficulties" that conspire to make the poor even poorer. In passages D and E, a rich heir has gained property as an inheritance. By mere right of succession, perhaps with no further efforts, the heir has come to possess much more than need would justify. Even granting the investment of some labor in this property, still the very essence of the ethics of ownership demands that he or she share with the needy.

This thought is further clarified in a passage from a homily on Matthew 24, which John delivered to the general public at Antioch.

> **F.** Even though you have received an inheritance from your father, and have in this way all that you possess, even then, all are God's. Even you, for your part, would desire that whatever you have given should be carefully dispensed. Do you not think that God will require His own of us with greater strictness, or that He suffers them to be wasted at random? These things are not, they are not so. Because for this end He left these things in your hand, in order "to give them their meat in due season." But what does it mean, "in due season"? To the needy, to the hungry.[16]

No matter how legal the manner in which the few rich may have acquired their property, ultimately the only ethically correct view of the ownership right, according to Chrysostom, is that it is subordinate to God's absolute dominion. The human right to own is subsidiary to the *purpose of the Supreme Owner*. The following passages neatly point up this teleology, which constitutes an essential note of John Chrysostom's philosophy of property.

5. The Few Who Are Rich Are Accountable to All: Their Manner of Accumulating Wealth May Class Them with Murderers

> **A.** Even though you are rich, if you spend more than you need to, you shall have to render an account of the money entrusted to you. . . . You have received more than others

not that you may use it for yourself alone, but that you may be a good steward for those others.[17]

B. The Scriptures are full of warnings: Today a rich man, tomorrow a pauper. For that reason I have often laughed while reading documents that say: That one has the ownership of fields and house, but another has its use. For all of us have the use, and no one has the ownership. . . . Having received only its use, we pass to the next life bereft of its ownership.[18]

C. But perhaps someone may say, "Why then has he given to me, a rich person, and not also to the poor person?" . . . He has not willed your riches to be unproductive, nor the other's poverty to be without its reward. He has given to you, rich person, that you be rich in almsgiving, and make distribution in justice.[19]

D. We do all things ignoring the fact that we shall have to give account of everything that goes beyond our use, for we thus misuse the gifts of God. For he has not given us these things that we alone may use them, but that we may alleviate the need of our fellow human beings.[20]

E. But if you are rich, reflect that you shall be giving an account . . . and not only of your expenditures, but also of how you acquired your property: whether you gathered money by just labor, or by robbery and avarice; whether it was an inheritance from your father, or the result of your exploiting orphans when you ejected them from their homes, or by robbing widows.[21]

Chrysostom repeatedly implies that to be the owner of material goods does not mean to have the unrestricted right of control over these goods—contrary to what prevailing Roman law prescribed and society accepted. First, all of us must sooner or later part with all the things we use. Therefore no one can ever have absolute control over property. Second, whatever property one may have remains a gift of God and does not cease to belong to the Absolute

Lord. One will have to give an account of whatever one has received. "He has given to you, rich person, that you may be rich in
almsgiving, and make distribution in justice." Wealth accumulated in the hands of a few is the opportunity for these wealthy few
to rectify the injustice that has made such accumulation possible
in the first place. The control over property which ownership
brings is essentially related to this purpose of achieving social justice.

Passage B registers Chrysostom's amusement with the legal fic-
tion of ownership. Documents of ownership are meaningless to
him because of his moral approach to the concept of ownership.
Legal papers cannot void the ethics of ownership, nor therefore
its essence. If the owner of house or fields has ceased to have need
of the use of such property, then his or her actual ownership,
regardless of what the law may say, has ceased—again, because of
the ethical determinant of what possession is in actual fact. *Despoteia*, or ownership, is justified by and reducible to *chrēsis*, or
use, of the property concerned.

In passage E, John adds that the accounting every owner will
one day have to render to the Absolute Owner will include not
only an account of the disposition made of his or her property,
but one of the acquisition of that property, as well. It is not
enough to recognize that the right of ownership implies the duty
of sharing one's superfluous goods with the needy, if one came to
one's "right" by exploiting others. In this case, ownership becomes doubly unjust: in itself, and by reason of the unjust manner of its acquisition.

> **F.** I do not ask you mercifully to render from what you have
> plundered, but to abstain from fraud. . . . For, unless you
> desist from your robbery, you are not actually giving alms.
> Even though you should give ever so much money to the
> needy, if you do not desist from your fraud and robbery you
> shall be numbered by God among the murderers.[22]

Distribution of wealth in an ongoing context of oppression is
but the height of self-deception and hypocrisy. The many are
poor because they have been oppressed by the rich few. If the
heirs of the latter wish to rectify social injustice, as of course they

should, it is not enough to appear charitable or merciful by token, or even substantial, almsgiving. What is essential is to "desist from your robbery," to desist from a continuation of the concentration of your wealth, which debases the poor and renders them dependent. To refuse to undertake this task is tantamount to the murder of those whom you deprive of a worthy human life.

6. The Root of Accumulated Wealth Must Be Injustice: Private Ownership Causes Antagonisms, As If Nature Itself Were Indignant

In the following passages, Chrysostom explicitly speaks of land ownership, and of what may be described as the communal character of land and other natural wealth-producing resources.

John Chrysostom delivered eighteen homilies on the First Epistle of Paul to Timothy, probably at Antioch before he became bishop. Passages A and B, however, represent an excursus into a consideration of Luke 16:1-9, the parable of the Unjust Steward. John asks why Christ calls riches the "mammon of unrighteousness." How unrighteous is wealth, then? Is it unrighteous of its very nature? It is in the context of this question that John reviews the origin of wealth, and draws the following conclusion.

A. Tell me, then, how did you become rich? From whom did you receive it, and from whom he who transmitted it to you? From his father and his grandfather. But can you, ascending through many generations, show the acquisition just? It cannot be. The root and origin of it must have been injustice. Why? Because God in the beginning did not make one man rich and another poor. Nor did He afterwards take and show to anyone treasures of gold, and deny to the others the right of searching for it: rather He left the earth free to all alike. . . .

Why then, if it is common, have you so many acres of land, while your neighbor has not a portion of it . . . ? But I will not urge this argument too closely. Let us grant that your riches are justly gained, and not from robbery. For you are not responsible for the covetous acts of your father . . .

or granting that he did not obtain it by robbery, that his gold was cast up somewhere out of the earth. . . .

What then? Is wealth, therefore, good? By no means. At the same time it is not bad, you say, if its possessor be not covetous; it is not bad, if it be distributed to the poor; otherwise it is bad; it is ensnaring. "But if he does no evil, though he does no good, it is not bad," you argue. True. However, is this not an evil, that you alone should enjoy what is common? Is not "the earth God's and the fullness thereof"? If then our possessions belong to one common Lord, they also belong to our fellow-servants. The possessions of one Lord are all common.[23]

B. Mark the wise dispensation of God. . . . He has made certain things common, as the sun, air, earth, and water, the sky, the sea, the light, the stars, whose benefits are dispensed equally to all as brethren. . . . And mark, that concerning things that remain common there is no contention but all is peaceable. But when one attempts to possess himself of anything, to make it his own, then contention is introduced, as if nature herself were indignant.[24]

Roman law, which embodied the accepted philosophy of ownership in fourth-century Antioch, provided for an action called *vindicatio*.[25] Here the possessor of a piece of property vindicated, or asserted, his or her right over it in the face of the claim of someone else, who claimed to be the actual lawful proprietor of the same piece of property. Possession itself was prima facie proof of ownership: it was the burden of the non-possessor, then, to prove ownership; and if he or she failed to do so, the property remained in the possession of the current possessor.

In the texts before us, the great rhetorician refuses to recognize possession as any kind of proof of ownership at all. Rather, he would impose on the possessor the burden of proving that the acquisition of the property in question has been just. In other words, Chrysostom is boldly re-examining the prevailing concept of property by using an altogether new approach—a moral-historical approach, as we might term it. The "root and origin" of current property, John contends, "must have been injustice": otherwise how explain its concentration in the hands of a few, in the face of an original divine disposition placing all things in common ownership, so that there could be neither rich nor poor? Legal facts, Chrysostom contends, come second. And in this instance, law merely legitimizes an unjust situation—a situation which, in his view, needed to be changed.

Unless the present property-owners, then, can show a posteriori that their property had been justly acquired, Chrysostom will contend a priori that it must have been unjustly acquired somewhere in the course of the generations. His stunningly simple assertion rests on the fact that "in the beginning God did not make one man rich and another poor." Thus, in a situation in which so much wealth lies in the hands of a few, while so many are impoverished, the burden of proof of just acquisition lies with the wealthy.

Chrysostom's indictments will not go beyond reason. He grants that, after all, present owners may not be responsible for the covetous deeds of their forebears. Still, he emphasizes, the wealth that has accumulated in their hands throughout generations of unjust practices is in any case not truly theirs to do with as they like. Rather they should open their eyes to the fact that "our possessions belong to one common Lord," and that "they also belong to our fellow-servants. The possessions of one Lord are all common." The wealth of creation is not evil. What is evil is "that you alone should enjoy what is common."

Indeed, Chrysostom argues that the equal right of all to the use of the wealth of the earth is as clear as their equal right to breathe the air—a right proclaimed by the fact of their existence, and by the equal and equalizing gift of the Creator—a right natural and inalienable, vested in all persons as they enter the world, and which, so long as they continue in the world, can be limited only by the equal rights of others. No one of us can rightfully make a grant of exclusive and absolute ownership in land or other wealth-producing resources, because no one of us has made the earth, that we should determine the rights of those who shall have tenancy of our creation after us. All are equally "fellow-servants" of the one Lord, whose possession all things are, and who makes them available to all. To recognize the robbery and injustice of past owners is only a first step that must lead to rectifications in the present social arrangement. If restitution is not made, then indeed, property is nothing but a continuing and fresh robbery.

In passage B, Chrysostom invites people to lift their eyes to the larger horizon: "Mark the wise dispensation of God. . . . He has made certain things common." Social justice is natural justice, he seems to say, and conversely, social injustice is against nature. When some appropriate to themselves exclusively the things that are given in common, then antagonism ensues, "as if nature herself were indignant."

Chrysostom has scant respect for Roman legalization of ownership. To him, absolute ownership is meaningless, because God alone is true owner. As he says in another passage:

C. We have received all things from Christ. Both existence itself we have through him, and life, and breath, and light and air, and earth. . . . "We are sojourners and pilgrims." And all this about "mine" and "thine" is mere verbiage, and does not stand for reality. For if you say the house is yours, it is a word without a reality: since the very air, earth, matter, are the Creator's; and so are you too yourself who have framed it; and all other things also.[26]

For Chrysostom, then, everything is, in the most realistic sense, God's property. Human arrangements of ownership should merely be actualizing God's intention to place all material goods at the disposition of everyone. There should be no longer any strictly "mine" and "thine," because everything is profoundly "ours" to use. As John has already said, "When one attempts to possess oneself of anything, to make it one's own, then contention is introduced, as if nature herself were indignant." Human ownership-arrangements should never be regarded as absolute. This would only render them meaningless. Nor may they be viewed as exclusive. Rather, they should be seen as a way to attain the purpose of the world's wealth, which Chrysostom sees as being essentially ordained for the requirements of all human kind.

"We are sojourners and pilgrims," John reminds us. We are but tenants for a day. As we travel through history in a common pilgrimage, we shall surely find enough along the way for the requirements of all—if only we do not allow some to rob others of what belongs to all. A new consciousness of reality must supersede the socially and legally accepted notion of ownership, which merely legitimizes and perpetuates robbery by a few, resulting in the degradation of many.

7. Where Is the God-Given Dignity of All, When the Poor Rank Beneath the Dogs of the Rich?

In the last year of his episcopal tenure at Constantinople, John Chrysostom delivered thirty-four homilies on the Epistle to the Hebrews. The following passage, from one of these homilies, is a digression on Psalm 41:1: "Happy is he who has regard for the lowly and the poor."

A. When you see a poor man, do not hurry by, but immediately reflect what you would have been, had you been he. . . . Reflect that he is a freeman like yourself, and shares the same noble birth with you, and possesses all things in common with you; and yet, oftentimes, he is not on a level with your dogs. On the contrary, while they are satiated, he oftentimes sleeps hungry. . . . But you say that dogs perform needful services for you? What are these? Do they serve you well? Suppose then I show that this poor one too performs needful services for you far greater than your dogs do. For he will stand by you in the Day of Judgement, and will deliver you from the fire.[27]

B. Do you give to the poor? What you give is not yours but your Master's, common to you and your fellow-servants. For which cause you ought especially to be humbled, in the calamities of those who are your kindred. . . . And after all, what is wealth? "A vain shadow, a dissolving smoke, a flower of the grass," or rather something meaner than a flower (cf. Isaiah 40:6–8).[28]

C. Let us set to work all the different kinds of almsgiving. Can you do alms by money? Be not slack. Can you by good offices? Say not, because I have no money, this is nothing. This is a very great point: look upon it as if you had given gold. Can you do it by kind attention? Do this also. For instance, if you be a physician, give your skill: for this is also a great matter. Can you by counsel? This service is much greater than all.[29]

In these passages one sees the basic underpinning of Chrysostom's social philosophy: God-given human dignity. Chrysostom emphatically posits both the dignity of the individual and that of the human species as a whole. Every human person "shares the same noble birth." Hence also, all humanity possesses all things in common.

But the accumulation of wealth by the propertied few has wounded human dignity. The poor are poor because they have been oppressed and deprived of common resources. The concentration of wealth in the hands of a few has afflicted them. They live in a permanent state of anxiety, without the requirements for decent human life—"not even on the level of the dogs" of the rich. All suffer, *including the wealthy*. For there is no escape from "the Day of Judgement." And wealth, in the end, no matter how huge the accumulation, is nothing but "a vain shadow, a dissolving smoke."

However, Chrysostom notes optimistically, this degradation, this unjust state of affairs, can be remedied—by our common awakening to the reality of human dignity, which awakening must necessarily lead to acts of sharing. "Let us set to work all the different kinds of almsgiving." The wealth accumulated in the hands of the rich must be shared, for "what you give is not yours" after all, but must be returned, to meet the requirements of the dignity of all. And this sharing is to be not only of money or gold, but of skills, time, talent, and counsel, in human solidarity—in one family under God. Thus we shall have respite from our anxiety to lord it over one another, for we have one Lord alone, who has given us everything in common for the realization of the dignity of all. We shall all be sharing, just as the Lord himself has shared.

8. The Dispersion of Property Is the Cause of Expense and Waste, and So of Poverty

In a major homily to the Christian community of Constantinople on the fourth chapter of the Acts of the Apostles, John Chrysostom argues, in concrete, realistic economic terms, for the need to practice *koinōnia*.

"And great grace," it says, "was upon them all; for neither was there any among them that lacked." Grace was among them, since nobody suffered want, that is, since they gave so willingly that no one remained poor. For they did not give a part, keeping another part for themselves; they gave everything in their possession. They did away with inequality and lived in great abundance; and this they did in the most praiseworthy fashion. They did not dare to put their offering into the hands of the needy, nor give it with lofty condescension, but they laid it at the feet of the apostles and made them the masters and distributors of the gifts. What a man needed was then taken from the treasure of the community, not from the private property of individuals. Thereby the givers did not become arrogant.

Should we do so much today, we should all live much more happily, rich as well as poor; and the poor would not be more the gainers than the rich. And if you please, let us now for a while depict it in words, and derive at least this pleasure from it, since you have no mind for it in your actions. For at any rate this is evident, even from the facts which took place then, that by selling their possessions they did not come to be in need.

Let us imagine things as happening in this way: All give all that they have into a common fund. No one would have to concern himself about it, neither the rich nor the poor. How much money do you think would be collected? I infer—for it cannot be said with certainty—that if every individual contributed all his money, his lands, his estates, his houses (I will not speak of slaves, for the first Christians had none, probably giving them their freedom), then a million pounds of gold would be obtained, and most likely two or three times that amount. Then tell me how many people our city (Constantinople) contains? How many Christians? Will it not come to a hundred thousand? And how many pagans and Jews! How many thousands of pounds of gold would be gathered in! And how many of the poor do we have? I doubt that there are more than 50 thousand. How much would be required to feed them daily? If they all ate at a common table, the cost could not be very great. What could we not undertake with our huge treasure! Do you believe it could ever be exhausted?

And will not the blessing of God pour down on us a thousand-fold richer? Will we not make a heaven on earth? Would not the grace of God be indeed richly poured out?

If this turned out so brilliantly for three or five thousand (the first Christians) and none of them was in want, how much more would this be so with such a great quantity? Will not each newcomer add something more?

The dispersion of property is the cause of greater expenditure and so of poverty. Consider a household with husband and wife and ten children. She does weaving and he goes to the market to make a living; will they need more if they live in a single house or when they live separately? Clearly, when they live separately. If the ten sons each go his own way, they need ten houses, ten tables, ten servants and everything else in proportion. And how of the mass of slaves? Are these not fed at a single table, in order to save money? Dispersion regularly leads to waste, bringing together leads to economy.

This is how people now live in monasteries and how the faithful once lived. Who died of hunger then? Who was not fully satisfied?

And yet people are more afraid of this way of life than of a leap into the endless sea. If only we made the attempt and took bold hold of the situation! How great a blessing there would be as a result! For if at that time, when there were so few faithful, only three to five thousand, if at that time, when the whole world was hostile to us and there was no comfort anywhere, our predecessors were so resolute in this, how much more confidence should we have today, when by God's grace the faithful are everywhere! Who would still remain a heathen? Nobody, I believe. Everyone would come to us and be friendly.

But yet if we do but make fair progress, I trust in God that even this shall be realized. Only do as I say, and let us successfully achieve things in their regular order; if God grant life, I trust that we shall soon be progressing to this way of life.[30]

SUMMARY

It is not difficult to see why John Chrysostom was said to have a golden tongue. How eloquently he enunciated the Christian vision! In the matter of private property, he speaks, as we have seen, most compellingly of the need to eliminate oppression and poverty, and to build a more just, more humane social order. It is likewise easy to see why he was persecuted. He was oppressed for denouncing oppression. The vision of the world to which he so eloquently sought to raise the consciousness of his auditors seared the sensitivities of the privileged and the mighty. Propertied officials of state and Church, and all the large landowners, who represented less than one-tenth of the total population, smouldered with resentment. That this person should thunder before them like an Old Testament prophet, lashing them with his "golden tongue" to expose the accumulation of wealth, which impoverished the many, as "robbery" and "murder," while yet admonishing people to say yes to life and sharing, inevitably made him eligible for early retirement!

Essentially what did this simple, serious person have to say on the troublesome topics of property and social justice?

Throughout our selection of passages, the *theistic factor* is dominant. John looked at the prevailing social order and saw that it did not seriously, practically recognize the Creator as the Absolute Owner of all things. So John went "back to basics" and emphasized that all wealth, primarily and essentially, belongs to God, the one Lord. That God, for Chrysostom, is Lord in the sense of "owner" is evinced by his use of the word *despotēs* for God. (*Despoteia*, we recall, is his word for "dominion," "ownership.")

Second, Chrysostom emphasizes the *solidarity of humankind*. We all have the same destiny, we are all "sojourners and pilgrims" together. Further: we are all the *sundouloi*, fellow servants, of the one, true Lord and owner of all things. Now, as fellow servants of one Lord, called to a common destiny, we may not be allowed to lord it over one another, but must rather assist one another along the way of this common pilgrimage. Human ownership, then, human lordship over material goods, is but a means to ensuring the availability of these goods for all our co-pilgrims. We cannot stay, we have to move on. We should not hoard, then, but share.

Finally, Chrysostom invests his reflections on property with a peculiarly Christian personalist tone. He restores the phenomenon of ownership to the universe of person-to-person relationships. The prevailing view of the right to ownership conceived that right simply as a legalized relationship of exclusion, a relationship whereby an owner excluded others from access to his or her possessions. Thus the relationship of ownership was a negative one and one fixed in a world of "it"—a world that ignored the ethically negative consequences of this relationship for the dignity of the human person. In other words, the Roman law notion of ownership precisely promoted the wounding of other, genuine, human relationships by legitimizing the robbery, spoliation, and oppression that made so many people poor and dependent and kept them in a state of continual anxiety and resentment.

The notion of ownership as "mine" and "not mine," Chrysostom held, was meaningless. To him, the notion of an absolute and exclusive right of ownership was a caricature of its true nature, which was essentially that of a means serving to deepen genuine human relationships among fellow pilgrims and fellow servants of the same Lord. Chrysostom conceived the nature of ownership essentially as that of a dynamic function of sharing the world's wealth to meet the requirements of a life of dignity for all.

Thus Chrysostom questions the project of a person's amassing wealth, and keeping it for the security of future generations, in the face of the present cry for liberation arising from the many who have been reduced to poverty by the oppressive practices that concentrate wealth in the hands of a few. We might say that, for Chrysostom, the phenomenon of inheritance was tantamount to wresting property from its essentially dynamic function and fixing it in a static order.

Again and again John returned to the unquestionably communal character of all the natural sources of wealth—these *koina* of land, water, air, light, and sky. They had been intended to be "free to all alike," he thundered—but private ownership had concentrated some of them in the hands of a wealthy few, and this was nothing but "robbery, greediness, deprivation," and "murder." The larger picture was ever before his eyes. His main efforts, then, centered on awakening people to the obvious fact that all had an equal right to breathe the air, till the land, use water, and bask in the rays of the sun. This natural, inalienable right of every person to nature's resources could be limited only by the duty to respect the equal rights of others. Indeed, there was enough of these for all, if force and fraud were no longer to be used by some to deprive others of their birthright.

For, in the last analysis, God's was the sole ownership and dominion: "The very air, earth, matter, are the Creator's; and so are you yourself . . . ; and all other things also."

Chapter 7

Augustine:
What You Have Is Not Your Own

Aurelius Augustinus, usually considered the most influential of all the philosophers of the patristic age, was born November 13, 354, at Tagaste, in Roman (northern) Africa, in today's Tunisia. His mother, Monica, was a Christian, but his father, Patricius, was not.

Augustine's family, while occupying a respectable place in society (Patricius was a municipal officer), was not a wealthy one. Nevertheless, after the boy's success with his early education at Tagaste and Madaura, Patricius determined to send him to Carthage for a legal career. During the several months it took Patricius to gather the necessary funds, then, Augustine had to pass much of his sixteenth year in idleness at Tagaste, where, according to the great bishop himself, writing in later years, he gave himself to various pleasures with all impetuosity and passion.

Arrived in Carthage at last, the young man settled down to his studies. In 373, he tells us, his curriculum prescribed a study of Cicero's *Hortensius*. This dialogue aroused in Augustine a desire for a philosophical foundation for his life. Indeed, he resolved to give up everything for the truth. "Immortalitatem sapientiae," he tells us, "concupiscebam aestu cordis incredibili—I yearned with unbelievable ardor for the immortality of wisdom."[1] He became a Manichaean while still a student at Carthage.

At the termination of his course of studies, he would normally have entered a legal practice in the courts, but he preferred a literary career and returned to Tagaste to teach grammar. Then, after some years, he returned to Carthage to lecture in rhetoric. Here he decided to transfer to Rome because he had heard that instruction there was conducted in more orderly fashion.

After some months in Rome, Augustine moved to Milan, in response to an appeal from that city for a professor of rhetoric. Here he became acquainted with the great Ambrose, and thus with his mother's religion—which he had much earlier dismissed as "an old wives' tale." Here, too, he was actually joined by his mother, who played a powerful role in hurrying the last steps of his conversion to Christianity.

Augustine was baptized by Ambrose himself, in 387, together with Augustine's son, Adeodatus, and a close friend. Several months later he returned to Africa, via Rome (during his Roman sojourn his mother died at Ostia), and upon his arrival in Tagaste sold all his goods and gave the proceeds to the poor.[2] Retiring with some friends to one of his former estates, he now undertook to live a life of poverty, prayer, and the study of Scripture.[3]

Suddenly called to the priesthood at Hippo, Augustine consoled himself for the loss of his retirement by gathering another contemplative community around himself, on some property belonging to the Church. At the death of Bishop Valerius, who had already made him his coadjutor, Augustine became Bishop of Hippo.

Now Augustine left his second monastic community behind and moved to the episcopal residence—only to turn it, too, into a monastery, where members lived a life of sharing and religious discipline. With his life of contemplation and prayer, however, Augustine combined an extraordinary activity in the most varied fields: preaching, innumerable writings, and the administration of his diocese, which laid heavy cares upon him and took up a great deal of his time. In spite of his little personal interest in building, he undertook the construction of almshouses for the poor and increased the number of basilicas for people to gather in worship.

Augustine died at Hippo, on August 28, 430, as the city lay under seige at the hands of the Vandals.

Augustine passed the greater part of his life in northern "Africa," a fourth-century Roman province that thrived on agriculture. City life flourished too, but it was only a superstructure based on a developed rural and agricultural life. City residents formed but a minority in comparison with the large numbers of tillers of the soil who lived in the outlying villages.

The *latifundia* were an outstanding feature of agricultural life in the Africa of Augustine's time. It has been asserted that six landowners possessed half of Africa—which may be a simplification of the facts, but it is indicative of the very high degree of concentration of land in the hands of just a few proprietors.[4]

After the conquest of Carthage, Rome had decided that the land of the new province was to be the property of the Roman state, the *Senatus Populusque Romanus* (*SPQR*). Individuals, therefore, held their land *precario*, that is, without guarantee that it would not be taken from them by the state and given, sold, or leased to someone else.

Eventually, however, land seems to have begun to be sold outright to certain large Roman investors, under condition of regular payment to the state of a tax or rent called the "vectigal." It was probably thus that such large tracts passed into the hands of Roman financiers and that the foundations of the African *latifundia* were laid. Moneyed people were eager to invest in the rich virgin soil of Africa, of course, and the state was willing to accommodate them, for their investment promised increased production of grain for Italy, as well as a more productive tax base. Thus large estates, both imperial and private, came to be fostered and encouraged.

Residents on an estate would live in villages (*vici*). They cultivated the land as tenants (*coloni*), paying the owner part of the produce of the land and giving him or her certain days of their own and their animals' labor. The rent which they paid was collected by the "farmers general" (*conductores*) of the estate, who at the same time leased from the owners such lands as were not let out to the *coloni*. For their cultivation, the *conductores*, like the owners, probably made use of slaves and certainly used hired labor and the obligatory services (*operae*) of the tenants of the estate.

The owners of the estate never worked the land with their own hands. They resided in the cities. There may have been small landowners of the independent peasant type living on the municipal territories themselves, in the native *civitates*; but by and large, land, and therefore wealth, was concentrated in the hands of a few rich proprietors.

The peasants, mostly natives, formed the vast majority of the population and the economic backbone of the country.

Such were the socioeconomic conditions in the Roman Africa of Augustine's time.

Roman laws of ownership were the same for Augustine as for Ambrose, who was but a dozen years older than he. Like Ambrose, Augustine was altogether conversant with these laws, which he had studied ex professo. But he never directly concerns himself with the legal reform of property rights and laws. Instead he explores what ownership ought to mean and how it should be ethically regarded by all.

THE TEXTS

Augustine's theory of property cannot be considered in isolation from his general moral theory. The first foundation of his moral philosophy is that the purpose of human life is to be found only in God, the Supreme Good.[5] The whole of morality, then, consists in directing the free choice of our will explicitly or implicitly toward God. This basic principle of moral science is first developed by Augustine in his earliest works.[6] Later this is the thought that dominates the *Confessions*.[7] He returns to it in *On the Trinity*[8] and in *The City of God*,[9] and it also appears in other works.[10] Augustine's point of departure here is the undeniable psychological fact of our soul's insatiable yearnings for happiness. Building on this premise, Augustine now identifies the ultimate object of happiness with God himself: in virtue of the Platonic axiom that good is identified with being and that evil is but the lack or privation of being, perfect and absolute Good will exist only where there is complete Being without limits—consequently, immutable and eternal Being. God alone, then, is the perfect good—subsistent Goodness.

A corollary of this conclusion, and the guiding principle of all Augustine's ethical considerations, including those upon the ownership of goods, is his distinction between *frui*, "to enjoy," and *uti*, "to use." A good place for us to begin our own considerations, then, will be in the following passage from *On Christian Doctrine*.

1. Some Terms Defined: *Frui, Uti, Pecunia*

A. There are some things which are to be enjoyed, others which are to be used, others which are enjoyed and used. . . . To enjoy anything means to cling to it with affection for its own sake. To use a thing is to employ what we have received for our use to obtain what we want, provided that it is right for us to want it. An unlawfully applied use ought rather to be termed an abuse. . . . If we wish to return to our native country where we can be happy, we must use this world and not enjoy it.[11]

God alone may be loved for his own sake. Him alone may we "enjoy," in the full, proper sense of the word. Created goods—wealth and everything else—must only be "used," for they are but the means by which we go to God. They are not meant to be "enjoyed," in the refined philosophical sense which Augustine gives this word. "Fruition" is permitted only where an absolute value is concerned, for fruition is only of that which is loved for its own sake, and in Augustine's moral philosophy, love has the primacy. *Frui* is thus contrasted with *uti* ("to use"), the object of the latter being that set of interdependent subordinate values which, as they converge, continuously point to something higher—which is why these lower values of themselves cannot give us peace.[12] Hence the great moral rule of Augustine: "Solo Deo fruendum"; and this is the context in which we must read the great father's ethical views on property and ownership.

Another term whose meaning for Augustine it will be important to determine from the outset is *pecunia*—which in an earlier parlance, at least, meant simply "money." But Augustine assigns the word a more general meaning:

B. . . . *Pecunia*, in which single name are contained all things of which we are owners by right, of which we are considered to have the power to sell and to give.[13]

C. Everything that men possess on earth, everything of which they are owners, is called *pecunia*. Be it a slave, a vessel, a piece of land, a tree, a herd—anything of this kind—it is called *pecunia*. . . . *Pecunia* is so called because all that the ancients had, they possessed in cattle herds. *Pecunia* is derived from "cattle" (*a pecore*).[14]

From these texts it is clear that *pecunia* for Augustine is a generic term denoting all property, and not just what we call "money." We may even conjecture, from the impersonal style here, that this was a common meaning of the word in Augustine's time.

2. Theocratic "Communism"? Law Should Be Ruled by Ethics

The first and second passages of our second text are from a letter of Augustine to a certain Macedonius, dealing with restitution of property badly shared with one's neighbors. The third is from a major work, the *In Ioannis Evangelium*, actually a concatenation of several homilies.

A. And now, if we look carefully at what is written: "The whole world is the wealth of the faithful person, but the unfaithful one has not a penny," do we not prove that those who seem to rejoice in lawfully acquired gains, and do not know how to use them, are really in possession of others' property? Certainly, what is lawfully possessed is not another's property, but "lawfully" means justly, and justly means rightly. The one who uses his wealth badly possesses it wrongfully, and wrongful possession means that it is another's property.

B. You see, then, how many there are who ought to make restitution of another's goods, although those to whom restitution is due may be few; wherever they are, their claim to just possession is in proportion to their indifference to wealth. Property is wrongfully possessed by evil persons; while good persons who love it least have the best right to it. In this life the wrong of evil possessors is tolerated, and among them certain laws are established, called civil laws, not because they bring human beings to make a good use of their wealth, but because those who make evil use of it become thereby less injurious.[15]

C. Whence does anyone possess what he or she has? Is it not from human law? For by divine law, the earth and its fullness are the Lord's (cf. Psalm 23:1); the poor and the rich God has made from one mud, and the poor and the rich he sustains on one earth. Nevertheless, by human law, one says, "This estate is mine, this house is mine, this servant is mine." This is by human law therefore—by the law of the Emperors.[16]

Passages A and B above have been analyzed by Augustinian scholars with different results. Some have attributed to Augustine a "theocratic communism," according to which the Christian who believes in God would be the sole subject of property rights, while the unbeliever (or sinner) would be deprived of all such rights.[17] Others have vehemently dissented from this interpretation, pointing out that Augustine explicitly teaches in all his works that God gives earthly goods to the wicked as he does to the good. "He gives this to the good and the evil,"[18] or, "Lest these things be considered evil, they are given to the good; lest they be considered the great or chief goods, they are given to the evil."[19] According to this latter interpretation, then, Augustine holds that in civil society the right to property is ultimately derived from a divine right, since all wealth is a means provided by God for fulfilling our destiny. In society, the exercise of this right is sanctioned by civil laws. This, then, would be the whole extent of what Augustine wishes to say in this passage from the *Commentary on John.*[20]

What are we to think of this conflict of interpretations? It is clear that Augustine does distinguish two viewpoints to be taken with regard to ownership and property: the viewpoint of factual legal arrangements governing ownership, and the viewpoint of the inner meaning or essential ethic of ownership—the moral, or philosophical point of view.

When Augustine speaks of "lawfully acquired gains," of things that are "lawfully possessed" and are therefore "not another's property," he is clearly taking the factual legal viewpoint—what civil law in fact sanctions or permits. But this is not his central concern. He is more concerned with ownership from a higher point of view, to which he seeks to raise the consciousness of his community of hearers. This is clear from his conclusion, in which he states: "You see, then, how many there are who ought to make restitution of another's goods. . . . Property is wrongfully possessed by evil persons."

Thus Augustine's direct concern is with the moral or ethical meaning of ownership, as distinguished from the legal viewpoint—which in any case is a matter of who has the power to make and impose the law. Thus it is a matter of factual contingency whether the human legal arrangement is just. If it were to be unjust, in Augustine's words, "What would the great empires be but teeming broods of robbers?"[21]

But—and this is the point—the legal should be directly governed by the ethical. A proprietor should reflect on what it means to own—on what ownership ought to be—and not just what is actually allowed legally. "What is lawfully possessed is not another's property" (true enough from a legal viewpoint), but lawfully should mean justly, and justly should mean rightly.

The true meaning of ownership, then, for Augustine, is to be found in putting property to right use. If owners use property badly, for example by squandering it in luxurious living while others have barely enough for physical survival, they really possesses "others' property." According to the laws of the state, that is, the laws of the power-holders who are of course themselves proprietors, those who misuse their property still own it; but ethically speaking and in reality, they are actually bound "to make restitution of another's goods." The right of ownership does not imply the right to abuse what one owns (as in the Roman legal conception of absolute ownership), but only the right to use it well. "You see, then, how many there are who ought to make restitution of another's goods."

The Creator, who alone is Absolute Owner, did not make us human beings so many "islands," without any relation to each other, but one human family, "made from one mud" and sustained "on one earth." Elsewhere, Augustine examines more systematically the eminently social character of the person and distinguishes the three societies to which the person belongs: the family (*domus*), the state (*civitas*), and humanity.[22] And so in our present text he must conclude: human law may allow you to say, "This estate is mine, this house is mine"; but, beyond a certain point, everything is ours, to use on our pilgrimage, in dignity, toward a common destiny—the Supreme Good.

3. Superfluities Are Others' Property

The following passages deal with need as the most basic *title* to property and as determining the *extent* of the right to property.

A. You have a common universe with the rich. You may not have a common house with them, but you do have a common sky, a common light. Seek sufficiency, seek what is enough, and more do not seek. . . . Have you brought along anything hither? No, not even you rich people have brought anything. You have found everything here. With the poor, you were born naked.[23]

B. But we possess many superfluous things, unless we keep only what is necessary. For if we seek useless things, nothing suffices. . . . Consider: not only do few things suffice for you, but God himself does not seek many things from you. Seek as much as he has given you, and from that take what suffices; other things, superfluous things, are the necessities of others. The superfluous things of the wealthy are the necessities of the poor. When superfluous things are possessed, others' property is possessed.[24]

C. The rich person actually *has* nothing of his or her riches except that which the poor demand of him or her: nourishment and covering. Hence what do you *have*, of all the things you have? You have received food and necessary covering. (I say necessary—not useless, not superfluous.) Why do you take more from your riches? Tell me! Surely all your possessions are superfluous. The superfluous things you have may be the necessaries of the poor.[25]

D. He sought to satisfy his soul with superfluous things and too lavish banquets and most proudly despised so many hungry stomachs of the poor. He did not know that the stomachs of the poor are safer than his storerooms. For what he has hidden in those storerooms of his has perhaps been stolen by robbers by now: but if he had hidden it in the stomachs of the poor . . . it would be preserved more safely in heaven.[26]

In passage 3A, like Chrysostom and Ambrose, Augustine points out that all possess in common whatever nature offers— the sky, the air, the light, the whole universe. But human-made things are not possessed in common. Here, the rule for the property one may keep is self-sufficiency.

He cites the natural poverty of our birth. Whatever we have, we have found here, all ready for us. Our common essence and natural conditions entitle us to the wealth of earth in basically the same way. Both the person to whom a wealthy inheritance has fallen, and the one who has happened on impoverished conditions, have the same fundamental claim to the goods of earth, which neither of them originally possessed. For both, the most basic rule to consider in ownership is what one really needs. If one therefore keeps more than what is sufficient, ethically speaking one is really keeping others' property, because these others, by virtue of their need, have a fundamentally greater right to those material goods.

It is evident that when Augustine speaks of "need" here, he is speaking of it in the strict sense. "If we seek useless things, nothing suffices." And: "The rich person actually *has* nothing of his or her riches except that which the poor demand of him or her: nourishment and covering." Augustine's argumentation is consistent here with his moral philosophy of *uti* and *frui*. To "seek useless things" would evidence an attitude of *frui* toward created goods, which Augustine, as we have seen, considers unethical.

The powerful rhetorician concludes on a note of spiritual

pragmatism. "The stomachs of the poor are safer than store-rooms," he says, for sharing one's wealth with the poor guaran-tees one a reward in the next life.

Here, as so often, the source of Augustine's ethical doctrine is not always perfectly easy to determine. It may be in the Pla-tonists, or the Stoics, or the other schools of Greek philosophy, where, as Thomas Aquinas says, whenever Augustine "found in their teaching something consistent with faith, he adopted it: and those things which he found contrary to faith he emended."[27] The reflections on our having "a common universe" and sharing a comon nature may be of Stoic influence. The doctrine that un-derscores our natural poverty at birth and death may perhaps be traced to 1 Timothy 6:7–8: "We brought nothing into this world, nor have we the power to take anything out. If we have food and clothing we have all that we need."

4. Do Not Think You Are Giving from What Is Yours

The following passages further expound on the commual character of property and wealth.

A. God gives the world to the poor as well as to the rich. Will the rich person have two stomachs to fill because of being rich? Consider, and see to it that from the gifts of God the poor sleep satisfied. He who feeds you feeds them also, through you.[28]

B. Speaking through Haggai, the Lord said, "Mine is the silver and mine the gold" (Haggai 2:8), so that those who do not wish to share what they have with the needy . . . should understand that God commands [this] sharing not as being from the property of them whom he commands [this sharing], but as being from his own property; so that those who offer something to the poor should not think that they are doing so from what is their own.[29]

C. Gold and silver therefore belong to those who know how to use gold and silver. For even among human beings them-selves, each must be said to possess something [only] when he or she uses it well. For what a person does not treat justly, that person does not possess rightly. If one should call one's own what one does not possess rightly, this will not be the voice of a just possessor.[30]

Once more we find the theistic element coming to the fore. It is God the Creator who has given us everything. Human owners must imitate the Supreme Owner in this attitude of giving: just as God manifests absolute dominion by giving the world as a gift, so too the subordinate human owner is to recognize that the essential function of the right to ownership lies in giving to those in need— to oneself first of all and then to others. The human owner participates in God's ownership so that "those who offer something to the poor should not think that they are doing so from what is their own."

The thought in 4C is a conclusion drawn from the foregoing considerations, in a context of Augustine's general moral theory. One ought not have an attitude of *frui* toward anything but God, who is the human being's perfect happiness. Toward all other things, one must have an attitude of *uti*, because all other things are but means to attaining to God. When one uses (*uti*) anything well as a means, *then* one is said to be master or mistress of that thing, to possess that thing: "Each must be said to possess something when he or she uses it well." Otherwise things are topsy-turvy: the owner is possessed by the possession. In Augustine's view, the true and genuine owner is only the one who uses property rightly. If one exercises the legal right of ownership without justice, one is nothing more than a robber.[31] "Gold and silver *therefore* belong to those who know how to use gold and silver." Legal dimensions notwithstanding, those who know only how to *abuse* property (in reality—that is, according to moral considerations) have forfeited their participation in God's true ownership.

5. Private Property Is Loss

This set of passages treats the Augustinian idea that the phenomenon of property must be situated in the context of humanity's solidarity.

A. What is the burden of poverty? Not having. What is the burden of riches? Having more than necessary. . . . Bear with [the poor person the burden of] not having, and let him or her bear with you [the burden of] having more, so that your burden may be equal. . . . The two of you are walking the way of God in the pilgrimage of this world. You are carrying great, superfluous provisions; but the other has no expenses. . . . Do you not see how much you carry? Give something, then, to one who bears nothing and has nothing. You will help a companion, and you will relieve yourself of a burden.[32]

B. Let the rich who do not wish to be merciful hear: let them hear that we are all born under one law, live by one light, breathe one air, and die one death—which if it did not intervene, not even the poor man himself would last.[33]

C. "The love of money is the root of all evil" (1 Timothy 6:10)—if [by "love of money"] we mean general avarice, by which each desires something beyond what is appropriate, for its own sake, and a certain love of one's own property— which the Latin language has wisely called "private," for it connotes more a loss than an increase. For all privation is a diminution.[34]

D. Whence the discords among brethren?. . . Whence one womb, and not one soul?—if not for the fact that as long as their soul is crooked, those who possess a share with their brother or sister consider that share, and strive to enrich and increase it and wish to consolidate everything in their possession. . . . What could be more unjust than to wax rich at the expense of another's growing poor?[35]

The members of the human species all have the same essence and the same destiny. We enjoy the same natural conditions: "born under one law, living by one light, breathing one air, and dying one death." The conclusion Augustine draws from this given natural solidarity is that we should share one another's wealth and poverty. People travelling together through history are divided into rich and poor. This is a challenge to each group to come to the assistance of the other. Rich and poor can share each other's "burden"—the burden of having nothing and the burden of having too much—and both will have relief along the road of their pilgrimage. Of course, there may be some who would prefer to abandon the human journey—to "settle down"—and thus be nothing more than victims of a grand self-deception. For, sooner or later, every human being must set out on that great, last journey of death. As we are a human family, journeying toward the same goal, human ownership acquires the character of a means, to be used for the advantage of the whole family.

In passages C and D, Augustine asserts that the cause of the discord in this family of pilgrims is that some impoverish others in order to accumulate wealth for themselves: "waxing rich at the expense of another's growing poor." The rich deprive others of what they need. Instead of ownership being used to foster community, it becomes a means to destroy human solidarity. In the Roman law concept of private property, then, a means has become an end. It has ceased to be relative and inclusive, and has become absolute and exclusive.

In these passages, Augustine is teaching us that ownership can be neither quantitatively absolute (absolute with regard to how much one may possess), because there comes a point at which one begins to deprive others if there is no limit to the wealth one can amass for oneself, nor qualitatively absolute, as Roman law tolerated: that is, one may not be allowed to do with one's property just as one wills, but must do as one ought, because each of us is a member of the one great human family. It is therefore "unjust" to wish to "wax rich at the expense of another's growing poor."

In proclaiming these principles on property, Augustine has Paul's admonition in mind: "Help carry one another's burdens; in that way you will fulfill the law of Christ" (Galatians 6:2). He considered it a burden for the rich to have "more than necessary." He knew that "those who want to be rich are falling into temptation and a trap" (1 Timothy 6:9). Again, not only the Christian Scriptures, but the Stoic philosophers, too, may be having a direct influence on Augustine here. "Fundamental concepts as the doctrine of eternal law . . . were clearly Stoic categories."[36]

6. Do Not Entrust Your Children to Your Patrimony Rather Than to Your Creator

Our next reading is from a long sermon of Augustine on the Ten Commandments.

> He who made you, himself feeds you from the things which he has made. He feeds your children himself, too. For you do not entrust your children to your patrimony better than to your Creator. . . . Why does such a one not give alms? Because he is saving for his children. It happens that he loses one. If he was saving for his children's sake, let him send on the share that belongs to that one! . . . Give that one what is his! Give that one what you were saving up for him! "He is dead," comes the reply. So he has gone ahead to God? His share is due the poor.[37]

Once again Augustine underscores the now familiar principle that God as Creator is the Absolute Lord, and that God exercises absolute dominion in a paternal providence exercised toward all, of course not excluding the children of the present generation. He concludes that the rich, who participate in a limited way in God's ownership, ought to consider it safer to entrust their children to the Creator than to their wealth.

There is no excuse for the rich not to share. No wealth anywhere ceases to be God's property, and the poor remain under God's care. Therefore the rich are duty-bound to part with their superfluous wealth in favor of the poor.

7. Private Ownership Begets Manifold Miseries

As for the subjective attitude we ought to have toward private property:

> **A.** And nevertheless Christ says to you: Give to me from what I have given you. For what did you bring when you came here? All that I have created, you found here when you yourself were created. You brought nothing, you shall take nothing hence. Then why do you not give to me from

what is mine? You are full, and the poor person is empty.
Consider your origins: both of you were born naked. And
you, therefore, you were born naked. You have found many
things here—did you bring anything with you?[38]

B. Those who wish to make room for the Lord must find
pleasure not in private, but in common property. . . . Re-
double your charity. For, on account of the things which
each one of us possesses singly, wars exist, hatreds, discords, strifes among human beings, tumults, dissensions,
scandals, sins, injustices, and murders. On what account?
On account of those things which each of us possesses
singly. Do we fight over the things we possess in common?
We inhale this air in common with others, we all see the sun
in common. Blessed therefore are those who make room for
the Lord, so as not to take pleasure in private property.[39]

C. Let us therefore abstain from the possession of private
property—or from the love of it, if we cannot abstain from
possession—and let us make room for the Lord. . . . In
property which each possesses privately, each necessarily
becomes proud. . . . The flesh of the rich person pushes out
against the flesh of the poor person—as if that [rich] flesh
had brought anything with it when it was born, or will take
anything with it when it dies.[40]

D. The Good Master distinguished the commandments of
the Law from this more excellent perfection: for there he
said, "If you wish to enter into life, keep the commandments . . ." (Matthew 19:17); here, however, [he said,] "If
you seek perfection, go, sell your possessions," and so on
(Matthew 19:21). Why do we therefore deny that the rich,
although they abstain from that perfection, can nevertheless "enter into life" if they have kept the commandments,
and have given as it has been given to them, and forgiven as
they have been forgiven (cf. Luke 6:37–38)?[41]

The institution of private property was legalized by Roman law
and socially accepted as a legitimate approach to the use of the

earth's goods. Augustine, however, rejects this institution as undesirable and dangerous. In his view, private property is the chief enemy of peace. Wars and discords, injustices and murders, are caused by private property. "Do we fight over the things we possess in common?" he asks.

Augustine also warns that private property occasions an unrealistic, prideful bloating of the self: "The flesh of the rich person pushes out against the flesh of the poor person—as if that [rich] flesh had brought anything with it when it was born, or will take anything with it when it dies."

Private property tends to lead one's consciousness away from the conception of worldly goods as family goods. They all belong to God primarily, and only in a subsidiary way to us: "Give to me from what I have given you. . . . Why do you not give to me from what is mine?"

Further, far from fostering community, private property tends to destroy it. It tends to make relationships of love among people more difficult and to promote an individualism that insists on keeping excessive wealth for itself—inevitably frustrating the original intention of the Creator that material goods be communal. Thus Augustine clearly favors the disappearance of private property as an institution in order to make room for communal ownership arrangements.

And yet, even while condemning private property as such, Augustine issues no blanket condemnation of proprietors who recognize that their private ownership of goods is an opportunity for them to restore to others what the Supreme Owner intended everyone to have in the first place. It seems to us that this forbearance on his part stems from his realization that, evidently, private property arrangements cannot be expected to disappear overnight. Augustine thus accommodates those transitional owners "who have given as it has been given, and forgiven as they have been forgiven." The urgent thing to discard, for Augustine, is the absolutist and exclusivist Roman law idea of ownership, because it legalizes not the proper use but rather the abuse of property.

Thus Augustine takes no absolutist position against material goods or property:

E. Some men make evil use of these things, and others make good use. And the man who makes evil use clings to them with love and is entangled by them, that is, he becomes subject to those things which ought to be subject to him, and creates for himself goods whose right and proper use require that he himself be good; [however, one] must be ready to possess and control them. . . . Since this is so, you do not think, do you, that silver or gold should be blamed because of greedy men, or food and wine because of gluttons and drunkards, or womanly beauty because of adulterers and fornicators?[42]

The abuse of property, as encouraged by the prevailing Roman law idea and practice of private ownership, tends to inhibit an appreciation of the splendor of nature's wealth. Now that wealth becomes the object of a *frui*, and thereby the occasion of self-infatuation or pride. With the accumulation of excessive wealth through private property, owners sought to satisfy useless "needs," and this placed them in a new dependence. Private ownership then tended to erase true ownership—the proper possession and control of property. Thus, while refraining from a blanket condemnation of proprietors, and surely from one of wealth per se, neither, clearly, does Augustine hold any ethical basis for private ownership per se.

SUMMARY

Augustine lived in fourth-century Roman Africa, where the Roman law theory and practice of private property had led, quite naturally, to the possession by a very few persons of very great wealth, at the price of the dispossession and impoverishment of very many other persons. This theological giant of the patristic age saw the prevailing oppression, the blatant injustices perpetrated against the poor, as an assault on Christ: "Christ says to you: Give to me from what I have given you."

He saw that the poor are poor because they have been deprived by the propertied few of the wealth that should belong to all. And he laid the blame for this unjust situation squarely on the doorstep of an absolutist and exclusivist legal right of private ownership. He argued that this legalized right was an affront, in theory and in practice, to the absolute dominion and paternal providence of the Creator, who had willed all of creation to be for all in common, according to each person's need, as a means toward our common goal in God, our Supreme Happiness, as we journey together through this life of pilgrimage.

He reminded his audience that they were all "made from one mud" and sustained "on one earth," under the same natural conditions, having the same essence, and called to the same destiny.

He rejected the legalized status quo as inappropriate for human living. Holding that legal arrangements of property rights were of human origin, he asserted that they should be changed, in theory and in practice, in function of a faith-informed ethic based on the true meaning of ownership.

An exaggerated individualism distorts human wholeness. The communal purpose of nature's wealth is frustrated, as private ownership tends to deprive the many through the accumulation of that wealth in the hands of a few, inevitably leading to hatreds, dissensions, murders, and wars. Augustine saw humanity as divided into warring groups by an absolutist concept of ownership that enabled a few to dispose of the resources of others through their private appropriation of what belonged to all.

Ownership arrangements should be made with a view to the proper use of goods and should preclude license or abuse. A person is owner only by participation in God's ownership, having received from God the goods of earth for use according to need. "Gold and silver therefore belong to those who know how to use gold and silver."

In fact, Augustine emphasizes over and over again, created goods must only be used, and not turned into idols, for they are but means on our journey toward the perfect and absolute Good.

In keeping with this philosophy of property, which he opposed to the prevalent exploitative concept, Augustine founded a number of monastic sharing-communities, as well as a number of almshouses to serve as an organized vehicle for the sharing of goods.

The revolution Augustine advocated in the concept and practice of ownership was not simply a revolution in the material conditions of the poor, who were deprived of the wealth appropriated by a few. This was a part of his ethic, to be sure. But more significantly, he also underscored the importance of assuring each human person a life of dignity consonant with what he perceived as humanity's destiny—not the intermediate little destinies of various historical epochs, but the one permanently imbedded in a restless human nature, that could find its home and "rest" only in eventual union with God, the Supreme Good.

This revolution, he emphasized, could be accomplished only by human beings who were capable and moral, committed to the proper use of created goods. Hence, we may conclude, it could be accomplished only by the abrogation of the prevailing, absolutist and exclusivist, Roman-law conception of private ownership.

Chapter 8

The Patristic Response:
Attack on an Ideology,
and an Alternative Program

*On account of the things which each
one of us possesses singly, wars exist,
hatreds, discords, strifes among human beings, tumults, dissensions,
scandals, sins, injustices, and murders.*
—Augustine

*Let us imagine things as happening
in this way: All give all that they have
into a common fund. . . . The dispersion of property is the cause of
greater expenditure and so of poverty. . . . And yet people are more
afraid of this way of life than of a
leap into the endless sea. If only we
made the attempt and took bold hold
of the situation! How great a blessing there would be as a result!*
—John Chrysostom

Promoted and legitimized by the absolutist and exclusivist Roman law conception of ownership, the concentration of private

125

property in the hands of a few, which had begun very early in Rome, continued apace under the Emperors. The resultant deprivation and misery of the peasant majority and the urban poor were matched only by the luxurious consumerism of the propertied few. They whose few hands had accumulated the surplus product of the efforts of the majority through ownership of natural resources, now found their function in society reduced to the spare one indeed of competing with one another in enjoyment and lavish expenditure. The limits of enjoyment sometimes led to the most "unnatural" vices and intricate cruelties or to despair and a death-wish—or to shame and the longing for a new and better life.

It is true that a small but perhaps significant portion of the population was eventually molded into a middle class, midway between the very wealthy few and the extremely poor majority. Earlier, the luxurious, ostentatious lifestyles of the large landholders had been facilitated by their ownership of great numbers of household slaves, even after the supply of agricultural slave labor had begun its decline. Slaves were cooks, clerks, musicians, physicians, teachers, actors, and even philosophers. Often they shared the lifestyles of their masters and mistresses. Eventually, many of them not only gained their freedom, but became actually better off than the peasant majority and the dispossessed rural folk who had been driven to the urban areas.

As time went on, however, a new class began to emerge. Those who had been uprooted from their towns and cast adrift had not all been reduced to beggary or to the status of a *Lumpenproletariat* or rabble. An increasing number—small enough, to be sure, as compared with the whole population—became respectable artisans, successful business people, administrators, or professionals of one kind or another. There were even women among their number, for the status and education of women had been slowly improving.[1]

The typical member of the urban middle class, however, sat between two chairs, afflicted with the insecurity of the poor majority, and at the same time enjoying the extravagance of the wealthy few. He or she was generally at least as earnest a subscriber, then, to the dominant ownership ideology as anyone else. For the moment, at least, this ideology permitted them the privileged status of the, shall we say, "have-somethings," awkwardly positioned between the classic haves and have-nots. Torn up from their towns, these new "citizens of the world" often found their new world to be a lonely and impersonal place. Their peculiar problem was to devise ways of dealing with the anxieties and uncertainties of their new position.

The peasant masses, on the other hand, composed of tenants bound to the land, agricultural slaves, and heavily indebted free peasants, continued with their toil and travail, groaning behind their primitive plows or toiling at their looms, and knowing that their labor and pain were not for themselves but for the urban rich. The socioeconomic gap between their world and that of the wealthy was as day and night. However, the two worlds were related: the wealthy were related to the dispossessed as exploiters to the exploited, as aggressors to the victims. The oneness of these opposed worlds was essentially provided by the prevailing Roman law theory-and-practice of private ownership. The task of making people *aware* of the causal relationship of wealth to poverty has never been an easy one, and the patristic age was no exception, as its prophets and moral leaders who undertook the task were often persecuted.

THE CHRISTIAN MOVEMENT

The movement which later came to be known as Christianity had begun in one of the Eastern provinces of the Empire early in the fourth decade of the first century. The movement initiated by Jesus of Galilee was a visionary one, seeking to realize what it called "God's kingdom" of justice and peace in the province of Palestine. In his programmatic declaration to villagers of Galilee, Jesus had stated that his aims were to be summed up in the words of a bygone prophet of his culture: "to bring glad tidings to the poor, to proclaim liberty to captives, recovery of sight to the blind and release to prisoners." His movement, however, in its sociohistorical context, did not seek to confront Roman imperial authority directly and immediately. In Jesus' view, the immediate and greatest obstacles to the realization in Palestine of God's kingdom of justice and peace were the Pharisees in Galilee and the priests in Jerusalem.[2] These were the ideologues and beneficiaries of the tributary class system on which the authority of imperial Rome was superimposed. Jesus' movement was basically a Galilean peasant movement, and the exploitation of the Galilean peasants, the appropriation of their surplus labor, was perpetrated by the priests, by means of the trade and taxes of the temple.

After Jesus' execution, the Palestinian movement as a sociohistorical phenomenon in Galilee lost its momentum and was eventually wiped out. However, the story of Jesus and how he had preached God's kingdom of justice and peace did not die, but merely changed its sociohistorical character. It ceased to be a movement of Galilean peasants. Instead it became a heterogeneous international movement throughout the cities and provinces of the Roman Empire, cutting across class lines of rich, middle-class, and poor. Adapting to its new heterogeneous class composition and the diverse historical aspirations of its new adherents, the movement's message now appeared more and more "in a spiritual form—as a heavenly hope," rather than as a historical project with a common aim.[3] In early third-century Rome, the Christian community "included a powerful freedman chamberlain of the emperor; its bishop was the former slave of that freedman; it was protected by the emperor's mistress, and patronized by noble ladies."[4]

However, the early Christian communities were always theoretically egaliterian. Among them there was "no difference between Jew and Greek"; and they "shared all things in common; they would sell their property and goods, dividing everything on the basis of each one's need."[5] Probably the appeal of the new faith was partly owing to its contrast with some of the other cults of the time, which were often so exclusive, and, while offering special means of salvation in the next world, rarely paid a great deal of attention to the position of their devotees in this world. The new faith appealed to those areas of society which were the most fluid—people who felt marginalized, economically, ethnically, or just personally, whether they were have-nots, have-a-littles, or even haves who longed for a new life. During inflationary periods, Christians put their monies not in dead monuments, but in living people. During emergencies they were often the only united group in the town organizing food supplies and arranging the burial of the dead. The state had often washed its hands of the poorer provincials. Its laws declared that even Roman citizens who had been enslaved by barbarians would remain slaves after being bought back by Romans. Thus an increasing number of people felt that to be a Christian offered more protection—because it meant more solidarity with one's "fellows," one's *socii* or *koinōnoi*—than to be a Roman citizen. The persecutions themselves showed that something was gravely amiss in the life of Roman towns, a lack which the new *koinōnia* seemed likely to be able to fill. Thus even on the defensive, even persecuted, Christianity was both a vision and a movement that seemed ready to animate, if not absorb, a whole society. It was putting down firm roots in all the great cities of the Mediterranean, and rapidly becoming the most powerful movement of the time.

However, as it grew, it also became "well-organized" and institutionalized. Even as early as the second century A.D. it often tended to imitate the structure, and sometimes the ideological values, of the Roman state. (Christianity's acceptance of the Roman ownership ideology is a case in point.) Through a growing number of its members, it also showed itself increasingly capable of swimming with the intellectual mainstream and of identifying with the culture, outlook, and needs of the average well-to-do pagan citizen. A new age was heralding Christ as the "Divine Schoolmaster," as Clement of Alexandria called him when lecturing at *didaskaleia*, or study groups, on themes for a new way of living in this world.

The internationalized Christian movement was predominantly urban in its sociological base—an important factor hindering its koinonic society from starting right out as a community of production.[6] The practical *koinōnia* of the first Christians was one of service and consumption, not one of production, conditions for comradely city industry being absent. In agriculture, a *koinōnia* of production would have been more practicable, as earlier Essenism and later monasticism demonstrate.

A salient characteristic of Christian service-*koinōnia* was *eleēmosunē*, or "compassion." The term originally meant the feeling from which the act of giving alms sprang. In time, however, it came to mean almsgiving itself. In the patristic age it signified a substantial transfer of one's own income or property to a fund designed to enable the destitute and socially marginalized to live without suffering absolute want or degradation. A fervent

Christian community, embracing the ideal of *koinōnia*, would undertake a sharing and common management of goods contributed by haves and have-a-littles and destined for the needs of all, especially the sick, the widowed, the orphaned, the aged, the abandoned, and those condemned to the mines or to exile for the faith. While there were no fixed quotas, offerings were expected to be made monthly and were to be proportioned to the donor's income. Thus wealthy members were expected to contribute more, but without having more authority over the disposition of the funds which they contributed: it was the role of the clergy, not that of the donors, to administer the common fund, which eventually came to be the source not only of food, clothing, and shelter for the destitute, but also of cemeteries, houses of worship, and the needs of the clergy themselves.

The longer a Christian community continued to exist, however, the greater its chance to absorb and replicate in itself and its organization the prevailing ideology and practice of the larger society. Once more the Roman law theory-and-practice of ownership is an instance of this, and its acceptance within Christian groups fostered a tendency to transform the primitive Christian concept of an earthly kingdom of God into a heavenly one, to be realized not in this world but beyond it, in "heaven," in "eternal life," after death, or perhaps in an impending millennium. The palpable deterioration of the Empire in the fourth century contributed to a heightened eschatological consciousness in Christian communities. The Last Judgment could be any minute now, and the great ecclesiastical leaders at the end of the fourth and early fifth centuries—Basil, Ambrose, Chrysostom, Augustine—took their responsibility for the readiness of their flock altogether seriously. It is not difficult to sense the urgency of their moralizing, for instance in their strictures on the prevailing, accepted ethic of ownership, which, as we have seen, they viewed very largely as an economics of sin. Shortly now, all might well be standing together before the "fearful judgment seat of Christ."

A sense of the "last things," however, did not incline these leaders to degrade their faith-vision to a religious opiate for a suffering people. Instead of an opiate, eschatology became a leaven for a new ideological attack on injustice, as the fathers confronted the "sinful" gap between the few rich and the many poor. With the earnestness, force, courage, and lucidity of the old prophets, they took a "radical" stance—they went straight to the *root* of the problem, which was the Roman law conception of ownership and wealth, and proposed an alternative consistent with both common sense and their faith-vision.

THE PATRISTIC PHILOSOPHY OF OWNERSHIP

Wealth in Itself Is Good, but the Wealthy Are Thieves

Wealth per se, wealth taken absolutely—the simple abundance of goods—receives no condemnation in patristic thought. "Goods are called goods," Clement of Alexandria says, "because they do good, and they have been provided by God for the good of humanity."[7] "It is not wealth that is evil," says Chrysostom, "for every creature of God is good."[8] And Basil the Great: "Things of this kind are from God: the fertile land, moderate winds, abundance of seeds, the work of the oxen, and other things by which a farm is brought to productivity and wealth."[9] Likewise Ambrose of Milan: "Everything belongs to God—both the seeds and the seedlings that grow at his nod, and are multiplied for the use of humankind. It is God who gives these things."[10] Wealth in itself is not bad, says Augustine, for, in fact "by divine law, the earth and its fullness are the Lord's (Ps. 23:1)."[11] And continuing, as it were, the same thought: "Do you think, then, that it is the fault of silver or gold that people are greedy, or the fault of food and wine that people are gluttons and drunkards, or the fault of female beauty that people are adulterers and fornicators?"[12] Finally, against the exaggerated ascetics of his time who condemned wealth and material goods per se, Clement of Alexandria argued *ad absurdum*, saying that it was God who commanded us "to give drink to the thirsty and bread to the hungry, to receive the homeless and to clothe the naked. And if it is not possible to satisfy these needs except with riches, what else would the Lord be doing than exhorting us to share and not to share? But that would be the height of unreason."[13] Thus the fathers are clear: absolute wealth, riches, or material goods are in themselves good. They are "gifts of God," provided by "God the Giver."

However, while patristic thought considered absolute wealth good in itself, good as all of God's creation is good, it denounced, in the harshest terms, the phenomenon of relative wealth: that is, it denounced the appropriated wealth that differentiated humanity into rich and poor. It could think of the rich-poor cleavage only in terms of a relationship between exploiters and exploited, expropriators and dispossessed.

"Tell me, then," John Chrysostom asks the wealthy, "how did you become rich?"

> From whom did you receive [that large estate], and from whom [did he receive it] who transmitted it to you? . . . The root and origin of it must have been injustice. Why? Because God in the beginning did not make one man rich and another poor. . . . He left the earth free to all alike. Why, then, if it is common, have you so many acres of land, while your neighbor has not a portion of it? . . . Is this not an evil, that you alone should enjoy what is common?[14]

Chrysostom was unwilling to blame contemporary owners for the thefts of their forebears. Nonetheless he denounced them for continuing the act of robbery in the present: "I do not ask you mercifully to render from what you have plundered, but to abstain from fraud. . . . For unless you desist from your robbery, you are not actually giving alms. Even though you should give ever so much money to the needy, if you do not desist from your fraud and robbery you shall be numbered by God among the murderers."[15]

The words are strong, and they did not make Chrysostom popular with the large landowners. Still he kept on: "This is robbery: not to share one's resources. Perhaps what I am saying astonishes you. . . . Not only to rob others' property, but also not to share your own with others, is robbery and greediness and theft. . . . The rich . . . are in possession of the property of the poor, even if it is a patrimony they have received, even if they have gathered their money elsewhere."[16]

Ambrose, too, stressed the causal relationship between wealth and poverty. "Do spacious halls exalt you? They should rather sting you with remorse, because, while they hold crowds, they exclude the cry of the poor. . . . You cover your walls, you strip men naked. . . . A man asks for bread, and your horse champs gold under his teeth. . . . The people are starving, and you close your barns; the people weep bitterly, and you toy with your jewelled ring."[17] Because the few rich have kept their wealth instead of redistributing it, the poor, whose deprivation is the cause of this wealth, have remained poor and miserable.

Basil takes the same position:

Do you think that you who have taken everything into the unlimited compass of your avarice, thereby depriving so many others, have done injury to no one? Who is avaricious? One who is not content with those things which are sufficient [*autarkeia*]. . . . Are you not a robber? You who make your own the things which you have received to distribute? . . . That bread which you keep, belongs to the hungry; that coat which you preserve in your wardrobe, to the naked; . . . that gold which you have hidden in the ground, to the needy.[18]

The approach to ownership taken in patristic thought is primarily a moral-philosophical one. The fathers merely note the purely factual-legal approach to reject it, because they find it inadequate for purposes of changing the unjust reality of so much poverty caused by the accumulation of so much wealth in the hands of so few. Thus Augustine said: "Do we not prove that those who seem to rejoice in lawfully acquired gains, and do not know how to use them, are really in possession of others' property? . . . He who uses his wealth badly possesses it wrongfully, and wrongful possession means that it is another's property. . . . You see, then, how many there are who ought to make restitution of another's goods."[19] These may still be owners from a legal point of view, but in reality they are thieves. "You have received food, and necessary covering. (I say necessary—not useless, not superfluous.) Why do you take more than your riches? Tell me! Surely all your possessions are superfluous. The superfluous things you have may be the necessities of the poor."[20]

Augustine's view had been voiced earlier by Basil the Great: "Do you gird yourself with costly vestments? Is a tunic of two cubits not enough for you . . .? Do you use your riches for mere sumptuous living? And yet one loaf of bread is sufficient to satisfy your stomach. . . ."[21]

Thus the fathers of the Christian Church refused to see wealth and poverty separately. They saw them as a unity of opposites, in causal relationship. The many are poor because a few have succeeded in depriving them.

It has been argued that a widespread belief in the reality of "fate" has helped to separate wealth and poverty in so many minds over so many centuries. Believing that riches were a gift of destiny, both rich and poor could intellectually accept the status quo—the unjust structures which they had inherited and which were maintained and legitimized by the Roman law concept of ownership. Patristic thought, however, ignored mere legality. It was making a moral judgment and proposing a new way of looking at things-as-they-were, from the point of view of things-as-they-ought-to-be.

Individual Ownership of the *Koina* Is Robbery

To our early Christian moral philosophers, then, the relationship between wealth and poverty was most concrete: it was the relationship between the wealthy and the poor. This unbalanced and unjust relationship was maintained by what patristic thought exposed as an essentially unjust concept and practice—the right to and appropriation of the *koina*, the things that should be common to all, by a privileged few.

The fruits of one's labor may be justly appropriated by the laborer. John Chrysostom says, "If you are rich, reflect that you shall be giving an account . . . not only of your expenditures, but also of how you acquired your property: whether you gathered money by just labor, or by robbery and avarice."[22] Basil, too, admits a certain right of laborers to the product of their labor; but he asks the landlords by what right they exercise ownership over their vast estates: "Which things, tell me, are yours? Whence have you brought them into being?" Whatever you have produced, or brought into being, may justly be yours. However, it is land that has made the landlords rich, and land is not something they have brought into being. They have merely "gotten there first," so to speak.

> You are like one occupying a place in a theatre, who should prohibit others from entering, treating that as one's own which was designed for the common use of all. . . . If each one would take that which is sufficient for one's needs, leaving what is in excess to those in distress, no one would be rich, no one poor. Did you not come naked from the womb? Will you not return naked into the earth?[23]

Basil distinguished between *ta idia*, "one's own"—what is one's private property in virtue of one's having brought it into being, as the product of one's labor—and *ta koina*, "common goods," which are just "there," which have been created by God for the use of all. Natural productive elements are not "there" due to anyone's merit or labor. Hence under no conditions may they rightly be treated as *idia*. When certain individuals so treat them, their action, in Basil's view, constitutes nothing less than robbery. Whether by "first occupancy" or force of conquest, they take into their private ownership what should be treated as common for the use of all. Thus they rob others of their common property.

Clement of Alexandria had pointed out much earlier that food, clothing, and shelter-producing resources are there as God's gifts for all, and that their products should therefore be brought "into the common stock for those in need." No one made these resources, he said. "They have been provided by God for the good of all. Indeed, they lie at hand" (they are just "there") "and are put at our disposal as a sort of material and as instruments to be well used."[24]

In Milan, the great Ambrose fulminated from the pulpit: "The story of [land seizures] is old in time but daily in practice. For who of the rich does not daily covet the goods of others?" Mere ownership of the land already puts them in unjust possession of others' property. "Why do you cast out the fellow sharers of nature, and claim it all for yourselves? The earth was made in common for all. . . . Why do you arrogate to yourselves, you rich, exclusive right to the soil?"[25]

In John Chrysostom's words, "God generously gives all things that are much more necessary than money, such as air, water, fire, the sun—all such things. . . . That we may live securely, the causes of virtue are given to us in common.''[26] In Chrysostom's view, then, the fact that the majority of the populace do not ''live securely'' is due to their being deprived of the ''causes of life''— what nature's bounty or nature's God has given for the use of all. Augustine, too, said: ''You have a common universe with the rich. . . . You do have a common sky, a common light. . . . Have you brought along anything hither? No, not even you rich people have brought anything. You have found everything here. With the poor, you were born naked.''[27] Elsewhere Augustine wrote, ''God gives the world to the poor as well as to the rich. Will the rich person have two stomachs to fill because of being rich?''[28]

Inheritance: Transmission and Accumulation of Stolen Goods

Our patristic authors looked at the contemporary situation and then looked into the past. They saw that the laws of inheritance, reflecting the traditional Roman absolutist, exclusivist conception of ownership, provided the vehicle by which stolen *koina* were transmitted to and accumulated in the hands of a few. They rejected the familiar position of the wealthy that the poor were poor because they did not work. John Chrysostom speaks more honestly: ''We accuse the poor of laziness. This laziness is often excusable. We ourselves are often guilty of worse idleness. But you say, 'I have my paternal inheritance!' Tell me, just because he is poor and was born of a poor family possessing no great wealth, is he thereby worthy to die? . . . You are often idling. . . . And do you condemn this poor and miserable person who lives the whole day in entreaties, tears, and a thousand difficulties?''[29]

John goes on: ''Is it by working that you have what you have? Have you not received it as an inheritance from your father? . . . Are all the poor poor through idleness? None from being robbed? None from catastrophe? None from illness? None from any other difficulties?''[30]

The patristic defense of the poor offended and angered the upper classes of the later Roman Empire. The fathers declared that owners had the luxury of idleness because they made their tenants and slaves produce surpluses for their accumulation and lavish consumption. On the other hand, the dispossessed had the shame of idleness because their talents and energy had no access to the natural and social wealth which had been expropriated (legally, of course) by the wealthy few.

Chrysostom was careful not to reject a work ethic altogether. In fact, patristic thought generally emphasized that people are called by God to be "co-creators"; and Chrysostom, for his part, arrestingly pointed out that the children of the rich, too, need a chance to co-create—to produce for themselves and for others, and not be condemned to wallow in the wealth which a private ownership system handed down to them.[31]

Augustine joins John in attacking the easy wealth of inheritance. "For you do not entrust your children to your patrimony better than to your Creator. . . . Why does such a one not give alms? Because he is saving for his children."[32]

Restitution

Patristic thought never discussed a so-called "just compensation" to expropriated landlords. There is nothing to be "compensated." It was a matter of simple justice. "Not from your own do you bestow upon the poor man," said Ambrose, "but you make return from what is his. For what has been given as common for the use of all, you appropriate to yourself alone. The earth belongs to all, not to the rich. . . . Therefore you are paying a debt. . . ."[33] Whatever form it takes, this restitution is a demand of justice, "because the giver knows that God has given all things to all in common. . . . They are just, therefore, who do not retain anything for themselves alone, knowing that everything was given for all."[34] In the Eastern Roman Empire, John Chrysostom concurred: "Do you give to the poor? What you give is not yours, but your Master's, common to you and your fellow-servants."[35] In Africa, Augustine told the people of Hippo: "God gives the world to the poor as well as to the rich. . . . Those who offer something to the poor should not think that they are doing so from what is their own."[36]

Legality is not the question. Justice is the question. The early Christian moral philosophers held that there could be no justice in the matter of private property unless the expropriating rich were to restore to the poor the common goods which they had stolen from them.

Condemnation of Private Ownership

It may come as something of a surprise to us today, but the fact is inescapable: the early Christian moral philosophers simply never held up private property as the ideal way of producing, using, or disposing of wealth. Their voices ring like those of the prophets of old in whose religious tradition they stand: possessions are not a help to salvation.

The reason is clear. Relative wealth is injustice. Indeed, when we come to examine their position more closely, we see that it is not only private ownership in great abundance, but private ownership itself that is reprehended and proscribed. Private ownership caused poverty (it may not have been the only cause, but it was a cause), and it caused poverty by "robbery," "violence," "avarice," "deprivation," "spoliation," and "injustice." Land, after all, was the source of everyone's wealth, not just of that of a few; that was why it had been given by God to be possessed in common by all.

The fathers knew the social and economic situation around them. They knew that whoever (seemingly) owned land, privately, was necessarily the beneficiary of its produce, while the non-owners, who tilled that land which should have been the source of their wealth too, received less than the full amount of that produce of their own hands—indeed, as anyone could see, often only enough to stay physically alive in order to be able to do more tilling. In other words, the unjust differentiation between rich and poor was the product of the expropriation of both the land and the labor power of the workers on the land.

Evil, then, was necessarily at the root of private ownership. But evil was its fruit, as well. Owners were constantly motivated to extend the area of their exploitation by going to war or by other land-seizing enterprises. Augustine, for instance, taught that private ownership was the source of all kinds of "discords."[37] Through the centuries, conflicts—be they wars and revolutions, or the private quarrels of individuals—had in the main centered around having and owning, around "mine" and "thine": for "on account of the things which each one of us possesses singly, wars exist, hatreds, discords, strifes among human beings, tumults, dissensions, scandals, sins, injustices, and murders. . . . Let us therefore abstain from the possession of private property. . . ." And anticipating, as it were, the modern expression "pride of ownership," he adds: "In property which each possesses privately, each necessarily becomes proud. . . . The flesh of the rich person pushes out against the flesh of the poor. . . ."[38]

In the view of John Chrysostom, private ownership was not even natural. "When one attempts to possess himself of anything, to make it his own, then contention is introduced, as if nature herself were indignant."[39] Ambrose, insisting along with our other authors that "avarice must be the cause of our need," explains: "We lose the things that are common when we claim things as our own."[40] Augustine, too, considered private possession a "diminishment" of the possessor, a burden. "The Latin language has wisely called [one's own property] 'private,' for it connotes more a loss than an increase. For all privation is a diminution."[41]

For Ambrose, the notion of private right in the matter of property was unnatural to the point of striking at the root of justice itself. He disputed the traditional Stoic "first duty of justice," considering it as falling too short: "not to harm anyone unless provoked by injury." No, the Gospel, he insisted, had abrogated this, referring to Luke 9:55, where Jesus reprimands his followers for wishing to call down fire from heaven to destroy the Samaritans who had refused to welcome them. Then he went on to reject as well the traditional Stoic "duty of justice to consider the things that are common . . . as public property indeed, and those that are private as private." No, Ambrose said, the possession of private property "is not according to nature, for nature has brought forth all things for all in common. . . . Nature therefore is the mother of common right, usurpation [in the sense of private appropriation] of private right."[42] Private distribution, then, as Augustine was to say, is "by human law, by the law of the Emperors,"[43] and is an abuse.

Private Ownership As Idolatry

How ironic that, only a few score years ago, people who advocated a life of community of goods for society at large tended almost to take it for granted (as of course did their adversaries) that their position was somehow implicitly atheistic, or at least agnostic. After all, it surely seemed to be at odds with institutional religion. How surprised these people would have been had they known that, a millennium-and-a-half before them, the early Christian philosophers had held precisely the contrary. It was private ownership, in the view of the fathers of the Christian Church, that was "atheistic" or "idolatrous." These early social critics never forgot the perfect disjunction that Jesus had set before his own followers: "You cannot give yourself to God and money" (Luke 16:13). Property was a "false god." Property and money had become an object of worship, enslaving both the possessor and the dispossessed. The hoarding of wealth had become a passion that could not be satisfied, an unending process which always demanded more after each new acquisition. The hoarder was identified by these philosophers as the landgrabber, the usurer, the trader, and the political power-holder, and accused of sacrificing both nature and people on the altar of this newly developed god, money, and its veritable religion, the ideology and practice of absolute ownership. Patristic thought found it revulsive that God's creation had been made into property. They refused to make Mammon the supreme reality of human existence.

In the first two centuries of our era, when the new religion called Christianity had first become an international movement, Christians had often preferred torture and death, or the underground life, to the sin of idolatry. Patristic thought now challenged people to see that the Roman law idea of absolutist and exclusivist ownership was just as much a direct affront to the Christian faith-view, that God alone is absolute, and that God alone has absolute *dominium* or *despoteia*. God alone is the one absolute *dominus* or *despotēs* of all things.

Chrysostom tells us that the idea of an absolute human right of ownership amused him to the point of laughter.[44] To him, as we have seen, the notion itself was meaningless.[45] All things were God's—only God's, whose servants we all are together, *sun-douloi* of his. He will require an accounting of our stewardship over his possessions.[46] "Existence itself we have through him, and life, and breath, and light and air, and earth."[47] For "is not 'the earth's God's and the fullness thereof'? If then our possessions belong to one common Lord, they also belong to our fellow servants. The possessions of one Lord are all common."[48] Augustine agreed: "God commands sharing not as being from the property of them whom he commands, but as being from his own property."[49]

How foolish, then, to allow the chattel to usurp the place of the Master. And how insidious: Ambrose held that "just as idolatry endeavors to deprive the one God of his glory, so also avarice extends itself into the things of God, so that, were it possible, it would lay claim to his creatures as exclusively its own. . . ."[50] Basil taught that those who took an exclusivist and absolutist view of property were in fact playing the part of atheists, or godless ones, by leaving God out of their practical life.[51]

Affirmation of Human Equality: Common Origin, Common Nature, Common Destiny

The private ownership by a few of the natural wealth which was made into useful products by the work of many had turned non-owner-workers into mere things. They had become the laboring machine of the privileged few. The workers on the land, for instance, had effectively become part of the landed property itself—an instrument to produce wealth for the few proprietors. As such, the poor were, at worst, carefully exploited and completely disregarded as human existents, or, at best, treated as *objects* of pity rather than as persons with an innate human dignity, the potential subjects of their own co-creative actions. The new idolatry of the propertied few had led to the sacrifice of human beings on the altar of Mammon—the endless pursuit of money or property. Things were thus accorded the dignity of persons, while persons were reduced to the status of things.

Quite in keeping with its tradition of revealed humanism, Christian patristic thought decried this inversion as basically unjust and inhuman, affirming in no uncertain terms the truth of basic human equality with all its consequences. Private property in land could be justifiable only if some human beings had a greater right to existence than others. But, said these moral leaders of long ago, we are all of us here by the equal permission of the Creator, hence we are all here with equal right to breathe the air and use the land and the other productive elements necessary for a decent human existence. Such rights must then be considered our birthright, both guaranteed and proclaimed by the fact of our existence. Our right to the use of the *koiná* must be considered a right vested in each human being entering the world, and limited only by the equal rights of others.

According to Ambrose, we are all "fellow sharers of nature"—*consortes naturae*. But "nature, which begets all poor, does not know the rich."[52] Further: we are all children of one Father. The poor, then, are our brothers and sisters.[53] The universe, for Ambrose as for the prophet Baruch (3:24–25), is "the house of God," and thus belongs to all of us, God's children. "Since therefore [the poor person] is your equal, it is unjust that he is not assisted by his fellow humans—especially since the Lord our God has willed this earth to be the common possession of all and its fruits to support all."[54] And John Chrysostom thundered: "[The poor person] shares the same noble birth with you, and possesses all things in common with you; and yet, oftentimes, he is not even on a level with your dogs."[55]

In northern Africa, Augustine told his people: "The poor and the rich God has made from one mud, and the poor and the rich he sustains on one earth," and it is not by divine or natural law, but "by human law, by the law of the Emperors," that one claims one's land, one's house, or one's servant as private property.[56] Then, on a familiar patristic note, he added: "Consider your origins: both of you [rich and poor] were born naked. . . . You have found many things here—did you bring anything with you?"[57]

In the patristic view, then, the notion of private ownership was contradicted by humanity's common origin and common nature. But humanity has a common destiny, too, and it may have been the heightened eschatological sense of so many Christians of the time—a time of the perceptible decline of Roman imperial fortunes—that occasioned their pastors' emphasis on the destiny of the human species: the destiny of human nature as such, then, and not merely of concrete humanity as historically modified by the manner of life of a particular historical epoch or historical mode of production. Thus the fathers often dwelt on the absolute moral summons of God to humanity: to care for one another, to travel together, to build community. "We are sojourners and pilgrims," said John Chrysostom.[58] "And after all, what is wealth? 'A vain shadow, a dissolving smoke, a flower of the grass,' or something meaner than a flower."[59] It is not lasting, not worth pursuing with all one's might; it is only something useful, and should be used not to divide and destroy common humanity, but to help it, the humanity of each one of us, all co-pilgrims, all down the course of this historical journey of ours, in a manner worthy of our common human dignity.

Augustine said that we must therefore avoid "clinging" to property and learn to *use* it, in a manner consonant with our pilgrim state—for, like it or not, we all must move on. Wealth and poverty are equally burdens, and both burdens should be shared equally by all.[60]

Thus, far from using eschatology as an opiate to help and encourage a suffering people to endure the status quo, patristic thought used it as a premise from which to deduce the need to change the status quo. The injunction to bear one another's burdens, of course, meant a rejection of oligopoly in ownership and an endorsement of *koinōnia*, as we have seen time and again in our texts. Thus it did not mean merely a bit of a lessening in the wealth of the rich few and a weakening of their exclusive control over the *koina*, with a corresponding alleviation of the burden of the poor and the partial restoration of their access to these *koina*. It meant a blanket emancipation of the many poor from conditions of impoverishment, a blanket emancipation of society at large—of all humanity travelling together toward their common destiny—from the burden of wealth and ownership. For this, after all, is what *koinōnia* is.

And if indeed we can overcome our exploitative divisions and achieve human wholeness, "will not the blessing of God pour down on us a thousand-fold richer?" asked John Chrysostom. "Will we not make a heaven on earth?"[61]

No dualistic eschatology of deliverance in another world, this. This is a call for a practical utopia in the here and now.

Twin Goals of Ownership: *Autarkeia* and *Koinōnia*

Our early Christian philosophers had seen that, with each expropriation of nature's bounty and the fruits of workers' labor, owners had gradually accumulated wealth and increased their dominion to a point where that wealth and that dominion enslaved workers and owners alike. For the latter had become slaves of what they owned and of the drive to own more and more. Surely this could not be the right order of things. In the words of Chrysostom: "Money is called *chremata* [from *chraomai*, "I use"] so that we may use it, and not that it may use us. Therefore possessions are so called that we may possess them, and not they possess us. Why do you invert the order?"[62] Augustine, too, held that the owner of money and property falls in love with them, and becomes so enmeshed in them as actually to become subject to them, when of course they ought to be subject to him or her.[63]

And the first power that owners ought to have over their possessions is the capacity to part with them voluntarily—the power to share. But owners have lost this power.

> With that gold you have buried your heart in the earth. . . . Whosoever, therefore, does not use his patrimony as a possession, who does not know how to give and distribute to the poor, is the servant of his wealth and not its master. . . . The man belongs to his riches, not the riches to the man.[64]

The Herculean task of patristic thought was to confront the established ownership concept and stand it on its head. From being an instrument of exclusion and separation it was to become one of inclusion and community building. Instead of an unlimited and absolute power it was to be a limited one, related to genuine human values. Instead of being considered an end in itself it was to be considered a means to certain ends.

"There is, if I may say so," Ambrose declares, "a law of nature that one should seek only what suffices. . . ."[65] Clement of Alexandria, a good century-and-a-half before, had already given a name to this terminal limit. He called it *autarkeia*. "All property," Clement had said, "is ours to use and every possession is for the sake of self-sufficiency [*autarkeia*], which anyone can acquire by a few things."⁶⁶ Property is a means to the relative end of self-sufficiency and self-reliance which keeps one from being a perpetual burden to others. One achieves a degree of self-determination—one becomes relatively self-insured, so to speak, and thereby morally independent, so as to be free for service to others. *Autarkeia* denotes a standard of living that enables one to live a life consonant with human dignity.

Autarkeia can mean a frugality which, paradoxically, as Clement says, "is not at all reluctant to spend money on things it requires and that need to be paid for, for as long a time as the need exists."⁶⁷ Nevertheless, "just as the foot is the measure of the sandal, so the physical needs of each are the measure of what one should possess."⁶⁸ Beyond the limits of *autarkeia*, the holding of property makes no sense in the patristic view. *Autarkeia* implies that ownership of property be subordinated to use, and not be for the sake of "holding" or "keeping" or showing off. Clement says, "Expensiveness should not be the goal in objects whose purpose is usefulness. Why? Tell me, does a table knife refuse to cut if it be not studded with silver or have a handle of ivory?"⁶⁹ And Augustine: "Seek sufficiency, seek what is enough, and more do not seek."⁷⁰ Indeed, "if we seek useless things, nothing suffices."⁷¹

However, the purpose of property, and of wealth, is not only to achieve individual *autarkeia*, but also to attain *koinōnia*, the equal fellowship that abolishes the differentiation between the few rich who live in luxury and, in the words of Clement, "the many who labor in poverty." Patristic thought considered the individual person essentially social. An individual who in no sense lives in society is not truly living at all. In a fundamental sense, it is our relationship with one another that makes us human. "It is God Himself," says Clement, "who has brought our race to a *koinōnia*, by sharing Himself, first of all, and by sending His Word to all alike, and by making all things for all. Therefore everything is common, and the rich should not grasp a greater share."⁷² Or, as Augustine would later say, the wealthy should certainly not be wealthy at the expense of others being poor. In his view, nothing could be more unjust, divisive, and thus destructive of *koinōnia,* than that.

This is the fundamental reason why patristic thought rejected private property: it essentially attacked the social nature of the human being and the personalist character of social relations. The fathers viewed material things as essentially a means of fostering living community. Instead, however, private property had only imposed the impersonal character of things themselves on social relations, especially between owners and those whom the owners excluded from their wealth. Thus, in order to cement *koinōnia,* people would now have to renounce their private ownership of the natural productive elements so that all could share them in common. Their monopoly was no longer to be permitted. If the owners were to have the will, they could help restore the true essence of ownership under God, the one Absolute Owner and Lord.

But realistically, private property was too great a temptation. In fact, not only the upper class landlords themselves, but also the up-and-coming have-a-littles were going to dislike such a "new" style of ownership—*koinōnia*, this "new" way of using and producing the wealth that all people needed equally.

Chrysostom's Practical Program

Their pastors knew people's reluctance where *koinōnia* was concerned, as can be gathered from Chrysostom's major homily on the Acts of the Apostles to the people of Constantinople. Commenting on Acts 4: ". . . Nor was there anyone needy among them, for all who owned property or houses sold them and donated the proceeds"—part of the description of the early Christian movement's life of common ownership—John said:

> Nobody suffered want, that is . . . they gave so willingly that no one remained poor. For they did not give a part, keeping another part for themselves; they gave everything in their possession. They did away with inequality and lived in great abundance; and this they did in the most praiseworthy fashion.

Then, after further describing the early Christian practice of *koinōnia*, Chrysostom added: "Should we do as much today, we should all live much more happily, rich as well as poor; and the poor would not be more the gainers than the rich." Perhaps it was with a patient smile that he continued:

> And if you please, let us now for a while depict it in words, and derive at least this pleasure from it, since you have no mind for it in your actions. . . . Let us imagine things as happening in this way: All give all that they have into a common fund. No one would have to concern himself about it, neither the rich nor the poor. How much money do you think would be collected? I infer . . . a million pounds of gold would be obtained, and most likely two or three times that amount.

"The dispersion of property," Chrysostom now went on to argue "is the cause of greater expenditure and so of poverty."

> Consider a household with man and wife and ten children. . . . Will they need more if they live in a single house or when they live separately? Clearly when they live separately. If the ten sons each go his own way, they need ten houses, ten tables, ten servants, and everything else in proportion. . . . Dispersion regularly leads to waste, bringing together leads to economy. This is how people now live in monasteries and how the faithful once lived. Who died of hunger then? Who was not fully satisfied?

But Chrysostom sensed resistance:

> And yet people are more afraid of this way of life than of a leap into the endless sea. If only we made the attempt and took bold hold of the situation! For if at that time when there were so few faithful, only three to five thousand, if at that time when the whole world was hostile to us and there was no comfort anywhere, our predecessors were so resolute in this, how much more confidence should we have today, when by God's grace the faithful are everywhere!

Chrysostom knew, of course, that his program, however practical and realistic it might be in itself, would scarcely be met with
general enthusiasm. "But yet," he said with optimism, "if we do
but make fair progress, I trust in God that even this shall be realized. Only do as I say, and let us successfully achieve things in
their regular order; if God grant life, I trust that we shall soon be
progressing to this way of life."[73]

The Christian "Social Dropout" Movement

The patristic philosophy of ownership, as we have seen it in
these pages, may have been very far from being matched in
general Christian practice. Nevertheless it was surely uncontested
as the traditional teaching on the subject. People had no doubts
that, originally, this was what Christianity had both taught and
practiced. Nor was there ever a time, during those early centuries
of the Christian era, when any well-informed Christians doubted
that this vision of *koinōnia*, which vision they held as integrally
pertaining to the full practice of their faith and their ideals, of
itself called for implementation in life. It was the kind of vision
whose truth had to be *done*. But even before Constantine had
commandeered the institutional element in the Christian movement in a state Church, that Church had itself, as early as the
middle of the third century, "lowered her standard of life."[74] The
practice of *koinōnia*, while not dead, had begun fading away. It
was becoming a matter of constant, hence indefinite, postpone-
ment. The apparatus of external culture with which the institutional Church had enriched itself had begun to weaken its resistance to the new and more insidious form of idolatry later to be
exposed by Ambrose of Milan.

Another factor undermining the practice of Christian *koinōnia*
was that, in the course of the third century, the Christian movement had become so much more heterogeneous in its sociological
character. Significant Christian elements had entered the Roman
social system and had begun to engage in a dialogue with Greek
philosophy. Christians now tended to be ready to concede things,
to compromise, in so many aspects of life and thought.

But there was a positive facet of all this, as well: in accommo-
dating to the heterogeneity of its members, the Christian move-

ment had opened up to different styles of living out the *koinōnia* that they felt to be implied in their faith-vision. Even scholarly, allegorical Alexandria had failed to prevent simple folk from taking the Gospel literally. Now, as it happened, the Egyptians had a particular term for villagers who had "dropped out" of society in times of oppression or depression: they were called "anchorites," or "displaced persons," as they practiced *anachōrēsis*, or removal to another place, in order to remove themselves from society. They had left their villages to live in the wasteland. Then suddenly they began to do the same thing for what they saw as Christian reasons. One remarkable Egyptian, called Anthony, meditating on the Gospel precepts, concluded that, given society as it was, one would now have to "drop out" of it merely in order to live the Christian life. Others agreed, and a whole movement of Christian "dropouts" began, motivated by Christian faith and ideals. This is the movement that eventually became Christian monasticism. It was based on the idea that the only really effective way to resist the "god Mammon" and embrace true *koinōnia* was to drop out of the "civilized" life of the Empire and start afresh.

The movement we are describing coincided with the general awareness of the age that a great epoch in human history was passing away. The Roman Empire was dying. The great moral leaders of the fourth century—Basil the Great, Augustine of Hippo, and John Chrysostom among them—themselves actively promoted this "dropout movement," and thousands upon thousands of people began to lead a communal life and renounce private property. Thus monasteries served to sharpen popular consciousness of both the Christian koinonic ideal and the social character of the human being as such. They recruited the unemployed and the chronically underemployed and gave them a life of contemplation and *koinōnia*, affording them the opportunity to work in the service of the larger community besides. Hospitals, food-supply centers, and burial associations sprang up, all products of the grassroots labor of the "monks and nuns," as they had come to be called. During the barbarian invasions it was they who organized the ambulance services, to remove the wounded from the field of battle and nurse them back to health as best they could.[75] Basil the Great, for example, as we have seen, established communities within cities, or near them, for a remarkable work

of social service. He also established centers for the laity alongside his monasteries, both to serve as schools for training recruits
and for active work in the community at large. For Basil, as for so
many other pastors and earnest lay Christians, "dropping out"
of Roman society was not to be a substitute for work. Indeed,
Basil taught, one could actually pray while working—in agriculture, weaving, shoemaking, woodworking, metal-working, and
building.[76]

As time went on, the endeavors of the monks and nuns broad-
ened. They began to clear forests, turn deserts into fertile fields,
and even study the "heathen" poets, historians, and philosophers. Settlement after settlement became the center of vibrant
Christian life in a whole countryside.[77]

Bound to embrace but a small part of society, as it comported a
life of celibacy, the great monastic movement nonetheless became
a mighty force in history. Indeed, there were times when it included a large minority of the population indeed. But most important for our purposes, it became one way of demonstrating the
practicability of the koinonic ideal. To be sure, the experiment
would eventually be marred by authoritarianism, as well as by an
elitism springing in part from its minority status in society. Still, it
was one epoch's practical expression of the patristic philosophy
of ownership, and it was an expression that has well outlived the
epoch. If Christian society at large refused to answer the call of
the fathers to a life of *autarkeia* and *koinōnia*, at least a part of
that society did not.

Conclusion

> *They shall live in the houses they*
> *build,*
> *and eat the fruit of the vineyards*
> *they plant;*
> *They shall not build houses for*
> *others to live in,*
> *or plant for others to eat.*
> *—Isaiah 65:21*

The fourth century of the Christian era is no more than a mere twenty-five human lifetimes away. But during those twenty-five human lifetimes humanity has seen many different forms and degrees of producing and reproducing its material life. These means have changed in so many ways—from oxen and primitive ploughs to tractors and combines, from carts and chariots to trains, jets, and space shuttles, from fragile parchments to sophisticated computers, from manual piecework to assembly lines, mechanization, and cybernetics.

With few exceptions, however, the relationships of production underlying these tremendous productive forces have remained basically the same as they were during the patristic period of the Roman Empire. In other words, through all the dramatic changes in the means of production, the substance of ownership has remained unchanged. For the most part, in fact, we in the last quarter of the twentieth century are still mired in the old Roman law theory and practice of ownership.

From primitive accumulation to the development of industrial capital, the evolution of private ownership itself has been an extensive process. But the process has been a continuous one, from the Roman *latifundia* to present-day monopoly-capital as exemplified in the global hegemony of transnational corporations. First, nonowner-worker-producers were denied free access to the *koina*; then they were denied the product of their intellectual and physical energies; then they were denied the tools of their trade. Through those centuries, the original form of profit, which was rent on land, was compounded by other forms of surplus extraction from the nonowner-workers. The stored-up labor of past worker generations became the property or capital of the heirs of past owners. Together with the monopoly of the natural productive elements, "dead labor," labor as a thing, labor as property, became the chief means of expropriating the surplus labor power of the living persons who are workers. As owners of nothing, the latter could only sell their labor power as the price of material survival. Thus property accumulation by the owners increased, giving them even more power over the nonowner-producers—a theme which became the subject of treatises by the political economists of the eighteenth, nineteenth, and twentieth centuries.

This accumulation of property or capital necessarily involved force—violence, enslavement, robbery, murder—exactly as Augustine of Hippo had said it would. It meant, as Ambrose saw, that a few would try to own the whole world themselves. And, as so many feared, the new idolatry—the supremacy of Property or Capital—replaced people-to-people relationships with relationships between human beings and things (commodities). Nature itself, as John Chrysostom intoned, was becoming indignant at being turned into property—used, abused, endlessly violated in the extraction of wealth by the insatiable avarice of owners whose total disregard for natural thresholds had become a threat to the very life of natural systems, indeed of the earth itself.

Thus an attack was mounted on the absolutist and exclusivist ideological conception of ownership as set forth in Roman law. The political and social form of the early Christian movement was really communism or socialism—communism (from the Latin *communis*, in Greek *koinos*) if you emphasize the common nature of property, socialism (from the Latin *socius*, in Greek *koinōnos*) if you underscore the fellowship or community which common proprietorship furthered. Long before the twentieth-century status quo found an excuse in "atheistic materialism" for an attack on socialism, it was precisely the rejection of *koinōnia,* or socialism, that Christianity had considered to be practically atheistic and idolatrous. However, the earliest Christian experiments in *koinōnia* did not endure, because the first Christians were too few in number to bring about the transformation of the whole socioeconomic system in which they lived.

By the fourth century, Christian numbers had grown, however, as John Chrysostom pointed out in his practical outline for the realization of socialism in Constantinople. And yet at the same time the institutional aspect of the Christian movement had now begun to be converted into Roman power, Roman organization, and Roman law. Fatigued by three centuries of intermittent persecutions, with their tortures and executions, and generally leading, or preparing to lead, an underground life, the institutional leaders of the Christian movement decided to accept an alliance of power with the Roman Empire. This tragic decision, ironically, may have been based in part on Pope Sylvester's suspicion that Christ would take more time than had previously been thought to come back to judge the living and the dead. To be sure, belief in the return of Christ would always be part of the faith, and, under certain conditions, would assume a warped, millenarianist shape among the elements of that faith for certain Christians. Nonetheless, pragmatic ecclesiastical leaders were simply unable to refuse this unholy alliance, and probably for the "holiest" of reasons, namely, the more expeditious propagation of the faith. But in time, as Church properties accumulated and political and even military powers were assumed by Church authorities, it was inevitable that the essentially socialist content of their faith-vision would fade away.

Thus the message of the primitive Church and the patristic philosophy of ownership, both of which contradicted the practices of the institutional Church, were progressively buried and forgotten, or else relegated to a world of uncrucifiable generalities and highly spiritualized realities. In any case, now the early Christian socialist doctrine would become one of institutional Christianity's best-kept secrets.

But the Spirit breathes where it wills, as Jesus said it would, and the message has been taken up and proclaimed again and again, by other prophets of other times and places, prophets as differently regarded by the institutional Churches as Thomas More and Karl Marx. Indeed, as humanity travels through the last part of the twentieth century, it seems to be becoming more and more aware of the danger that the logic of private property may lead the species, and planet Earth, to total destruction. There would thus seem to be no escaping the warning of these prophets through the centuries that the welfare of human *being* depends on the justice of human *having*.

The signs are clear now. The peasantry of the Third World seek liberation from landlordism and corporate farming. Urban factory workers seek a direct people's control of the means of production. Both of these sectors of the masses demand the kinds of tools that respect natural thresholds, or the balance of nature. People are weary of being reduced to the status of things, and will have liberation from all manner of slavery, even slavery with golden chains. Workers in industrial countries see only a difference of form and degree between their enslavement and that of the bonded laborers of India or the migrant workers of the Philippines. Nations look for liberation from the clutches of all manner of imperialism and neo-colonialism. In short, the Roman law theory and practice of ownership, which has formed the basis successively of the slave-owning, the feudal, the private capitalist, and the state capitalist economic systems, today is being rejected with increasing determination. The alternative ideal of a new dispensation based on a view of property as a means to the ends of *autarkeia* and *koinōnia* is fast receiving a welcome from peoples, nations, and whole regions of the earth. Area by area—in agriculture, forestry, fisheries, industry, commerce, and the services, in the tools which produce both tangible commodities and intangible ones like education and health, and across the gamut of institutions fundamentally twisted and distorted by avarice—the unjust, obsolete concept of private property is being questioned and concrete alternatives are being explored.

Ever louder and clearer has the clamor become to establish a new economy of relative permanence—an economy whose foundation and goals rest upon activities generating goods and services essential to a life of human dignity, rather than one mainly geared to the production of consumer commodities peripheral to human life or, worse still, to the destruction of life. Such a new economy, that would be totally involved with life-sustaining productivity will be the only stable one. In fact, it will be as sound and strong as the undeniable aspiration of every man and woman for greater life and freedom.

Indeed the awareness is becoming more widespread that the physical and spiritual goods and services essential to life are more than mere fads, and therefore have a lasting urgency transcending all pressures and fluctuations, even those caused by natural catastrophes and the tragic foolishness of war. Hence, that economy alone will enjoy relative permanence which is based on the demand for life-sustaining productivity—an economy in which individual persons are allowed to achieve *autarkeia*, and in which society as a whole has become a *koinōnia*, that is, a community of communities that is finally in charge of its own human destiny rather than being merely determined by the mad drive of exploitative property/capital toward limitless growth at whatever cost.

Justice will then be realized when humanity has effectively rejected the idolatry of property; and with justice, the exciting project of freedom and peace can have a realistic chance.

The Old Testament "prophets of doom" were arrestingly optimistic, as were the Christian philosophers of the patristic age. Perhaps they deserve to be listened to, for perhaps indeed the people "shall live in the houses they build, and eat of the fruit of the vineyards they plant" (Isaiah 65:21).

Notes

CHAPTER 1

1. Ugo Vigilino, I.M.C., "The Social Function of Property and Its Metaphysical Foundation," *Theology Digest* 1-2 (1953-54): 164.

2. *Encyclopedia Americana* (New York: Americana, 1963), 21:67.

3. Austin Fagothey, *Right and Reason* (Saint Louis: Mosley, 1953), p. 334.

4. Ibid.

5. *Encyclopedia Americana*, 22:660.

6. Cf. Henry George, *Progress and Poverty* (New York: Schalkenbach Foundation, 1954), passim. This monumental work, subtitled, "An Inquiry into the Cause of Industrial Depressions and of Increase of Want with Increase of Wealth . . . the Remedy," was first published in January 1880. It was translated into the chief languages of Europe and may have sold more than five million copies through the years. The past three decades, however, had fairly consigned it to oblivion, except perhaps for esoteric use on the part of professional political economists. On first reading Henry George, almost twenty years ago when doing research for this volume, I was particularly struck by the similarity of his arguments, and even analogies, to those of the fourth-century Christian social philosophers on the topic of land ownership.

7. Cf. Stephen Fuchs, *Social Origins* (Bombay: Gyaneyatan, 1957), pp. 94 ff.

8. Emile de Laveleye, *Primitive Property,* cited in George, *Progress and Poverty,* p. 370.

9. Hilaire Belloc, "Land Tenure in the Christian Era," in *The Catholic Encyclopedia* (New York: Universal Knowledge Foundation, 1913), 8:775.

10. De Laveleye, *Primitive Property.*

11. John C. H. Wu, *Fountain of Justice* (New York: Sheed and Ward, 1955), p. 4.

12. Benjamin Cardozo, *The Growth of the Law* (New Haven, Conn.: Yale University Press, 1924), pp. 23-26.

13. Cf. George, *Progress and Poverty,* pp. 364–67.

14. Bertrand Russell, *A History of Western Philosophy* (New York: Simon and Schuster, 1965), p. 335.

15. Berthold Altaner, *Patrology,* translated by Hilda C. Graef (Freiburg: Herder and Herder, 1960), p. 1.

16. "What is philosophy? Philosophy is not easily identified as a single and distinct branch of study, and philosophers themselves have never agreed upon any clear definition of their subject. Instead, the question, 'What is philosophy?' is itself a philosophic question, likely to be answered in somewhat different ways by philosophers belonging to different schools of thought." C. I. Lewis, "Philosophy," in *Encyclopedia Americana,* 21:67.

17. Ryan mentions Bebel's *Die Frau*, de Laveleye's *Le socialisme contemporain*, and Nitti's *Catholic Socialism* (John A. Ryan, *Alleged Socialism of the Church Fathers* [Saint Louis: Herder, 1913] in the Foreword).

18. Ibid.

19. F. Klueber, *Eigentumstheorie und Eigentumspolitik* (Osnabruck: Fromm, 1963), p. 86.

20. L. W. Countryman, *The Rich Christian in the Church of the Early Empire* (New York, Toronto: Mellen, 1980).

21. Case belonged to the so-called Chicago School of sociohistorical scholarship, which insisted that no dichotomy could be made between faith and history, and that early Christian faith must be seen in relationship to sociocultural factors.

22. To be acknowledged at the outset are Michael Rostovtzeff, *The Social and Economic History of the Roman Empire* (London: Oxford University Press, 1957); A. H. M. Jones, *The Later Roman Empire, 284–602: A Social, Economic and Administrative Survey,* 2 vols. (Norman, Oklahoma: University of Oklahoma Press, 1964); Ramsay MacMullen, *Roman Social Relationships: 50 B.C. to A.D. 284* (New Haven, Conn.: Yale University Press, 1974); John B. Bury, *A History of the Later Roman Empire* (London, New York: Macmillan, 1889); Peter Brown, *The World of Late Antiquity: A.D. 150–750* (London: Thames and Hudson; New York: Harcourt Brace Jovanovich, 1971); and Abraham J. Malherbe, *Social Aspects of Early Christianity* (Baton Rouge: Louisiana State University Press, 1977).

CHAPTER 2

1. The Emperor Justinian's commissioners, in preparing their legal digest, "read close to 2,000 separate works, written by about forty authors and ranging from short treatises on special topics to great com-

mentaries covering the whole field of law: the whole material totalled 3,000,000 lines or over twenty times the length of the digest" (Jones, *Later Roman Empire*, 1:470).

2. Alan Watson, *The Law of the Ancient Romans* (Dallas: Southern Methodist University Press, 1970), p. 3.

3. Ibid.

4. H. F. Jolowicz and Barry Nicholas, *Historical Introduction to the Study of Roman Law*, 3rd ed. (Cambridge: Cambridge University Press, 1972), p. 139.

5. Ibid. Cf. also George, *Progress and Poverty*, passim.

6. Jolowicz and Nicholas, *Roman Law*, passim.

7. Ibid., p. 140.

8. Fritz Schulz, *Classical Roman Law* (Oxford: Clarendon, 1954), p. 339.

9. W. W. Buckland and Peter Stein, *A Textbook of Roman Law from Augustus to Justinian* (Cambridge: Cambridge University Press, 1966), p. 188.

10. Ibid.

11. Watson, *Law of the Ancient Romans*, passim.

12. Ibid.

13. Jolowicz and Nicholas, *Roman Law,* p. 138.

14. Ibid.

15. Cf. Karl Kautsky's excellent *Der Ursprung des Christentums: Eine historische Untersuchung*, translated by Henry F. Mins as *Foundations of Christianity* (New York: Russell and Russell, 1953).

16. Ibid.

17. There were few restrictions on the rights of even this mode of proprietorship. Romulus, Rome's legendary founder, it was held, had decreed that the *paterfamilias* might not put to death any of his children under the age of three except malformed newborns who had been exhibited to at least five neighbors, and this prohibition was still in force. Otherwise Roman law gave the father absolute power of life and death over his children and their children. He could sell them into slavery, command or veto a marriage, or insist on a divorce. All property of children belonged to their father until his death. This *patria potestas* was wielded over children both natural and adopted, and even if a son attained to the highest offices of state he was still in the absolute power of his father. This power could be terminated only by death or emancipation. Emancipation was accomplished by ritually selling the son three times to a consenting friend and seeing him "freed" after each sale. At the last repurchase—for the father must "buy him back" each time—the father would "manumit" the son just as he would free a slave, and thus empower the

son to become a *paterfamilias* in his own right. Only one ritual sale-and-repurchase was needed for daughters and other descendants. Cf. Watson, *Law of the Ancient Romans.*

The patriarchal character of Roman law was in marked contrast to the economic society of earlier agrarian peoples from about 2,300 B.C. on, according to Merlin Stone, *When God Was a Woman* (New York: Harcourt Brace Jovanovich, 1978). Material produced by extensive archaeological excavation in the twentieth century in the Near and Middle East tends to confirm the theory advanced by late nineteenth- and early twentieth-century scholars like Johann Bachofen, Robert Briffault, and Edward Hartland that matrilineality was a specific stage in the evolutionary development of the phenomenon of property. In many early societies, the mother or female kin structure, which was the polyandric producer of offspring and the producer of food and shelter, naturally led to a matrilineal code of descendancy of name and property.

18. Cf. Kautsky, *Foundations*, pp. 36–44.

19. Cf. Bury, *Later Roman Empire*, 1:25–28.

20. Ibid.

21. Jones, *Roman Empire*, 2:769–70.

22. Ibid.

23. Ibid., 2:781.

24. Ibid., 2:772.

25. As quoted ibid., 2:797, from *Codex Justiniani,* XI, *lviii*, 1, 371.

26. Bury, *Later Roman Empire*, 1:27.

27. Jones, *Roman Empire*, 1:358.

28. Ibid., 1:802.

29. John Chrysostom, *In Matthaeum Homilia*, 61–63, *PG* 58:591, quoted in Jones, *Roman Empire*, 2:805. See our Appendix, pp. 186–87.

30. Libanius as quoted in Jones, *Roman Empire*, 1:811.

31. E. Thompson, *Past and Present,* 2:18–19. Cited in Jones, *Roman Empire*, 2:812.

32. Ambrose, *De Officiis Ministrorum,* 3, 7, *PL* 16:158–59.

CHAPTER 3

1. Johannes Quasten, *Patrology* (Westminister, Md.: Newman, 1950), 2:6.

2. F. Cayré, *Manual of Patrology and History of Theology* (Tournai: Desclee, 1936), p. 178.

3. Igino Giordani, *The Social Message of the Early Church Fathers* (Paterson, N.J.: St. Anthony, 1957), pp. 285 ff.

4. Quasten, *Patrology*, 2:7.

5. Rostovtzeff, *Roman Empire*, p. 285.

6. Giordani, *Social Message*, p. 266.

7. Ibid.

8. "The Educator," 2, 3, *PG* 8:437 (in S. P. Wood, *Clement of Alexandria* [New York: Fathers of the Church, 1954], p. 128).

9. Cf. Wood, *Clement of Alexandria*, p. xvi. Cf. also Eduard Zeller, *Outlines of the History of Greek Philosophy* (New York: Meridian, 1955), pp. 237 ff.

10. Cf. Wood, *Clement of Alexandria*, p. xvii; C. P. Parker, "Musonius in Clement," *Harvard Studies in Classical Philosophy* 12 (1901):191–200; Emile Bréhier, *The Hellenistic and Roman Age* (Chicago: University of Chicago Press, 1965), pp. 236–38. "Clement casts Christianity in its entirety in the mold of Greek philosophical instruction. . . . And when we examine the details of his teaching, we see that his *Paedogogus* . . . is constructed like a Stoic treatise on ethics" (Bréhier, *Roman Age*, p. 237).

11. "The Educator," 2, 3, *PG* 8:436 (in Wood, *Clement of Alexandria*, p. 128—emphasis ours).

12. Ibid., 2, 12, *PG* 8:541 (Wood, *Clement*, p. 191).

13. Ibid., cols. 541–44 (Wood, *Clement*, pp. 192–93).

14. Jolowicz and Nicholas, *Roman Law*, pp. 142–43, 158. The right of ownership could also be conditioned extrinsically, when the convenience of the public necessitated some positive restriction. For instance, there were the so-called *iura in re aliena*, such as rights of way, rights of drawing water or taking it across the lands of another, rights of pasturage, or the right of preventing a neighbor from increasing the height of his or her house or obstructing access to light. By and large, however, the common mentality and the accepted ethic of property is accurately expressed by Clement in our passage 2B.

15. *Meditations*, 5, 1 (in Whitney J. Oates, ed., *The Stoic and Epicurean Philosophers* [New York: Random House, 1940], p. 517).

16. Cf. Johannes Hirschberger, *The History of Philosophy*, translated by Anthony N. Fuerst (Milwaukee: Bruce, 1958), 1:237.

17. Ibid., pp. 225–26.

18. Epictetus, *Discourses*, 1, 13 (in Oates, *Stoic and Epicurean Philosophers*, pp. 249–50).

19. *On the Gospel of John*, 13, 21 (in Bréhier, *Hellenistic and Roman Age*, p. 53).

20. "The Educator," 2, 12, *PG* 8:540 (in Wood, *Clement*, p. 191).

21. Cf. E. Bréhier, 63; Zeller, *Outlines*, pp. 237ff.

22. "The Educator," 3, 7, *PG* 8:609 (in Wood, *Clement*, p. 231).

23. Ibid., 3, 8, *PG* 8:612 (in Wood, *Clement*, p. 233).

24. G. W. Butterworth, tr., *Clement of Alexandria: The Exhortation to the Greeks; The Rich Man's Salvation; To the Newly Baptized* (London: Heinemann, 1953), p. 267.

25. Ibid., p. 271.

26. "The Rich Man's Salvation," 12-13, *PG* 9:616-17 (in Butterworth, *Clement,* p. 295).

27. Ibid., 13, *PG* 9:617 (Butterworth, p. 297).

28. Ibid., 14, *PG* 9:617 (Butterworth, p. 299).

29. Ibid., 16, *PG* 9:620 (Butterworth, p. 303).

30. Ibid., 31, *PG* 9:637 (Butterworth, p. 337).

31. Giordani, *Social Message,* p. 271.

32. Ibid., passim.

CHAPTER 4

1. Cayré, *Patrology,* p. 409.

2. Ryan, *Alleged Socialism,* p. 23.

3. Cayré, *Patrology,* p. 410.

4. Altaner, *Patrology,* p. 337.

5. Cayré, *Patrology,* pp. 409 and passim.

6. Jolowicz and Nicholas, *Roman Law,* p. 455.

7. *Homilia in illud Lucae, "Destruam . . . ,"* 7, *PG* 31:276 (translated in Ryan, *Alleged Socialism,* pp. 8-9).

8. Ibid., cols. 276-77 (translated in Ryan, *Alleged Socialism,* p. 9). Some of the same lines are to be found in *Sermo IV de Eleemosyna,* 3, *PG* 32:1158.

9. *Homilia in Divites,* 8, *PG* 31:281 (translated in Ryan, *Alleged Socialism,* p. 7).

10. *Homilia in illud Lucae, "Destruam . . . ",* 1, *PG* 31:261-64.

11. In his Foreword, for instance, Ryan writes: "Certain Socialists are fond of asserting that the Fathers of the Church denied the right of private property and defended common ownership. The only basis for the claim is some passages cited more or less correctly by Bebel, de Laveleye, and Nitti."

12. Consider, for instance, one paragraph that precedes the analysis proper: "None of the Fathers either explicitly or implicitly denied the right of private property. In the first place, all the doubtful passages can and should be explained in a sense consistent with the belief in private ownership; and, in the second place, there are other passages in the writings of these Fathers which show beyond question that such was their belief" (*Alleged Socialism,* p. 18).

13. W. F. Arndt and F. W. Gingrich, trs., *A Greek-English Lexicon of the New Testament and Other Early Christian Literature* (Chicago: University of Chicago Press, 1957). A translation of Walter Bauer's German original.

14. "The rich and the poor are easy to recognize: the former, by their excessive possession of the necessities of life, and the latter, by their want of them" (*Homilia in Psalmum XLVIII, PG* 29:433).

15. Arndt and Gingrich, *Lexicon.*

16. George, *Progress and Poverty*, passim.

17. Ibid., p. 344.

18. "Homily 2 on Psalm 14," 1, in Agnes C. Way, tr., *Exegetical Homilies* (Washington: Fathers of the Church, 1963), p. 183 *PG* 29:268.

19. *Sermo IV de Eleemosyna*, 1, *PG* 32:1153–56.

CHAPTER 5

1. The praetorian prefects were not merely chiefs of staff whose business it was to assist the emperor. They were to act, in principle, *vice versa:* not with the emperor, but in his stead. Cf. Jolowicz and Nicholas, *Roman Law*, p. 439.

2. This title did not imply that the bearer actually held the consulship, but merely denoted a governor, or *praeses*. Cf. ibid.

3. Augustine, *Confessions*, 6, 3.

4. Rostovtzeff straightforwardly calls them capitalists (*Roman Empire*, pp. 174, 205, 283, 536–39, 543, and passim—see his Index, p. 767), which may sound anachronistic for this period, and yet it is a fact that, although the mode of production in the Roman Empire could scarcely be considered to have been a capitalist one, nonetheless there were real capitalists investing in that production. At first the capitalistic enterprises were in the mines and quarries, where slave labor was used: no one maintains a mining industry for purposes of acquiring goods for one's personal needs alone, since no mine operation could be small enough for just this. Later, the *latifundia* were capitalist operations, maintained and cultivated to produce profit in the form of money for their owners, and not merely to produce goods for these owners' own consumption.

5. Martin R. P. McGuire, *S. Ambrosii De Nabuthe Jezraelita: A Commentary with an Introduction and Translation* (Washington, D.C.: Catholic University of America Press, 1927), pp. 2–3.

6. Ibid. McGuire mentions Schenkle in particular, who has indicated almost all the borrowed passages in his edition of the Vienna corpus—

and adds Forster, Ihm, and Kellner, who also observe Ambrose's indebtedness to classical authors, especially Sallust, Cicero, and Virgil, which "in the light of his training . . . is by no means surprising" (ibid., p. 6). Ryan, *Alleged Socialism*, p. 62, has noted the similarity of Ambrose's views and those of Basil.

7. *De Nabuthe*, 1, *PL* 14:731 (in McGuire, *De Nabuthe*, p. 47).

8. Ibid., col. 732 (McGuire, ibid.).

9. Hirschberger, *History of Philosophy,* p. 234.

10. Ibid., p. 233.

11. By "nature," the Stoics meant both the universe, and more particularly, human nature. Both senses are expressed by the same term. Cf. Frederick Mayer, *A History of Ancient and Medieval Philosophy* (New York: Americana, 1950), p. 238.

12. *Hexaemeron*, 5, 26, *PL* 14:217.

13. *De Nabuthe*, 5, *PL* 14:738 (McGuire, p. 63).

14. Ibid., 11, col. 748 (McGuire, p. 190).

15. McGuire, *De Nabuthe*, p. 189.

16. Ibid.

17. *De Nabuthe*, 3, *PL* 14:734 (McGuire, p. 53).

18. Ibid.

19. Ibid., 11, *PL* 14:747 (McGuire, p. 83).

20. Ibid., 14, *PL* 14:749 (McGuire, pp. 87-89).

21. Ibid., 15, *PL* 14:751 (McGuire, p. 93).

22. Ibid., 7, *PL* 14:741 (McGuire, pp. 69-70).

23. Ibid., cols. 741-42. (McGuire, p. 71).

24. *De Officiis Ministrorum,* 1, 11, *PL* 16:34.

25. Hirschberger, *History of Philosophy*, pp. 231-33.

26. *De Officiis Ministrorum*, 1, 11, *PL* 16:34-35.

27. *Hexaemeron*, 5, 26, *PL* 14:217 (in John J. Savage, *St. Ambrose: Hexaemeron, Paradise and Cain and Abel* [New York: Fathers of the Church, 1961], p. 181).

28. Ibid., 6, 52, *PL* 14:263 (in Savage, p. 265).

29. *Expositio Evangelii secundum Lucam*, 7, 124, *PL* 15:1731.

30. Cf. Hirschberger, *History of Philosophy*, pp. 233 ff.

31. Marcus Aurelius, *Meditations*, 5, 1 (in Oates, *Stoic and Epicurean Philosophers,* p. 517).

32. *In Psalmum CXVIII Expositio*, 8, 22, *PL* 15:1303 (translated in Ryan, *Alleged Socialism*, p. 15).

33. *De Officiis Ministrorum*, 1, 28, *PL* 16:61-62.

34. See "usurpo" and "usurpatio" in *Cassell's Latin Dictionary*, revised by J. R. V. Marchant and J. F. Charles (New York: Funk & Wagnall, 1959).

35. Therefore if an individual claims proprietorship of material goods to the exclusion of others, who enjoy the same basic right to nature's bounty, he or she distorts the essence of the right of ownership, which is but a means to an end: "Cur proprium id quod in saeculo est, putes, cum commune sit saeculum? Aut cur privatos terrae deputes fructus, cum terra communis sit?" ("Why do you deem what is in this world to be yours alone, when this world is common? Why do you consider the fruits of the earth as private, when the earth is common?") *De Viduis*, 1, *PL* 16:236.

36. *Commentarium in Epistolam II ad Corinthios*, 9, 9, *PL* 17:313–14.

37. Ibid.

38. This is the Ciceronian meaning of *retribuere*, which is most probably also Ambrose's. Cf. Cassell's Latin Dictionary.

39. *Commentarium in Epistolam ad Colossenses*, 3, 5, *PL* 17:435.

CHAPTER 6

1. Bury, *Later Roman Empire*, p. 95. The sources for the other biographical details here are Cayré, *Patrology*, pp. 461 ff.; Quasten, *Patrology*, 2:424 ff.; and Altaner, *Patrology*, pp. 373 ff.

2. *De Lazaro Concio*, 2, 4, *PG* 48:987–88.

3. Ibid., col. 988.

4. Cf. *In Ioannem Homilia*, 63, 1, *PG* 59:349.

5. *De Virginitate*, 68, *PG* 48:584–85.

6. *Ad Populum Antiochenum Homilia* 2, 6–7, *PG* 49:43.

7. *In Dictum Pauli, "Oportet Haereses Esse,"* 2, *PG* 51:255.

8. *Peccata Fratrum Non Evulganda*, 2, *PG* 51:355.

9. *In Inscriptionem Altaris et in Principium Actorum*, 1, 2, *PG* 51:69. Cf. *In Ioannem Homilia* 19, 3, *PG* 59:123–24.

10. Cf. Gerhard Kittel, *Theological Dictionary of the New Testament* (Ann Arbor, Mich.: Eerdmans, 1964–76), 9:261.

11. *In Epistolam ad Romanos*, 7, 9, *PG* 60:453.

12. *De Eleemosyna*, 6, *PG* 51:269.

13. Ibid.

14. *In Epistolam ad Hebraeos*, 11, 3, *PG* 63:94 (translated in Philip Schaff, ed., *A Select Library of the Nicene and Post-Nicene Fathers of the Christian Church* [New York: Scribner's, n.d.], p. 421).

15. Ibid.

16. *In Matthaeum*, 77, 4, *PG* 58:707 (Schaff, p. 466).

17. *De Lazaro Concio*, 2, 5, *PG* 48:988. Cf. *In Epistolam I ad Corinthios*, 10, 2, *PG* 61:84.

18. *Ad Populum Antiochenum*, 2, 6, *PG* 49:42.

19. *De Poenitentia*, 7, 7, *PG* 49:336.

20. *In Capitulum XV Genesis,* 37, 5, *PG* 53:348.

21. *De Decem Millium Talentorum Debitore,* 4, *PG* 51:22.

22. *De Verbis Apostoli, "Habentem Eumdem Spiritum,"* 3, 11, *PG* 51:299.

23. *In Epistolam I ad Timotheum,* 12, 4, *PG* 62:562–63 (in Schaff, *Nicene Fathers,* pp. 447–48).

24. Ibid., *PG* 62:563–64.

25. Cf. Jolowicz and Nicholas, *Roman Law,* p. 142.

26. *In Epistolam I ad Corinthios,* 10, 3, *PG* 61:85 (in Schaff, *Nicene Fathers,* p. 57).

27. *In Epistolam ad Hebraeos,* 11, 3, *PG* 63:93–94 (Schaff, p. 420).

28. *In Joannem,* 33, 3, *PG* 59:192 (Schaff, p. 118).

29. *In Acta Apostolorum,* 25, 4, *PG* 60:196 (Schaff, p. 166).

30. Ibid., 11, 3 *PG* 60:96–98. Cf. Kautsky, *Foundations,* pp. 357–59; Way, *Exegetical Homilies,* pp. 161–63.

CHAPTER 7

1. *Confessions,* 3, 4, *PL* 32:685.

2. Ibid., 9, 8, *PL* 32:771.

3. *Epistola CXXVI,* 7, *PL* 33:479–80.

4. Rostovtzeff, *Roman Empire,* pp. 311–42.

5. Eugene Portalie, *A Guide to the Thought of Saint Augustine* (London: Burnes and Oates, 1960), p. 241.

6. E.g., *De Beata Visione, PL* 32:959–76; *De Moribus Ecclesiae,* 1, 3–15, *PL* 32:1312–22.

7. *Confessions* 2, 6; 4, 12; 5, 4; 10, 1–43 (*PL* 32:680, 700–701, 708–709, 779–810).

8. *On the Trinity,* 12, 4–7, *PL* 42:1000–1005.

9. *City of God,* 14, *PL* 41:403–36; 19, *PL* 41:621–58.

10. E.g., *In Psalmum CXVIII Enarratio,* 1, 12, 13–14, 19 (*PL* 37: 1501–04, 1531–35, 1538, 1556).

11. *De Doctrina Christiana,* 1, 3–4, *PL* 34:20–21 (translated in John Gavigan, *Saint Augustine: Christian Instruction* [New York: CIMA, 1947] pp. 29–30).

12. Hirschberger, *History of Philosophy,* p. 333.

13. *De Libero Arbitrio,* 1, 15, 32, *PL* 32:1238. Cf. *Cassell's Latin Dictionary,* which gives *pecunia* a first meaning of "property." Eventually, to be sure, the most common meaning of the word came to be "money."

14. *Sermo de Disciplina Christiana,* 6, 6, *PL* 40:672.

15. Our passages A and B are from *Epistola CLIII,* 26, *PL* 33:665. Passage A has a biblical text as its starting point, which, according to the

Migne edition, is to be found "in the Septuagint, Proverbs 17, following verse 6," and has been cited as well by Jerome, Cassian, and Bernard.

16. *In Ioannis Evangelium*, 6, 25, *PL* 35:1437.

17. John Wycliff, *De Civili Dominio* (London: 1885), p. 5.

18. "Hoc dat bonis et malis" (*Sermo CCCXVII*, 1, *PL* 38:1435). Cf. *Sermo CCCXI*, 13–16, *PL* 38:1418–19.

19. "Sed ne putentur mala, dantur et bonis: ne putentur magna vel summa bona, dantur et malis" (*Epistola CCXX, PL* 33:996).

20. Portalie, *Thought of Saint Augustine*, p. 281.

21. *City of God*, 4, 4 *PL* 41:115.

22. *Enarratio in Psalmum LXXXVIII*, 2, *PL* 37:1134.

23. *Sermo LXXXV*, 5, 6, *PL* 38:522-23.

24. *Enarratio in Psalmum CXLVII*, 12, *PL* 37:1922.

25. *Sermo LXI*, 11, 12, *PL* 38:413.

26. *Sermo XXXVI*, 9, 9, *PL* 38:219.

27. *Summa Theologiae*, Prima Pars, 84, 5.

28. *Sermo XXXIX*, 2, *PL* 38:242.

29. *Sermo L*, 1, *PL* 38:326.

30. Ibid., 2 and 4, col. 327 .

31. Ibid. Cf. *City of God*, 4, 4, *PL* 41:115, where Augustine asks: without justice "what would the great empires be but teeming broods of robbers?"

32. *Sermo CXLIV*, 7, 9, *PL* 38:899.

33. *Sermo CCLXVII*, 11, *PL* 39:1651.

34. *De Genesi*, 11, 15, *PL* 34:436.

35. *Sermo CCCLIX*, 2, *PL* 39:1591.

36. Cf. Hirschberger, *History of Philosophy*, p. 330: "This is Stoic terminology. . . . In the background we can, none the less, discern Aristotle and Plato, as well as the cosmic law of Heraclitus."

37. *Sermo IX*, 12, 20, *PL* 38:89-90.

38. *Sermo CXXIV*, 5, 5, *PL* 38:686.

39. *Enarratio in Psalmum CXXXI*, 5, *PL* 37:1718.

40. Ibid., 6–7, cols. 1718–19.

41. *Epistola CLVII*, 25, *PL* 33:687.

42. *On Free Choice of the Will,* translated by A. S. Benjamin and L. H. Hackstaff (Indianapolis: Bobbs-Merrill, 1964), 1, 15, 33 (PL 32:1239).

CHAPTER 8

1. Brown, *Late Antiquity*, pp. 34–45.

2. A recent biblical study of the meaning of "Kingdom of God" is a landmark: George V. Pixley, *God's Kingdom* (Maryknoll, N.Y.: Orbis,

1981). Cf. José Miranda's *Marxism and the Bible* (1974), *Being and the Messiah* (1977), and *Communism in the Bible* (1982) (Maryknoll: Orbis); Fernando Belo, *A Materialist Reading of the Gospel of Mark* (Maryknoll: Orbis, 1981).

3. Pixley, *God's Kingdom*, p. 89.

4. Brown, *Late Antiquity*, p. 66.

5. Romans 10:12; Acts 2:44-45.

6. Cf. Kautsky, *Foundations*, pp. 351 ff. Cf. also Friedrich Engels, "On the History of Early Christianity," in Karl Marx and Friedrich Engels, *On Religion* (New York: Schocken, 1974), pp. 316-23.

7. "The Rich Man's Salvation," 14, *PG* 9:617 (in Butterworth, *Clement*, p. 299).

8. *In Inscriptionem Altaris et in Principium Actorum*, 1, 2 *PG* 51:69. Cf. *In Ioannem Homilia* 19, 3, *PG* 59:123-24.

9. *Homilia in illud Lucae, "Destruam . . . ,"* 1, *PG* 31:261-64.

10. *Commentarium in Epistolam II ad Corinthios*, 9, *PL* 17:331-32.

11. *In Ioannis Evangelium*, 6, 25, *PL* 35:1437.

12. *On Free Choice of the Will*, 1, 15, *PL* 32:1238.

13. "The Rich Man's Salvation," 13, *PG* 9:616 (in Butterworth, *Clement*, p. 297).

14. *In Epistolam ad Timotheum*, 12, 4, *PG* 62:562-63.

15. *De Verbis Apostoli, "Habentem Eumdem Spiritum,"* 3, 11, *PG* 51:299.

16. *De Lazaro Concio*, 2, 4, *PL* 48:988.

17. *De Nabuthe*, 11, *PL* 14:747 (in McGuire, *De Nabuthe*, p. 190).

18. *Homilia in illud Lucae, "Destruam . . . ,"* 7, *PG* 31:276-77. Cf. *Sermo IV de Eleemosyna*, 3, PG 32:1158.

19. *Epistola CLIII*, 26, *PL* 23:665.

20. *Sermo LXI*, 11, 12, *PL* 38:413.

21. *Sermo IV de Eleemosyna*, 1, *PG* 32:1153-58.

22. *De Decem Millium Talentorum Debitore*, 4, *PG* 51:22.

23. *Homilia in illud Lucae, "Destruam . . . ,"* 7, *PG* 31:276-77.

24. "The Rich Man's Salvation" 14, *PG* 9:617 (in Butterworth, *Clement*, p. 299).

25. *De Nabuthe Jezraelita*, 1, *PL* 14:741 (in McGuire, *De Nabuthe*, p. 47).

26. *Ad Populum Antiochenum Homilia* 2, 6-7, *PG* 49:43.

27. *Sermo LXXXV*, 5, 6, *PL* 38:522-23.

28. *Sermo XXXIX*, 2, *PL* 38:242.

29. *De Eleemosyna*, 6, *PG* 51:269.

30. *In Epistolam ad Hebraeos*, 6, *PG* 63:94 (in Schaff, *Nicene Fathers*, p. 421).

31. *In Epistolam ad Romanos*, 7, 9, *PG* 60:453.

32. *Sermo IX*, 12, 20 *PL* 38:90.

33. *De Nab. Jez.*, 11, *PL* 14:747 (in McGuire, *De Nabuthe*, p. 83).

34. *Commentarium in Epistolam II ad Corinthios*, 9, 9, *PL* 17:313-14.

35. *In Ioannem*, 23, *PG* 59:192 (in Schaff, *Nicene Fathers*, p. 118).

36. *Sermo L*, 1, *PL* 38:327.

37. *Sermo CCCLIX*, 2, *PL* 39:1591.

38. *Enarratio in Psalmum CXXXI*, 5, *PL* 37:1718.

39. *In Epistolam ad Timotheum*, 12, 4, *PG* 62:563-64 (in Schaff, *Nicene Fathers*, pp. 447-48).

40. *Expositio Evangelii secundum Lucam*, 7, 124, *PL* 15:1731.

41. *De Genesi*, 11, 15, *PL* 34:436.

42. *De Officiis Ministrorum*, 1, 28, *PL* 16:61-62.

43. *In Ioannis Evangelium*, 6, 25, *PL* 35:1437.

44. *Ad Populum Antiochenum*, 2, 6, *PG* 49:42.

45. *De Virginitate*, 68, *PG* 48:584-85.

46. *In Matthaeum*, 77, *PG* 58:707.

47. In *Epistolam I ad Corinthios*, 10, 3, *PG* 61:85 (in Schaff, *Nicene Fathers*, p. 57).

48. *In Epistolam ad Timotheum*, 12, 4, *PG* 62:562-63.

49. *Sermo L*, 1, *PL* 38:226.

50. *Commentarium in Epistolam ad Colossenses*, 3, 5, *PL* 17:435.

51. *In illud Lucae, "Destruam . . . ,"* 7, *PG* 31:276.

52. *De Nab. Jez.*, 2, *PL* 14:742 (in McGuire, *De Nabuthe*, p. 47).

53. *De Officiis Ministrorum*, 1, 11, *PL* 16:34.

54. *In Psalmum CXVIII Expositio*, 22, *PL* 15:1303.

55. *In Epistolam ad Hebraeos*, 11, 6, *PG* 63:93-94.

56. *In Ioannis Evangelium*, 6, 25, *PL* 35:1437.

57. *Sermo CXXIV*, 5, 5, *PL* 38:686.

58. *In Epistolam I ad Corinthios*, 10, 3, *PG* 61:85 (in Schaff, *Nicene Fathers*, p. 57).

59. *In Ioannem*, 23, *PG* 59:192 (Schaff, p. 118).

60. *Sermo CXLIV*, 7, 9, *PL* 38:899.

61. *In Acta Apostolorum*, 11, 3, *PG* 60:96-98.

62. *In Inscriptionem Altaris et in Principium Actorum*, 1, 2, *PG* 51:69. Cf. *In Ioannem Homilia* 19, 3, *PG* 59:123-24.

63. *On Free Choice of the Will*, 1, 15, *PL* 32:1238.

64. *De Nab. Jez.*, 14-15, *PL* 14:747, 751 (in McGuire, *De Nabuthe*, pp. 83, 87-89).

65. *Hexaemeron*, 5, 26, *PL* 14:217 (in Savage, *Ambrose,* p. 181).

66. "The Educator," 2, 3, *PG* 8:436 (in Wood, *Clement*, p. 128).

67. Ibid., 3, 8, *PG* 8:612 (Wood, *Clement*, p. 233).

68. Ibid., 3, 7, *PG* 8:609 (Wood, *Clement*, p. 231).

69. Ibid., 2, 3, *PG* 8:437 (Wood, *Clement*, p. 128).

70. *Sermo LXXXV*, 5, 6, *PL* 38:522–23.

71. *Enarratio in Psalmum CXLVII*, 12, *PL* 37:1922.

72. "The Educator," 2, 12, *PG* 8:541 (in Wood, *Clement*, pp. 191, 192).

73. *In Acta Apostolorum Homilia IX, PG* 60:96–98. We have amalgamated two translations here, while keeping the Migne text before our eyes: (1) *The Homilies of S. John Chrysostom on the Acts of the Apostles*, Library of Fathers of the Holy Catholic Church, Anterior to the Division of the East and West (Oxford: Parker; London: Rivington; 1851), pp. 161–63; and (2) Kautsky, *Foundations*, pp. 357–59.

74. Cf. Adolf von Harnack, *Monasticism: Its Ideals and History* (London, Oxford: Williams and Norgate, 1901), p. 32.

75. Brown, *Late Antiquity*, p. 110.

76. Cf. Ian C. Hannah, *Christian Monasticism, a Great Force in History* (New York: Macmillan, 1925), pp. 39–55.

77. Cf. Harnack, *Monasticism*, pp. 96–97.

Following is an Appendix, reproduced photographically from Migne, *Patrologia Graeca* and *Patrologia Latina*, of all the Greek and Latin texts quoted in indented blocks and examined throughout our study, with loci cited following the texts. Citations of Ambrose from *PL* 14, 15, and 16 are from the 1845 editions.

Appendix

CLEMENT

Text 1

Χρὴ δὲ προειληφέναι τοὺς περὶ σωτη-
ρίᾳ σπεύδοντας, ὡς ἄρα χρήσεως μὲν ἔνεκεν ἡ πᾶσα
ἡμῖν (8) κτῆσις· αὐταρκείας δὲ χάριν ἡ κτῆσις (9),
ἣν καὶ ἐξ ὀλίγων ἄν τις περιποιήσαιτο. Μάταιοι γὰρ
οἱ δι' ἀπληστίαν ἐπ' αὐτοῖς χαίροντες κειμηλίοις·
« Ὁ δὲ συνάγων τοὺς μισθοὺς, » φησὶ, « συνήγαγεν
εἰς δεσμὸν τετρυπημένον. » Οὗτός (10) ἐστιν ὁ συνάγων
καὶ ἀποκλείων τὸν σπόρον, καὶ ἐλαττούμενος, ὁ μηδενὶ
μεταδιδούς.   [*Paid.*, 2, 3, *PG* 8:437]

Text 2

A
                                                    « Ὃν
καὶ ἔδειξεν (13) ὁ Θεός, διὰ τί μή χρησώμεθα ; » καὶ
« Πάρεστί μοι, διὰ τί μὴ τρυφήσω ; » καὶ, « Τίσιν οὖν
ταῦτα γέγονεν εἰ μὴ ἡμῖν ; » Τελέως δὲ ἠγνοηκότων
τὸ θέλημα τοῦ Θεοῦ αἱ τοιαῦται φωναί. Πρῶτον μὲν
γὰρ (14) τὰ ἀναγκαῖα, καθάπερ τὸ ὕδωρ καὶ τὸν
ἀέρα, προφανῆ πᾶσι χορηγεῖται· τὰ δὲ ὅσα μὴ ἀναγ-
καῖα, γῇ τε καὶ ὕδατι ἔκρυψε.   [*Paid.*, 2, 12 *PG* 8:541]

B
Παρήγαγε δὲ τὸ γένος ἡμῶν ἐπὶ κοινωνίᾳ ὁ Θεός,
αὐτὸς τὸν ἑαυτοῦ (19) πρότερος μεταδοὺς καὶ κοινὸν
πᾶσιν ἀνθρώποις τὸν ἑαυτοῦ ἐπικουρήσας Λόγον,
πάντα ποιήσας ὑπὲρ πάντων. Κοινὰ οὖν τὰ πάντα,
καὶ μὴ πλεονεκτούντων οἱ πλούσιοι. Τὸ οὖν, « Πάρεστί
(20) μοι, καὶ πλεονάζει μοι· διὰ τί μὴ τρυφήσω ; » οὐκ
ἀνθρώπινον, οὐδὲ κοινωνικόν. Ἐκεῖνο δὲ μᾶλλον ἀγα-
πητικὸν, « Πάρεστί μοι, διὰ τί μὴ μεταδῶ τοῖς δεο-

μένοις ; ὁ γὰρ τοιοῦτος τέλειος, ὁ τὸ, « Ἀγαπήσεις
τὸν πλησίον σου ὡς σεαυτὸν , » πληρώσας .

[Paid., 2, 12 PG 8:541-44]

C   Ἡ δὲ εἰς τὰς ματαίους (21) ἐπιθυμίας ἀνά-
λωσις ἀπωλείας οὐ δαπάνης ἐπέχει λόγον. δέδωκε γὰρ
ὁ Θεὸς, οἶδ' ὅτι, τῆς χρήσεως ἡμῖν τὴν ἐξουσίαν,
ἀλλὰ μέχρι τοῦ ἀναγκαίου· καὶ τὴν χρῆσιν κοινὴν
εἶναι βεβούλευται (22). Ἄτοπον δὲ ἕνα τρυφᾶν, πε-
νομένων πλειόνων. Πόσῳ (23) μὲν γὰρ εὐκλεέστερον
τοῦ πολυτελῶς οἰκεῖν τὸ πολλοὺς εὐεργετεῖν ; πόσῳ
δὲ συνετώτερον τοῦ εἰς λίθους καὶ χρυσίον τὸ εἰς ἀν-
θρώπους ἀναλίσκειν........................τίνα
δὲ ἂν ἀγροὶ τοσοῦτον, ὅσον τὸ χαρίζεσθαι ὠφελήσειαν .

[Paid., 2, 12 PG 8:544]

Text 3

A   Μέτρον (3) δὲ, καθάπερ
ὁ ποῦς τοῦ ὑποδήματος, οὕτω καὶ τῆς κτήσεως ἑκάστου τὸ σῶμα. Τὸ δὴ περιττὸν, ἃ δή φασι (4) κό-
σμια, καὶ τὰ ἔπιπλα τῶν πλουσίων ἄχθος ἐστὶν, οὐ
κόσμος τοῦ σώματος. Χρὴ δὲ τὸν ἀναβαίνειν βιαζό-
μενον (5) εἰς τοὺς οὐρανοὺς καλὴν βακτηρίαν, τὴν
εὐεργεσίαν, περιφέρειν· καὶ τοῖς θλιβομένοις μετα-
δεδωκότα, τῆς ἀληθοῦς ἀναπαύσεως μεταλαμβάνειν.
Ὁμολογεῖ γὰρ ἡ Γραφὴ, « ὡς ἄρα λύτρον ἐστὶν ἀνδρὸς
ψυχῆς ὁ ἴδιος πλοῦτος· » τουτέστιν, ἐὰν πλουτῇ,
μεταδόσει σωθήσεται .

[Paid., 3, 7, PG 8:609]

B   Διὰ τοῦτό τοι πατρίδα ἐπὶ γῆς οὐκ
ἔχομεν ὡς ἂν καταφρονοῖμεν τῶν ἐπιγείων κτημά-
των. Πλουσιωτάτη δὲ ἡ εὐτέλεια (19), ἐξισοῦσα
ἀνελλιπέσι δαπάναις, ταῖς εἰς ἃ χρὴ, καὶ ἐφ' ὅσον
χρὴ, τελεῖσθαι προσηκούσαις· « τέλη » γὰρ τὰ δαπα-
νήματα.

[Paid., 3, 8, PG 8:612]

A   Ἀνέφικτον γὰρ καὶ ἀμήχανον, δεόμενον τῶν πρὸς τὸ βιοτεύειν ἀναγκαίων μὴ κατακλᾶσθαι τὴν γνώμην καὶ ἀσχολίαν ἄγειν ἀπὸ τῶν κρειττόνων, ὁπωσοῦν καὶ ὁθενοῦν ταῦτα πειρώμενον ἐκπορίζειν.

Καὶ πόσῳ χρησιμώτερον τὸ ἐναντίον, ἱκανὰ κεκτημένον αὐτόν τε περὶ τὴν κτῆσιν μὴ κακοπαθεῖν, καὶ οἷς καθῆκεν ἐπικουρεῖν; Τίς γὰρ ἂν κοινωνία καταλίποιτο παρὰ ἀνθρώποις, εἰ μηδεὶς ἔχει μηδέν.   [*Quis Div. Sal.*, 12-13, *PG* 9: 616-17]

B   Οὕτω τὴν χρείαν αὐτῶν ἐπαινεῖ, ὥστε καὶ μετὰ τῆς προσθήκης ταύτης τὴν κοινωνίαν ἐπιτάσσει, ποτίζειν τὸν διψῶντα, ἄρτον διδόναι τῷ πεινῶντι, ὑποδέχεσθαι τὸν ἄστεγον, ἀμφιεννύναι τὸν γυμνόν. Εἰ δὲ τὰς χρείας οὐχ οἷόν τε ἐκπληροῦν ταύτας μὴ ἀπὸ χρημάτων, τῶν δὲ χρημάτων ἀφίστασθαι κελεύει, τί ἂν ἕτερον εἴη ποιῶν ὁ Κύριος, ἤ...κοινωνεῖν καὶ μὴ κοινωνεῖν; ὅπερ ἀπάντων ἀλογώτατον.   [*Quis Div. Sal.*, 13, *PG* 9:617]

C   κτήματα γάρ ἐστι κτητὰ ὄντα καὶ χρήματα χρήσιμα ὄντα καὶ εἰς χρῆσιν ἀνθρώπων παρεσκευασμένα ὑπὸ τοῦ Θεοῦ. ἃ δὴ παράκειται καὶ ὑποβέβληται καθάπερ ὕλη τις καὶ ὄργανα πρὸς χρῆσιν ἀγαθὴν τοῖς εἰδόσι.....Δύνασαι χρῆσθαι δικαίως αὐτῷ; πρὸς δικαιοσύνην καθυπηρετεῖ. Ἀδίκως τις αὐτῷ χρῆται; πάλιν ὑπηρέτης ἀδικίας εὑρίσκεται. Πέφυκε γὰρ ὑπηρετεῖν, ἀλλ' οὐκ ἄρχειν.   [*Quis Div. Sal.*, 14, *PG* 9:617]

D   Ὁ μὲν γὰρ ἔχων κτήματα καὶ ....ὡς Θεοῦ μωρεάς...

.... καὶ εἰδὼς, ὅτι ταῦτα
κέκτηταί διὰ τοὺς ἀδελφοὺς μᾶλλον ἢ ἑαυτόν·.....
.............................οὗτος ὁ μα-
καριζόμενος ὑπὸ τοῦ Κυρίου, καὶ πτωχὸς τῷ πνεύ-
ματι καλούμενος, κληρονόμος ἕτοιμος οὐρανοῦ βασι-
λείας, οὗ ολούσιος ζῆσαι μὴ δυνάμενος.

[Quis Div. Sal., 16, PG 9:620]

E

« Ποιήσατε
ὑμῖν φίλους ἐκ τοῦ μαμμωνᾶ τῆς ἀδικίας, ἵνα, ὅταν
ἐκλίπητε, δέξωνται ὑμᾶς εἰς τὰς αἰωνίους σκηνάς · »
φύσει μὲν ἅπασαν κτῆσιν ἣν αὐτός τις ἐφ᾽ ἑαυτοῦ
κέκτηται, οὐκ ἰδίαν οὖσαν ἀποφαίνων. Ἐκ δὲ ταύτης
τῆς ἀδικίας ἐνὸν καὶ πρᾶγμα δίκαιον ἐργάσασθαι καὶ
σωτήριον, ἀναπαῦσαί τινα τῶν ἐχόντων αἰώνιον σκη-
νὴν παρὰ τῷ Πατρί.

[Quis Div. Sal., 31, PG 9:637]

BASIL

Text 1

A

Τίνα, φησὶν, ἀδικῶ συνέχων τὰ ἐμαυτοῦ (59) ;
Ποῖα, εἰπέ μοι, σαυτοῦ ; πόθεν λαβὼν εἰς τὸν βίον
εἰσήνεγκας ; Ὥσπερ ἂν εἴ τις, ἐν θεάτρῳ θέαν κα-
ταλαβών, εἶτα ἐξείργοι τοὺς ἐπεισιόντας, ἴδιον ἑαυτοῦ κρίνων τὸ κοινῶς πᾶσι κατὰ τὴν χρῆσιν προχεί-
μενον · τοιοῦτοί εἰσι καὶ οἱ πλούσιοι. Τὰ γὰρ κοινὰ
προκατασχόντες, ἴδια ποιοῦνται (60) διὰ τὴν πρό-
ληψιν. Ἐπεὶ εἰ τὸ πρὸς παραμυθίαν τῆς ἑαυτοῦ
χρείας ἕκαστος κομιζόμενος, τὸ περιττὸν ἠφίει τῷ
δεομένῳ, οὐδεὶς μὲν ἂν ἦν πλούσιος, οὐδεὶς δὲ ἐνδεής. Οὐχὶ γυμνὸς ἐξέπεσες τῆς γαστρός ; οὐ γυμνὸς
πάλιν εἰς τὴν γῆν ὑποστρέψεις ; Τὰ δὲ παρόντα σοι
πόθεν ; Εἰ μὲν ἀπὸ ταυτομάτου λέγεις, ἄθεος εἶ, μὴ
γνωρίζων τὸν κτίσαντα, μηδὲ χάριν ἔχων τῷ δεδω-

χότι· εἰ δὲ ὁμολογεῖς εἶναι παρὰ Θεοῦ, εἰπὲ τὸν λόγον ἡμῖν δι᾽ ὃν ἔλαβες. Μὴ ἄδικος ὁ Θεὸς, ὁ ἀνίσως ἡμῖν διαιρῶν τὰ τοῦ βίου ; Διὰ τί σὺ μὲν πλουτεῖς, ἐκεῖνος δὲ πένεται ; Ἢ πάντως, ἵνα καὶ σὺ χρηστότητος καὶ πιστῆς οἰκονομίας μισθὸν ὑποδέξῃ (61), κἀκεῖνος τοῖς μεγάλοις ἄθλοις τῆς ὑπομονῆς τιμηθῇ ;   [In illud Luc., "Destruam . . . ," 7, PG 31:276]

B   Σὺ δὲ, πάντα τοῖς ἀπληρώτοις τῆς πλεονεξίας κόλποις περιλαβών, οὐδένα οἴει ἀδικεῖν τοσούτους ἀποστερῶν ; Τίς ἐστιν ὁ πλεονέκτης ; Ὁ μὴ ἐμμένων τῇ αὐταρκείᾳ. Τίς δέ ἐστιν ὁ ἀποστερητής ; Ὁ ἀφαιρούμενος τὰ ἑκάστου. Σὺ δὲ οὐ πλεονέκτης ; σὺ δὲ οὐκ ἀποστερητής ; ἃ πρὸς οἰκονομίαν ἐδέξω, ταῦτα ἴδια σεαυτοῦ ποιούμενος ; Ἢ ὁ μὲν ἐνδεδυμένον ἀπογυμνῶν λωποδύτης ὀνομασθήσεται· ὁ δὲ τὸν γυμνὸν μὴ ἐνδύων, δυνάμενος τοῦτο ποιεῖν, ἄλλης τινός ἐστι προσηγορίας ἄξιος ; Τοῦ πεινῶντός ἐστιν ὁ ἄρτος, ὃν σὺ κατέχεις· τοῦ γυμνητεύοντος τὸ ἱμάτιον, ὃ σὺ φυλάσσεις ἐν ἀποθήκαις· τοῦ ἀνυποδέτου τὸ ὑπόδημα, ὃ παρὰ σοὶ κατασήπεται· τοῦ χρῄζοντος τὸ ἀργύριον, ὃ κατορύξας ἔχεις. Ὥστε τοσούτους ἀδικεῖς, ὅσοις παρέχειν ἐδύνασο.
[In illud Luc., "Destruam . . . ," 7, PG 31:276-77]

C   Εἰ γὰρ ὅπερ διεβεβαιώσω ἀληθὲς ἦν, ὅτι ἐφύλαξας ἐκ νεότητος τὴν ἐντολὴν τῆς ἀγάπης, καὶ τοσοῦτον ἀπέδωκας ἑκάστῳ ὅσον καὶ σεαυτῷ, πόθεν σοι ἡ τῶν χρημάτων αὕτη περιουσία ; Δαπανητικὸν γὰρ πλούτου ἡ θεραπεία τῶν δεομένων· ὀλίγα μὲν ἑκάστου πρὸς τὴν ἀναγκαίαν ἐπιμέλειαν δεχομένου, πάντων δὲ ὁμοῦ καταμεριζομένων τὰ ὄντα, καὶ περὶ αὐτοὺς (76) δαπανώντων. Ὥστε ὁ ἀγαπῶν τὸν πλησίον ὡς ἑαυτὸν οὐδὲν περισσότερον κέκτηται τοῦ πλησίον· ἀλλὰ μὴν φαίνῃ ἔχων κτήματα πολλά. Πόθεν ταῦτα (77); ἢ δῆλον, ὅτι τὴν οἰκείαν ἀπόλαυσιν προτιμοτέραν τῆς τῶν πολλῶν παραμυθίας ποιούμενός. Ὅσον οὖν πλεονάζεις τῷ πλούτῳ, τοσοῦτον ἐλλείπεις τῇ ἀγάπῃ. Ἐπεὶ πάλαι ἂν ἐμελέτησας (78) τῶν χρημάτων τὴν ἀλλοτρίωσιν, εἰ ἠγαπήκεις σου τὸν πλησίον.   [In Div., 8, PG 31:281]

D   Ἤνεγκε τοὺς ὄμβρους ἐπὶ τήν ὑπὸ τῶν πλεονεκτικῶν χειρῶν γεωργουμένην γῆν· ἔδωκε τὸν ἥλιον ἐκθάλπειν τὰ σπέρματα, καὶ πολυπλασιάζειν τοὺς καρποὺς διὰ τῆς εὐφορίας. Καὶ τὰ μὲν παρὰ Θεοῦ τοιαῦτα, γῆς ἐπιτηδειότης, ἀέρων εὔκρατοι καταστάσεις (9), σπερμάτων ἀφθονίαι, βοῶν συνεργίαι, τὰ ἄλλα, οἷς γεωργία πέφυκεν εὐθηνεῖσθαι· τὰ δὲ παρὰ τοῦ ἀνθρώπου οἷα; Τὸ πικρὸν τοῦ ἤθους, ἡ μισανθρωπία, τὸ δυσμετάδοτον. Ταῦτα τῷ εὐεργέτῃ ἀντεπεδείκνυτο. Οὐκ ἐμνήσθη τῆς κοινῆς φύσεως· οὐχ ἡγήσατο χρῆναι τὸ περιττεῦον τοῖς ἐνδεέσι καταμερίσαι.   [In illud Luc., "Destruam . . . ," 1, PG 31:261-64]

Text 2

Δέον παραμυθεῖσθαι τοῦ ἀνδρὸς τὴν πτωχείαν, σὺ δὲ πολυπλασιάζεις τὴν ἔνδειαν, ἐκκαρποῦσθαι ζητῶν τὴν ἔρημον. Ὥσπερ (30) ἂν εἴ τις ἰατρὸς πρὸς κάμνοντας εἰσιών, ἀντὶ τοῦ ὑγίειαν αὐτοῖς ἐπαναγαγεῖν, ὁ δὲ καὶ τὸ μικρὸν λείψανον τῆς δυνάμεως προσαφέλοιτο· οὕτω καὶ σὺ τὰς συμφορὰς τῶν ἀθλίων ἀφορμὴν πόρων ποιῇ. Καὶ ὥσπερ οἱ γεωργοὶ ὄμβρους εὔχονται εἰς πολυπλασιασμὸν τῶν σπερμάτων, οὕτω καὶ σὺ ἐνδείας καὶ ἀπορίας ἀνθρώπων ἐπιζητεῖς, ἵνα σοι ἐνεργὰ τὰ χρήματα γένηται. Ἀγνοεῖς πλείονα προσθήκην ταῖς ἁμαρτίαις ποιούμενος, ἢ τῷ πλούτῳ τὴν αὔξησιν ἀπὸ τῶν τόκων ἐπινοῶν [Homilia II in Ps. XIV, 1, PG 29:268]

Text 3

ἐσθῆτι

πολυτιμήτῳ περιβαλεῖς σεαυτόν ; Οὔκουν δύο μέν σοι πηχῶν χιτωνίσκος ἀρκέσει, ἑνὸς δὲ ἱματίου περιβολὴ πᾶσαν τῶν ἐνδυμάτων ἐκπληρώσει τὴν χρείαν ; Ἀλλ' εἰς τροφὴν καταχρήσῃ τῷ πλούτῳ ; εἷς ἄρτος ἱκανὸς ἀποπληρῶσαι γαστέρα·..................

..... ὁ δὲ ¦καλῶς καὶ κατα τὸν ὀρθὸν λόγον τὰ προσόντα μεταχειρίζων, καὶ οἰκονόμος τῶν παρὰ τοῦ Θεοῦ δεδομένων γινόμενος, μὴ οὐχὶ πρὸς ἰδίαν ἀπόλαυσιν θησαυρίζων, ἐπαινεῖσθαι καὶ ἀγαπᾶσθαι δίκαιός ἐστι, διὰ τὸ φιλάδελφον καὶ κοινωνικὸν τοῦ τρόπου. [Sermo IV, I de Eleem., 1, PG 32:1153-56]

AMBROSE

Text 1

A **1. Nabuthe historia tempore vetus est, usu quotidiana. Quis enim divitum non quotidie concupiscit aliena? Quis opulentissimorum non exturbare contendit agellulo suo pauperem, atque inopem aviti ruris eliminare finibus? Quis contentus est suo? Cujus non inflammet divitis animum vicina possessio?**

[De Nab., 1, PL 14:711]

B   **2. Quousque extenditis , divites , insanas cupiditates? Numquid soli inhabitabitis super terram? Cur ejicitis consortem naturæ? et vindicatis vobis possessionem naturæ? In commune omnibus divitibus atque pauperibus terra fundata est , cur vobis jus proprium soli, divites, arrogatis? Nescit natura divites, quæ omnes pauperes 566 generat. Neque enim cum vestimentis nascimur, nec cum auro , argentoque generamur. Nudos fudit in lucem, egentes cibo, amictu, poculo : nudos recipit terra quos edidit, nescit fines possessionum sepulcro includere.......**

..... Nescit ergo natura discernere quando nascimur , nescit quando deficimus. Omnes similes creat, omnes similes gremio claudit sepulcri.   [De Nab., 1, PL 14:732]

Text 2

A   Totus populus ingemiscit, et solus dives non flecteris, nec audis Scripturam dicentem : *Perde pecuniam propter fratrem , et amicum , et non abscondas eam sub lapide in mortem* (*Eccli*. xxix, 13). Et quia non audis, ideo exclamat Ecclesiastes dicens : *Est languor malus, quem vidi sub sole , divitias custodiri in malum possidentis eas* (*Eccle.* v, 12). Sed fortasse redeas domum et cum uxore conferas : illa te hortetur ut redimas venumdatum. Immo magis hortabitur ut mundum muliebrem conferas, unde potes [b] vel parvo pauperem liberare. Illa tibi imponet sumptuum necessitatem ; ut gemma bibat, **572** in ostro dormiat, in argentea sponda recumbat, auro oneret manus, cervicem monilibus.

[De Nab., 5, PL 14:738]

B   56. An vos ampla extollunt atria; quæ magis de-
bent compungere, quia cum populos capiant, vocem
excludunt pauperis? Quamquam nihil prosit audiri
eam, quæ etiam audita nihil proficit. Deinde non
ipsa vos pudoris aula admonet, qui ædificando ves-
tras vultis superare divitias, nec tamen vincitis. ᵈ
Parietes vestitis, nudatis homines. Clamat ante
domum tuam nudus, et negligis : clamat homo nudus, et tu sollicitus es quibus marmoribus pavi-
menta tua vestias.   [*De Nab.*, 11, *PL* 14:748]

C   Pecuniam pauper quærit, et non
habet : panem postulat homo, et equus tuus aurum
sub dentibus mandit. Sed delectant te ornamenta
pretiosa, cum alii frumenta non habeant. Quantum,
o dives, sumis tibi judicium ! Populus esurit, et tu
horrea tua claudis : populus deplorat, et tu gemmam
tuam versas. Infelix, cujus in potestate est tantorum
animas a morte defendere, et non est voluntas. ᵉ To-
tius vitam populi poterat annuli tui gemma servare.

                                 [*De Nab.*, 11, *PL* 14:748]

Text 3

A   Quid vos delectant naturæ
dispendia? Universis creatus est mundus, quem
pauci divites vobis defendere conamini. Non enim
terrena tantum possessio, sed cœlum ipsum, aer,
mare, in usum paucorum divitum vindicatur. ᶜ Hic
aer, quem tu diffusis includis possessionibus, quantos
alere populos potest?   [*De Nab.*, 3, *PL* 14:734]

B Non dabo? Non de tuo largiris pauperi, sed de suo
reddis. Quod enim commune est in omnium usum
datum, tu solus usurpas. Omnium est terra, non divitum : sed pauciores qui non utuntur suo, quam qui
utuntur. Debitum igitur reddis, non largiris indebi-
tum. Ideoque tibi dicit Scriptura : *Declina pauperi
animam tuam, et redde debitum tuum, et responde pa-
cifica in mansuetudine* (*Eccli.* iv, 8).   [*De Nab.*, 11, *PL* 14:747]

C   58. Custos ergo es tuarum , non dominus faculta·
tum, qui aurum terræ infodis, minister utique ejus,
non arbiter. Sed ubi thesaurus tuus, ibi et cor tuum.
Ergo in illo auro cor tuum infodisti terræ.......
Si vis perfectus esse, inquit, *omnia quæcumque habes
vende; et da pauperibus , et habebis thesaurum in cœlo*
(*Matth.* xix, 21). Et noli contristari, cum hæc audis;
ne dicatur et tibi , sicut et illi adolescenti diviti
dictum est : *Quam difficile qui pecunias habent, in
regnum Dei intrabunt* (*Ibid.*, 23) : magis cum hæc
legis, considera quia ista tibi potest mors eripere,
                                          [*De Nab.*, 14, *PL* 14:749]

D   Possessio enim possessoris debet esse,
non possessor possessionis. Quicumque igitur patri-
monio suo tamquam possessione non utitur , qui lar-
giri pauperi et dispensare non novit, **584** is sua-
rum servulus est, non dominus facultatum, qui alie-
nas custodit ut famulus , non tamquam dominus ut
suis utitur. In hujusmodi ergo affectu dicimus quod
vir divitiarum sit, non divitiæ viri.   [*De Nab.*, 15, *PL* 14:751]

Text 4

A 36. *Habes*, inquit , *multa bona*. Nescit avarus bona , nisi ea quæ quæstuosa sunt, nominare. Sed ac-
quiesco ei , ut bona dicantur quæ sunt pecuniaria.
Cur ergo de bonis facitis mala, cum de malis bona
facere debeatis? Scriptum est enim : *Facite vobis
amicos de mammona iniquitatis (Luc.* xvi, 9). Ei ergo
qui uti sciat, bona sunt : ei [b] qui uti nesciat, recte
mala. *Dispersit , dedit pauperibus , justitia ejus manet
in æternnm (Ps.* cxi, 9). Quid hoc melius? Bona sunt,
si **575** pauperibus largiaris, in quo tibi debitorem
Deum quadam pietatis feneratione constituas. Bona
sunt si aperias horrea justitiæ tuæ , ut sis panis pauperum , vita egentium, oculus cæcorum, orbatorum
infantium pater.   [*De Nab.,* 7, *PL* 14:741]

B   Habes multa bona in annos multos posita,
potes et tibi et aliis abundare. Habes fecunditatem
publicam, quid destruis horrea tua? Ostendo tibi ubi
melius tua frumenta custodias, ubi bene sepias, ut
fures ea tibi auferre non possint. Include ea in corde
pauperum , ... Dat enim tibi fecunditatem Deus, ut aut vincat aut condemnet avaritiam
tuam; quo excusationem habere non possis : tu vero
quod per te multis nasci voluit, tibi soli reservas ,
immo et tibi adimis ; magis enim servares tibi , si
dispertireris aliis........Si terra tibi reddit fructus
uberiores quam acceperit, quanto magis misericordiæ
remuneratio reddet multiplicatiora quæ dederis !
                              [*De Nab.,* 7, *PL* 14:741-42]

Text 5

Nihil tam commendat Christianam animam quam misericordia. g Primum in pauperes, ut communes judices partus naturæ, quæ omnibus ad usum generat fructus terrarum; ut quod habes, largiaris pauperi, et consortem et conformem tuum adjuves. Tu nummum largiris, ille vitam accipit: tu pecuniam das, ille substantiam suam æstimat. Tuus denarius, census illius est.

39. Ad hæc plus ille tibi confert, cum sit debitor salutis. Si nudum vestias, te ipsum induis justitiam. Si peregrinum sub tectum inducas tuum, si suscipias egentem : ille tibi acquirit sanctorum amicitias et æterna tabernacula. Non mediocris ista gratia. Corporalia seminas, et recipis spiritalia. Miraris judicium Domini de sancto Job ? Mirare virtutem ejus, qui poterat dicere : **12** *Oculus eram cæcorum, pes claudorum. Ego eram infirmorum pater, velleribus agnorum meorum calefacti sunt humeri eorum. Foris non habitabat peregrinus : ostium autem meum omni venienti patebat (Job* xxix, 15, 16). Beatus plane, de cujus domo numquam vacuo sinu pauper exivit; neque enim quisquam magis beatus, quam qui intelligit super pauperis necessitatem et infirmi atque inopis ærumnam. In die judicii habebit salutem a Domino, quem habebit suæ debitorem misericordiæ.

[*De Off. Minist.*, 1, 11, *PL* 16:34-35]

Text 6

A 26. An vero sine quadam dote naturæ manere piscibus etiam illam putamus gratiam, quod unum-.

quodque genus piscium præscripta sibi domicilia
habet, quæ sui generis nullus excedat, non incurset
alienus ? Quis geometra his divisit habitacula nullis
rumpenda temporibus ? Sed geometram audivimus,
thalassometram numquam audivimus ; et tamen·
pisces mensuram suam norunt , non muris urbium
portisque præscriptam, non ædificiis domorum, non
agrorum finibus limitatam, sed mensuram ejus quod
oporteat ; ut tantum satis sit unicuique , quantum
ad usum abundet, non quantum aviditas quædam
immoderata sibi vindicet. Lex quædam naturæ est
tantum quærere, ^ quantum sufficiat ad victum , et
alimentorum modo sortem censere patrimonii.

[*Hex.*, 5, 10, *PL* 14:217]

B   Omnibus in commune elementa
donata sunt, patent æque divitibus atque pauperibus
ornamenta mundi........ Unde ad eos qui domum
ad domum, et villam ad villam jungunt, dictum est :
Numquid soli habitabilis super terram (Esai. v, 8)?
.... Domus Dei diviti est communis ,
et pauperi .   [*Hex.*, 6, 52, *PL* 14:263]

C   *124. Considerate*, inquit, *volatilia cœli (Matth.* VI ,
26). Magnum sane et aptum quod fide sequamur
exemplum. Nam si volatilibus cœli quibus nullum
exercitium cultionis, nullus de messium fecunditate
proventus est, indeficientem tamen providentia di-
vina largitur alimoniam, verum est causam inopiæ
nostræ avaritiam videri. Etenim illis idcirco inela-
borati pabuli usus exuberat, quod fructus sibi com-

munem ad escam datos speciali quodam nesciunt vindicare dominatu; nos communia amisimus, dum propria vindicamus; nam nec proprium quidquam est, ubi perpetuum nihil est; nec certa copia, ubi incertus eventus. Cur enim divitias tuas æstimes, cum tibi Deus etiam victum cum cæteris animantibus voluerit esse communem? Aves cœli speciale sibi nihil vindicant, et ideo pabulis indigere nesciunt; quia non norunt aliis invidere. [*Exp. Ev. sec. Luc.*, 7, 124, *PL* 15:1731]

Text 7

A   22. Nunc de reliqua ipsius versus parte dicamus. *Miserere*, inquit, *mei secundum verbum tuum.* Misericordia quidem justitiæ portio est; ut si velis donare pauperibus, hæc misericordia justitia est, secundum illud : *Dispersit, dedit pauperibus : justitia ejus manet in æternum* (*Psal.* cxi, 9). Deinde quia conformis tuus injustum est ut non adjuvetur a socio; cum præsertim Dominus Deus noster terram hanc possessionem omnium hominum voluerit esse communem, et fructus omnibus ministrare : sed avaritia possessionum jura distribuit. Justum est igitur ut si aliquid tibi privatum vindicas, quod generi humano, immo omnibus animantibus in commune collatum est, saltem aliquid inde pauperibus aspergas : ut quibus juris tui consortium debes, his alimenta non deneges. [*In Ps. 118*, 8, 22, *PL* 15:1303]

B   130. Justitia ᶜ igitur ad societatem generis humani, et ad communitatem refertur. Societatis enim

ratio dividitur in duas partes, justitiam et benefi-
centiam, quam eamdem liberalitatem et benignitatem
vocant: justitia mihi excelsior videtur, liberalitas
gratior: illa censuram tenet, ista bonitatem.

131. Sed [d] primum ipsum quod putant philosophi
justitiæ munus, apud nos excluditur. Dicunt enim
illi eam primam esse justitiæ formam, ut nemini
quis noceat, nisi lacessitus injuria: quod Evangelii
auctoritate vacuatur (*Luc.* IX, 56); vult enim Scriptura, ut sit in nobis spiritus Filii hominis, qui venit
conferre gratiam, non inferre injuriam.

132. Deinde formam justitiæ putaverunt, ut quis
[e] communia, id est, publica pro publicis habeat,
privata pro suis. Ne hoc quidem secundum natu-
ram, natura enim omnia omnibus in commune pro-
fudit. Sic enim Deus generari jussit omnia [f] ut pastus
omnibus communis esset, et terra foret omnium
quædam communis possessio. Natura igitur jus
commune generavit, usurpatio jus fecit privatum.

[De Off. Minist., 1, 28, PL 16:61-62]

Text 8

A   (Vers. 9.) *Sicut scriptum est : Dispersit, dedit pauperibus, justitia ejus manet in æternum.* ....Mi-
sericordia ergo hæc, justitia appellata est; quia
sciens qui largitur, omnia Deum communiter omnibus dare, quia sol ejus omnibus oritur, et pluit omnibus, et terram omnibus dedit : idcirco dividit
cum iis, qui copiam terræ non habent ....
.... Justus ergo est, qui sibi soli
non detinet, quod scit omnibus datum : et justus non

solum hoc in tempore, sed et in æternum ; quia in
sæculo futuro hanc habebit secum in perpetuum.

[In Ep. II ad Cor., 9, 9, PL 17:313-14]

B   (Vers. 10, 11.) *Qui autem subministrat semen se-
minanti : et panem ad edendum ministrabit : et multi-
plicabit semen vestrum, et amplificabit fructum justitiæ
vestræ ; ut in omnibus locupletemini in omni simpli-
citate.* Omnia Dei sunt, et semina et nascentia Dei
nutu crescunt, et multiplicantur ad usus hominum :
Deus ergo qui hæc dat, ipse et jubet de his commu-
nicari eis, qui indigent ; . . . .
. . . . Hæc est justitia, ut quia Deus
dat, retribuat ex eo et homo ei, cui deest.

[In Ep. II ad Cor., 9, 9, PL 17:313-14]

Text 9

    . . . quia sicut idololatria uni Deo auferre
nititur gloriam, ne quod ejus peculiare est, solus
habeat nomen divinitatis sibi soli condignum ; ita et
avaritia in Dei se res extendit, ut si potest fieri,
unus et solus creaturam ejus sibi usurpet, quam Deus
communem omnibus fecit. Unde dicit Deus per pro-
phetam : *Meum est aurum, et meum est argentum*
(*Agæ.* II, 9). Utraque igitur Deo est inimica ; ambæ
enim Deo abnegant, quæ ejus sunt. [In Ep. ad Col., 3, 5, PL 17:435]

JOHN CHRYSOSTOM

Chapter 2, pp. 29–30

                Τοῖς γὰρ ἐν λιμῷ τηκομένοις,
καὶ δι' ὅλης πονουμένοις τῆς ζωῆς, καὶ τελέσματα δι-
ηνεκῆ καὶ ἀφόρητα ἐπιτιθέασι . . . .

.... οὗ τί γένοιτ' ἂν ἐλεεινό-
τερον, ὅταν δι' ὁλοκλήρου τοῦ χειμῶνος πονέσαντες, καὶ
κρυμῷ καὶ ὁμβρῷ καὶ ἀγρυπνίαις δαπανηθέντες, κεναῖς
ἀναχωρήσωσι ταῖς χερσὶν, ἔτι καὶ προσοφείλοντες, καὶ τοῦ
λιμοῦ τούτου καὶ τοῦ ναυαγίου τὰς τῶν ἐπιτρόπων βισά-
νους καὶ τοὺς ἐλκυσμοὺς καὶ τὰς ἀπαιτήσεις καὶ τὰς ἀπα-
γωγὰς καὶ τὰς ἀπαραιτήτους λειτουργίας · μᾶλλον δεδοικό-
τες καὶ φρίττοντες .   [*In Matt.*, 61-63, *PG* 58, 591]

Text 1

A   τοῦτο ἁρπαγὴ τὸ μὴ μεταδοῦναὶ τῶν
ὄντων. Καὶ τάχα ὑμῖν θαυμαστὸν εἶναι δοκεῖ τὸ λεγό-
μενον, ἀλλὰ μὴ θαυμάσητε · μαρτυρίαν γὰρ ὑμῖν
ἀπὸ τῶν θείων παρέξομαι Γραφῶν λέγουσαν, ὅτι οὐ τὸ
τὰ ἀλλότρια ἁρπάζειν μόνον, ἀλλὰ καὶ τὸ τῶν ἑαυτοῦ
μὴ μεταδιδόναι ἑτέροις, καὶ τοῦτο ἁρπαγὴ καὶ πλεον-
εξία καὶ ἀποστέρησίς ἐστι. Τίς οὖν ἐστιν αὕτη ; Τοῖς
Ἰουδαίοις ἐγκαλῶν ὁ Θεὸς διὰ τοῦ προφήτου, φησίν ·
*Ἐξήνεγκεν ἡ γῆ τὰ ἐκφόρια αὐτῆς, καὶ οὐκ εἰσ-
ηνέγκατε τὰ ἐπιδέκατα· ἀλλ' ἡ ἁρπαγὴ τοῦ* [753]
πτωχοῦ ἐν τοῖς οἴκοις ὑμῶν. Ἐπειδὴ τὰς προσφο-
ρὰς, φησὶ, τὰς εἰωθυίας οὐκ ἐδώκατε, ἡρπάσατε τὰ
τοῦ πένητος. Τοῦτο δὲ λέγει, δεικνὺς τοῖς πλουσίοις,
ὅτι τὰ τῶν πενήτων ἔχουσι, κὰν πατρῷον διαδέξων-
ται κλῆρον, κὰν ὁθενδήποτε συλλέξωσι τὰ χρήματα.

                                    [*De Lazaro*, 2, 4, *PG* 48:987-88]

B   Καὶ πάλιν ἀλλαχοῦ λέγει· *Μὴ ἀποστερήσῃς τὴν
ζωὴν τοῦ πτωχοῦ· ὁ δὲ ἀποστερῶν, τὰ ἀλλότρια
ἀποστερεῖ·* ἀποστέρησις γὰρ λέγεται , ὅταν τὰ ἀλλότρια λαβόντες κατέχωμεν. Καὶ διὰ τούτου τοίνυν παι-
δευόμεθα, ὅτι ὅταν ἐλεημοσύνην μὴ παράσχωμεν, ἐν
ἴσῳ τοῖς ἀποστεροῦσι κολασόμεθα ᶜ ....
.... σοι πλείονα ἔχειν συν-

εχώρησεν ὁ Θεὸς, οὐχ ἵνα εἰς πορνείαν, καὶ μέθην, καὶ ἀδηφαγίαν, καὶ ἱματίων πολυτέλειαν, καὶ τὴν ἄλλην βλακείαν ἀναλώσῃς, ἀλλ' ἵνα τοῖς δεομένοις αὐτὰ διανείμῃς. Καθάπερ γὰρ ὑποδέκτης· τις βασιλικὰ δεξάμενος χρήματα, ἂν ἀφεὶς οἷς ἂν κελεύηται διανεῖμαι, εἰς οἰκείαν καταναλώσῃ βλακείαν, εὐθύνας δίδωσι καὶ προσαπόλλυται· οὕτω δὴ καὶ ὁ πλούσιος, ὑποδέκτης τίς ἐστι τῶν τοῖς πένησιν ὀφειλομένων χρημάτων διανεμηθῆναι, ἐπιταχθεὶς αὐτὰ διανέμειν τῶν ἑαυτοῦ συνδούλων τοῖς πενομένοις. Ἂν οὖν πλέον τι τῆς χρείας εἰς ἑαυτὸν ἀναλώσῃ τῆς ἀναγκαίας, χαλεπωτάτας ἐκεῖ δώσει τὰς εὐθύνας. Οὐ γὰρ ἐστιν αὐτοῦ τὰ αὐτοῦ, ἀλλὰ τῶν συνδούλων τῶν ἑαυτοῦ.

[De Lazaro, 2, 4, PG 48:988]

Text 2

A
                                    Τί δέ ἐστιν
ὅλως, Ἐμὸς καὶ οὐκ ἐμός; Ταῦτα γὰρ ὅταν μετὰ ἀκριβείας ἐξετάσω τὰ ῥήματα, ῥήματα μόνον ὁρῶ ψιλά. Πολλοὶ μὲν γὰρ καὶ ζῶντες ἀποπηδῶντα αὐτὸν τῆς αὐτῶν δεσποτείας οὐκ ἴσχυσαν κατασχεῖν· οἷς δὲ μέχρι τέλους παρέμεινεν i, ἐν τῷ καιρῷ τῆς τελευτῆς καὶ ἐκόντες καὶ ἄκοντες αὐτοῦ τῆς ἐξουσίας ἐξέπεσον. Οὐκ ἐπὶ τοῦ ἀργύρου δὲ μόνον καὶ χρυσοῦ, ἀλλὰ καὶ ἐπὶ τῶν λουτρῶν, καὶ ἐπὶ τῶν παραδείσων, καὶ ἐν ταῖς οἰκίαις τὸ Ἐμὸν καὶ οὐκ ἐμὸν, τοῦτο ῥῆμα ἄν τις ἴδοι μόνον ψιλόν. Ἡ μὲν γὰρ χρῆσις κοινὴ πάντων ἐστὶν, πλεονεκτοῦσι δὲ οἱ δοκοῦντες αὐτῶν εἶναι κύριοι τῶν οὐκ ὄντων τὴν ὑπὲρ αὐτῶν φροντίδα. Οἱ μὲν γὰρ ἀπολαύουσι μόνον αὐτῶν, οἱ δὲ μετὰ τοῦ ποιεῖσθαι πολλὴν τὴν ἐπιμέλειαν τὸ αὐτὸ τοῦτο καρποῦνται, ὃ μετὰ τῆς ἀμελείας ἐκεῖνοι.

[De Virginitate, 68, PG 48:584-85]

B
                              Πάντα μετὰ
δαψιλείας δίδωσιν ὁ Θεὸς, τὰ πολλῷ τῶν χρημάτων

ἀναγκαιότερα, οἷον τὸν ἀέρα, τὸ ὕδωρ, τὸ πῦρ, τὸν
ἥλιον, ἅπαντα τὰ τοιαῦτα. Οὐκ ἔστιν εἰπεῖν ὅτι πλείονος ἀπολαύει τῆς ἀκτῖνος ὁ πλούσιος, ἐλάττονος δὲ ὁ
πένης· οὐκ ἔστιν εἰπεῖν, ὅτι δαψιλέστερον ἀέρα ἀνα-
πνέει τοῦ πένητος ὁ πλουτῶν· ἀλλὰ πάντα ἴσα καὶ κοινὰ
πρόκειται. . . . . Ἵνα
συγκροτῆται ἡμῶν ἡ ζωή, καὶ ἀρετῆς ἔχωμεν σκάμμα-
τα. Εἰ μὲν γὰρ μὴ ἦν τὰ ἀναγκαῖα ταῦτα κοινά, ἴσως
ἂν οἱ πλουτοῦντες, τῇ εἰωθυίᾳ κεχρημένοι πλεονεξίᾳ, τοὺς
πενομένους ἀπέπνιξαν ἄν· εἰ γὰρ ἐπὶ τῶν χρημάτων
τοῦτο ποιοῦσι, πολλῷ μᾶλλον ἐπ' ἐκείνων τοῦτο ἂν
ἐποίησαν· πάλιν εἰ καὶ τὰ χρήματα ἦν κοινά, καὶ πᾶσιν ὁμοίως προύκειτο, ἐλεημοσύνης ἀνήρητο πρόφασις,
καὶ φιλοφροσύνης ἀφορμή.

ξ'. Ἵνα οὖν ἀδεῶς ζῶμεν, κοινὰ γέγονεν ἡμῖν τὰ τῆς
ζωῆς αἴτια· πάλιν, ἵνα ἔχωμεν στεφάνων καὶ εὐδοκι-
μήσεων ἀφορμήν, οὐ κοινὰ γέγονε τὰ χρήματα, ἵνα
πλεονεξίαν μισοῦντες, καὶ δικαιοσύνην διώκοντες, καὶ τὰ
ὄντα τοῖς δεομένοις προϊέμενοι, παραμυθίαν τινὰ διὰ
τῆς μεθόδου ταύτης τῶν οἰκείων λαμβάνωμεν ἁμαρτη-
μάτων.   [Ad Pop. Antioch., 2, 6-7, PG 49:43]

C   Τὸ γὰρ ἐμὸν, καὶ τὸ σὸν, τοῦτο τὸ ψυχρὸν
ῥῆμα καὶ μυρίους πολέμους εἰς τὴν οἰκουμένην εἰσ-
αγαγὸν, ἐκ τῆς ἁγίας ἐκείνης Ἐκκλησίας ἐξώριστο,
καὶ τὴν γῆν ᾤκουν, καθάπερ οἱ ἄγγελοι τὸν οὐρανὸν, καὶ οὔτε ἐφθόνουν οἱ πένητες τοῖς πλουτοῦσιν·
οὐδὲ γὰρ ἦσαν πλούσιοι· οὔτε ὑπερεώρων οἱ πλούσιοι τῶν πενήτων· οὐδὲ γὰρ ἦσαν πένητες· ἀλλὰ
πάντα ἦν κοινά.   [Oportet Haereses, 2, PG 51:255]

Text 3

A   β'. Οὐ τῶν πλουτούντων ἁπλῶς κατηγορῶν ταῦτα
εἶπον, οὐδὲ τοὺς πένητας ἁπλῶς ἐπαινῶν· οὔτε γὰρ ὁ

πλοῦτος κακὸν, ἀλλὰ τὸ κακῶς κεχρῆσθαι τῷ πλούτῳ·
οὔτε ἡ πενία καλὸν, ἀλλὰ τὸ καλῶς κεχρῆσθαι τῇ πε-
νίᾳ. Ἐκολάζετο ὁ πλούσιος ἐκεῖνος ὁ ἐπὶ τοῦ Λαζά-
ρου, οὐκ ἐπειδὴ πλούσιος ἦν, ἀλλ' ἐπειδὴ ὠμὸς ἦν
καὶ ἀπάνθρωπος.　　　　　　　　[Peccata Fratrum, 2, PG 51:355]

B　　　　　Οὐ τοίνυν ὁ πλοῦτος κακὸν, ἀλλ' ἡ παρά-
νομος αὐτοῦ χρῆσις κακόν. Καὶ ὥσπερ πρῴην περὶ
μέθης λέγων, οὐ τὸν οἶνον διέβαλλον (πᾶν γὰρ κτί-
σμα Θεοῦ καλὸν, καὶ οὐδὲν ἀπόβλητον, μετ' εὐχα-
ριστίας λαμβανόμενον), οὕτω καὶ νῦν οὐ τῶν πλουτούντων κατηγορῶ, οὐδὲ τὰ χρήματα διαβάλλω, ἀλλὰ
τὴν κακὴν τῶν χρημάτων χρῆσιν, καὶ εἰς ἀσωτίαν
δαπανωμένην. Διὰ τοῦτο χρήματα λέγεται, ἵνα ἡμεῖς
αὐτοῖς χρησώμεθα, καὶ μὴ ἐκεῖνα ἡμῖν· διὰ τοῦτο
κτήματα λέγεται, ἵνα ἡμεῖς αὐτὰ κτησώμεθα, καὶ
μὴ ἐκεῖνα ἡμᾶς. Τί οὖν τὸν δοῦλον ἔχεις δεσπότην;
τί ἀντέστρεψας τὴν τάξιν.　　　　[In Inscrip. Altaris, 1, 2, PG 51:69]

Text 4

A　　　　　Εἰ τοίνυν βούλει καταλιπεῖν πλοῦτον τοῖς παι-
δίοις σου πολὺν, κατάλιπε τοῦ Θεοῦ τὴν πρόνοιαν. Ὁ
γὰρ, μηδὲν σοῦ ποιήσαντος, καὶ ψυχὴν δοὺς καὶ σῶμα
διαπλάσας καὶ ζωὴν χαρισάμενος, ὅταν ἴδῃ τοσαύτην
ἐπιδεικνύμενον φιλοτιμίαν, καὶ τὰ ἐκείνων αὐτῷ δια-
νέμοντα μετ' ἐκείνων, πῶς οὐ πάντα αὐτοῖς ἀνοίξει
πλοῦτον; . . . .
. . . . Μὴ τοίνυν καταλίπῃς πλοῦτον, ἵνα καταλίπῃς
ἀρετήν. Καὶ γὰρ ἐσχάτης ἀλογίας ζῶντας μὲν μὴ
ποιεῖν κυρίους αὐτοὺς ἁπάντων τῶν ὄντων, τελευτή-
σαντας δὲ πολλὴν τῇ τῆς νεότητος εὐκολίᾳ παρέχειν
τὴν ἄδειαν.　　　　　　　[In Ep. ad Rom., 7, 9, PG 60:453]

B Εἴ τις οὐ θέλει ἐργάζεσθαι, μηδὲ ἐσθιέτω ; ......
........Οἱ γὰρ τοῦ Παύλου νόμοι οὐχὶ τοῖς πένησι
μόνον, ἀλλὰ καὶ ἡμῖν κεῖνται. Εἴπω τι φορτικὸν καὶ
ἐπαχθές· οἶδα μὲν ὅτι ὀργιεῖσθε· πλὴν ἀλλ᾽ ὅμως
ἐρῶ· οὐδὲ γὰρ ὥστε πλῆξαι, ἀλλ᾽ ὥστε διορθῶσαι
τοῦτο λέγω. Τούτοις μὲν ἀργίαν ἐγκαλοῦμεν, πρᾶγμα
καὶ συγγνώμης πολλάκις ἄξιον· αὐτοὶ δὲ ἐργαζόμεθα
τοιαῦτα πολλάκις, ἃ πάσης ἀργίας ἐστὶ χαλεπώτερα.
Ἀλλ᾽ ἐγὼ πατρῷον ἔχω κλῆρον, φησίν. Ἐπεὶ οὖν
οὗτος πένης ἐστὶ, καὶ ἐκ πενήτων, καὶ οὐκ ἔσχε προ-
γόνους εὐπόρους, ἀπόλλυσθαι δίκαιος, εἰπέ μοι.
[De Eleem., 6, PG 51:269]

C   Σὺ μὲν γὰρ
πολλάκις διημερεύων τὴν ἡμέραν ἐν θεάτροις, ἢ ἐν
συνεδρίοις καὶ συλλόγοις οὐδὲν ἔχουσι κέρδος, καὶ
μυρίοις λέγων κακῶς, οὐδὲν ἡγῇ ποιεῖν δεινὸν, οὐδὲ
ἀργεῖν τὸν δὲ ἄθλιον τοῦτον καὶ ταλαίπωρον πᾶσαν
ἀναλίσκοντα τὴν ἡμέραν ἐν ἱκετηρίαις, ἐν δάκρυσιν,
ἐν μυρίᾳ ταλαιπωρίᾳ, κρίνεις, καὶ εἰς [258] δικαστή-
ριον ἕλκεις, καὶ εὐθύνας ἀπαιτεῖς ; Καὶ ποῦ ταῦτα
γνώμης ἀνθρωπίνης, εἰπέ μοι ;   [De Eleem., 6, PG 51:269]

D   Τί γὰρ οὐκ ἐργάζεται, φησί ; τί δὲ ἀρ-
γῶν τρέφεται ; Εἰπέ μοι, σὺ δὲ ἐργαζόμενος ἔχεις
ἃ ἔχεις, οὐχὶ κλῆρον πατρῷον παραλαβών ; Εἰ δὲ
καὶ ἐργάζῃ, διὰ τοῦτο ὀνειδίζεις ἑτέρῳ ; Οὐκ ἀκούεις
Παύλου λέγοντος, Ὑμεῖς δὲ τὸ καλὸν ποιοῦντες
μὴ ἐκκακήσητε ; μετὰ γὰρ τὸ εἰπεῖν, Ὁ μὴ ἐργαζόμενος μηδὲ ἐσθιέτω, τοῦτο ἐπήγαγεν.
[In Ep. ad Heb., 11, 3, PG 63:94]

E   Ἀλλ᾽ ἐπιθέ-
της, φησὶν, ἐστί.
   δ΄. Τί φῇς, ἄνθρωπε ; ἄρτου ἑνὸς ἕνεκεν καὶ ἱματίου

ἐπιθέτην καλεῖς ; Ἀλλ᾽ εὐθέως πωλεῖ αὐτὸ, φησί. Σὺ
δὲ πάντα τὰ σαυτοῦ καλῶς διοικεῖς ; Τί δέ ; πάντες
ἀπὸ ἀργίας πένονται; οὐδεὶς ἀπὸ ναυαγίων; οὐδεὶς ἀπὸ
δικαστηρίων; οὐδεὶς ἀπὸ κλοπῆς ; οὐδεὶς ἀπὸ κινδύ-
νων; οὐδεὶς ἀπὸ νόσων ; οὐδεὶς ἀπὸ ἄλλης περιστά-
σεως ;   [In Ep. ad Heb., 11, 3, PG 63:94]

F   Εἰ γὰρ καὶ πατρῷον διεδέξω κλῆρον,
καὶ οὕτως ἔχεις πάντα ἃ ἔχεις· καὶ οὕτω τοῦ Θεοῦ
πάντα ἐστίν. Εἶτα, σὺ μὲν ὅπερ ἔδωκας, οὕτω βούλει
μετὰ ἀκριβείας οἰκονομεῖσθαι· τὸν δὲ Θεὸν οὐκ οἴει τὰ
αὐτοῦ μετὰ πλείονος ἀπαιτήσειν ἡμᾶς τῆς σφοδρότητος,
ἀλλὰ ἀνέχεσθαι ἁπλῶς αὐτῶν ἀπολλυμένων ; Οὐκ ἔστι
ταῦτα, οὐκ ἔστι. Καὶ γὰρ διὰ τοῦτο καὶ παρὰ σοὶ ταῦτα
εἴασεν, ὥστε δοῦναι τὴν τροφὴν αὐτοῖς ἐν καιρῷ ²⁰. Τί
ἐστιν, ἐν καιρῷ; Τοῖς δεομένοις, τοῖς πεινῶσιν. Ὥσπερ
γὰρ σὺ τῷ συνδούλῳ ἔδωκας οἰκονομῆσαι, οὕτω καὶ σὲ ὁ
Δεσπότης βούλεται εἰς δέον ταῦτα δαπανᾷν.
                                          [In Matt., 77, 4, PG 58:707]
Text 5

A   κἂν εὔπορος
ᾖς, πλέον δέ τι τῆς χρείας ἀναλίσκῃς, λόγον δώσεις
τῶν ἐμπιστευθέντων σοι χρημάτων..............
.... Καὶ γὰρ ἔλαβες ἑτέρων
πλείονα, καὶ ὑπεδέξω, οὐχ ἵνα αὐτὰ ἀναλώσῃς μόνος,
ἀλλ᾽ ἵνα καὶ ἑτέροις οἰκονόμος γένῃ καλός.
                                          [De Lazaro, 2, 5, PG 48:988]
B   πλήρεις δὲ αἱ Γραφαὶ
τῶν διδαγμάτων· ὁ σήμερον πλούσιος, αὔριον πένης. Διὸ
καὶ πολλάκις ἐγέλασα διαθήκας ἀναγινώσκων λεγούσας·
Ὁ δεῖνα μὲν ἐχέτω τὴν δεσποτείαν τῶν ἀγρῶν, ἢ τῆς
οἰκίας, τὴν δὲ χρῆσιν ἄλλος· πάντες γὰρ τὴν χρῆσιν
ἔχομεν, τὴν δεσποτείαν δὲ οὐδείς. Κἂν γὰρ παρὰ πᾶσαν
ἡμῖν τὴν ζωὴν παραμένῃ μηδεμίαν μεταβολὴν ὁ πλοῦτος

δεχόμενος, καὶ ἑκόντες καὶ ἄκοντες ἐν τῇ τελευτῇ πα·
ραχωρήσομεν ἑτέροις, τὴν χρῆσιν αὐτοῦ καρπωσάμενοι
μόνον, τῆς δεσποτείας δὲ γυμνοὶ καὶ ἔρημοι πρὸς ἐκεί-
νην ἀποδημοῦντες τὴν ζωήν.   [Ad Pop. Antioch., 2, 6, PG 49:42]

C   Ἀλλ' ἐρεῖ τις ἴσως · Διὰ τί δὲ ὅλως ὥσπερ ἐμοὶ τῷ
πλουσίῳ δέδωκεν, οὐχὶ καὶ τῷ πένητι παραπλησίως δέδωκεν; Ἐδύνατο μὲν καὶ σοὶ δοῦναι ὁμοίως, καὶ τῷ
πένητι, ἀλλ' οὐκ ἠθέλησεν οὔτε σοῦ ἄκαρπον εἶναι τὸν
πλοῦτον, οὔτε ἐκείνου ἄμισθον τὴν πενίαν. Σοὶ τῷ πλου-
τοῦντι δέδωκε πλουτεῖν ἐλεημοσύνῃ, καὶ σκορπίζειν ἐν
δικαιοσύνῃ.   [De Poenitentia, 7, 7, PG 49:336]

D   ..... οὕτως ἡμεῖς ἅπαντα πράττομεν ᶜ, Οὐκ εἰδότες ὡς
πάντων τῶν ὑπὲρ τὴν χρείαν τὴν ἀναγκαίαν εὐθύνας
καὶ λόγον ὑφέξομεν, ὡς οὐ δεόντως κεχρημένοι τοῖς παρὰ
τοῦ Δεσπότου ἡμῖν παρασχεθεῖσιν. Οὐ γὰρ ἵνα εἰς ἀπόλαυσιν ἡμετέραν μόνον ἀποχρησώμεθα, ταῦτα ἡμῖν παρ-
έσχετο, ἀλλ' ἵνα καὶ τῶν ὁμογενῶν τὴν ἔνδειαν παρα-
μυθησώμεθα.   [In Cap. XV Gen., 37, 5, PG 53:348]

E   **Κἂν πλούσιος ᾖς, ἐννόησον ὅτι δώσεις λόγον,**
.... **Οὐχ ὑπὲρ τῆς δαπάνης δὲ**
μόνον, ἀλλὰ καὶ ὑπὲρ τῆς κτήσεως ἀπαιτηθήσῃ
λόγον, [7] **πότερον ἐκ δικαίων πόνων, ἢ ἐξ ἁρπαγῆς**
καὶ πλεονεξίας συνέλεξας, πότερον κλῆρον διαδεξάμε-
νος πατρῷον, ἢ τὰς τῶν ὀρφανῶν καταστρέψας οἰκίας,
καὶ τὰς τῶν χηρῶν διαρπάσας οὐσίας. Καὶ καθάπερ
ἡμεῖς τοῖς οἰκέταις τοῖς ἡμετέροις οὐχὶ τῆς ἐξόδου
μόνον τῶν χρημάτων, ἀλλὰ καὶ τῆς εἰσόδου ἀπαιτοῦ-
μεν τὸν λόγον, ἐξετάζοντες πόθεν ὑπεδέξαντο τὰ
χρήματα, καὶ παρὰ τίνων, καὶ πῶς, καὶ πόσα · οὕτω

δὴ καὶ ὁ Θεὸς οὐχὶ τῆς δαπάνης μόνον, ἀλλὰ καὶ τῆς κτήσεως ἡμᾶς ἀπαιτεῖ τὰς εὐθύνας.

[De Decem Mil. Talent., 4, PG 51:22]

F   Οὐ λέγω, ἵνα ἁρπάζων ἐλεῇς, ἀλλ᾽ ἵνα τῆς πλεονεξίας ἀποστὰς, πρὸς ἐλεημοσύνην [289] καὶ φιλανθρωπίαν ἀποχρήσῃ τῷ πλούτῳ. Εἰ γάρ τις μὴ παύσαιτο τῆς ἁρπαγῆς, οὐδὲ ἐλεημοσύνην ἐργάσεται· ἀλλὰ κἂν μυρία καταβάλῃ χρήματα εἰς τὰς τῶν δεομένων χεῖρας, τὰ ἑτέρων ἁρπάζων καὶ πλεονεκτῶν, τοῖς ἀνδροφόνοις ἐξίσης λελόγισται τῷ Θεῷ.

[Hab. Eumdem Spir., 3, 11, PG 51:299]

Text 6

A   Εἰπὲ γάρ μοι, πόθεν σὺ πλουτεῖς; παρὰ τίνος λαβών: τί δὲ ἕτερος πόθεν; Παρὰ τοῦ πάππου, φησὶ, παρὰ τοῦ πατρός. Δυνήσῃ οὖν μέχρι πολλοῦ τοῦ γένους ἀνιὼν, οὕτω δεῖξαι τὴν κτῆσιν δικαίαν οὖσαν; Ἀλλ᾽ οὐκ ἂν ἔχοις, ἀλλ᾽ ἀνάγκη τὴν ἀρχὴν αὐτῆς καὶ τὴν ῥίζαν ἀπὸ ἀδικίας εἶναί τινος. Πόθεν; Ὅτι ὁ Θεὸς ἐξ ἀρχῆς οὐ τὸν μὲν πλούσιον ἐποίησε, τὸν δὲ πένητα, οὐδὲ παραγαγὼν, τούτῳ μὲν ἔδειξε χρυσίου θησαυροὺς πολλοὺς, ἐκεῖνον δὲ ἀπεστέρησε τῆς ἐρεύνης, ἀλλὰ τὴν αὐτὴν πᾶσιν ἀνῆκε γῆν. Πόθεν οὖν κοινῆς οὔσης, σὺ μὲν ἔχεις πλέθρα τόσα καὶ τόσα, ὁ δὲ πλησίον οὐδὲ κύαθον γῆς;
.... Πλὴν ἀλλ᾽ οὐδὲ ὑπὲρ τούτων ἀκριβολογοῦμαι· ἔστω δίκαιος ὁ πλοῦτος, καὶ πάσης ἁρπαγῆς ἀπηλλάχθω· οὐ γὰρ δὴ σὺ ὑπεύθυνος περὶ ὧν ὁ πατὴρ ἐπλεονέκτησεν· ἔχεις μὲν γὰρ τὰ ἐκ τῆς ἁρπαγῆς, ἀλλ᾽ οὐχ ἥρπασας σύ. Πλὴν ἀλλὰ συγκεχωρήσθω μηδὲ ἐκεῖνον ἡρπακέναι, ἀλλά ποθεν ἀπὸ γῆς ἀναβλυσθέντα τὸν χρυσὸν ἔχειν·..............
.... Καλῶς· τοῦτο δὲ

οὐ κακὸν τὸ μόνον ἔχειν τὰ Δεσποτικά, τὸ μόνον ἀπο-
λαύειν τῶν κοινῶν; ἢ οὐχὶ τοῦ Θεοῦ ἡ γῆ καὶ τὸ
πλήρωμα αὐτῆς ; Εἰ τοίνυν τοῦ Δεσπότου τοῦ κοινοῦ
τὰ ἡμέτερα, ἄρα καὶ τῶν συνδούλων τῶν ἡμετέρων ·
τὰ γὰρ τοῦ Δεσπότου πάντα κοινά.

[In Ep. I ad Tim., 12, 4, PG 62:562-63]

B   Θέα γάρ μοι Θεοῦ οἰκονο-
μίαν · Ἐποίησεν εἶναί τινα κοινά, ἵνα κἂν ἀπ' ἐκείνων καταιδέσῃ τὸ ἀνθρώπινον γένος, οἷον τὸν ἀέρα,
τὸν ἥλιον, τὸ ὕδωρ, τὴν γῆν, τὸν οὐρανόν, τὴν θάλατ-
ταν, τὸ φῶς, τοὺς ἀστέρας, καθάπερ ἀδελφοῖς πάντα
ἐξ ἴσης διανέμει.............................
Καὶ θέα πῶς ἐν τοῖς κοινοῖς οὐδεμία μάχη, ἀλλὰ
πάντα εἰρηνικά. Ὅταν δέ τις παρασπάσαι τι ἐπιχει-
ρήσῃ, καὶ ἴδιον ποιήσῃ, τότε ἡ ἔρις ἐπεισέρχεται,
ὥσπερ αὐτῆς τῆς φύσεως ἀγανακτούσης.

[In Ep. I ad Tim., 12, 4, PG 62:563-64]

C   Πάντα γὰρ παρὰ τοῦ Χριστοῦ ἔχομεν b ·
καὶ αὐτὸ τὸ εἶναι δι' αὐτοῦ ἔχομεν, καὶ τὸ ζῆν καὶ
τὸ ἀναπνεῖν, καὶ τὸ φῶς καὶ τὸν ἀέρα καὶ τὴν γῆν ·
..... πάροικοι γάρ ἐσμεν καὶ παρεπίδημοι. Τὸ δὲ
ἐμὸν καὶ τὸ σὸν τοῦτο ῥήματά ἐστι ψιλὰ μόνον · ἐπὶ
δὲ πραγμάτων οὐχ ἕστηκε. Καὶ γὰρ εἰ τὴν οἰκίαν σὴν
εἶναι φῇς, ῥῆμά ἐστι πράγματος ἔρημον. Καὶ γὰρ
καὶ ὁ ἀὴρ καὶ γῆ καὶ ὕλη τοῦ Δημιουργοῦ, καὶ σὺ
δὲ αὐτὸς ὁ κατασκευάσας αὐτήν, καὶ τὰ ἄλλα δὲ
πάντα.   [In Ep. I ad Cor., 10, 3, PG 61:85]

Text 7

A   Ὅταν ἴδῃς πένητα, μὴ παρα-
δράμῃς, ἀλλ' εὐθέως ἐννόησον τίς ἂν ἦς, εἰ σὺ ἦς
ἐκεῖνος · τί οὐκ ἂν ἠθέλησας πάντας ποιεῖν ; Ὁ συ-

ριῶν, φησίν. Ἐνόησεν ὅτι ὁμοίως σοι ἐλεύθερός ἐστι,
καὶ τῆς αὐτῆς σοι κοινωνεῖ εὐγενείας, καὶ πάντα σοι
κοινὰ κέκτηται · ἀλλὰ τοῦτον τὸν οὐδὲν ἔλαττον
ἔχοντά σου, οὐδὲ τῶν κυνῶν πολλάκις τῶν σῶν ἴσον
ποιεῖς. Οἱ μὲν γὰρ ἄρτου κορέννυνται, οὗτος δὲ πολλάκις ἐκοιμήθη πεινῶν · καὶ δούλων τῶν σῶν ὁ ἐλεύ-
θερος ἀτιμότερος γέγονεν. Ἀλλ' ἐκεῖνοι ἡμῖν χρείαν
πληροῦσι, φησί. Ποίαν δὴ ταύτην, εἰπέ μοι; ὅτι δου-
λεύουσί σοι καλῶς; Ἐὰν οὖν δείξω καὶ τοῦτον χρείαν
σοι πληροῦντα πολλῷ μείζονα ἐκείνων, τί ἐρεῖς;
παραστήσεται γάρ σοι ἐν τῇ ἡμέρᾳ τῆς κρίσεως,
καὶ ἐξαιρήσεταί σε τοῦ πυρός. Τί τοιοῦτον οἱ δοῦλοι
ποιοῦσι πάντες;   [In Ep. ad Heb., 11, 3, PG 63:93-94]

B   Ἀλλὰ πένησι παρέχεις; Ἀλλ'
οὐ τὰ σά, ἀλλὰ τὰ τοῦ Δεσπότου, τὰ κοινὰ τῶν ὁμο-
δούλων. Καὶ διὰ τοῦτο μάλιστα ταπεινοῦσθαι χρή, ἐν
ταῖς τῶν ὁμογενῶν συμφοραῖς ....
.... Τί δὲ ὅλως καὶ ὁ πλοῦτός ἐστιν;
Σκιὰ ἀδρανής, καπνὸς διαλυόμενος, ἄνθος χόρτου,
μᾶλλον δὲ καὶ ἄνθους εὐτελέστερος.   [In Joann., 33, 3, PG 59:192]

C   Οὐκοῦν φέρε πάντα κινήσωμεν ἐπὶ τοῦ παρόντος τὰ
τῆς ἐλεημοσύνης εἴδη. Δύνασαι διὰ χρημάτων; Μὴ
ὄκνει. Δύνασαι διὰ προστασίας; Μὴ εἴπῃς, ἐπειδὴ χρήματα οὐκ ἔστι, τοῦτο οὐδέν ἐστι. Σφόδρα καὶ τοῦτο μέ-
γα· ὥσπερ χρυσίον δεδωκώς, οὕτω διάκεισο. Δύνασαι
διὰ θεραπείας; Καὶ τοῦτο ποίησον. Οἷον, ἰατρὸς εἶ τὴν
ἐπιστήμην; Ἐπιμελήθητι ἀρρωστούντων· καὶ τοῦτο
μέγα. Δύνασαι διὰ συμβουλῆς; Πολλῷ τοῦτο πάντων
μεῖζον·   [In Act. Apost., 25, 4, PG 60:196]

Text 8

Καλῶς δὲ εἶπε,
Χάρις ἦν ἐπὶ πάντας. Διὰ τοῦτο γὰρ ἡ χάρις, ὅτι
οὐδεὶς ἦν ἐνδεής· [93]τουτέστιν, ἀπὸ τῆς πολλῆς προθυ-
μίας τῶν ἐπιδιδόντων οὐδεὶς ἦν ἐνδεής. Οὐ γὰρ μέρει
μὲν ἐδίδοσαν, μέρει δὲ ἐταμιεύοντο · οὐδὲ πάντα μὲν,
ὡς ἴδια δέ. Τὴν ἀνωμαλίαν ἐκ μέσου ἐξήγαγον, καὶ
ἐν ἀφθονίᾳ ἔζων πολλῇ · καὶ μετὰ πολλῆς δὲ τῆς
τιμῆς τοῦτο ἐποίουν. Οὐδὲ γὰρ εἰς τὰς χεῖρας ἐτόλ-
μων δοῦναι, οὐδὲ τετυφωμένως παρεῖχον, ἀλλὰ παρὰ
τοὺς πόδας ἔφερον, καὶ αὐτοὺς οἰκονόμους ἠφίεσαν
γίνεσθαι, καὶ κυρίους ἐποίουν, ἵνα ὡς ἐκ κοινῶν
λοιπὸν ἀναλίσκηται, ἀλλὰ μὴ ὡς ἐξ ἰδίων. Τοῦτο καὶ
πρὸς τὸ μὴ κενοδοξεῖν αὐτοὺς συνεβάλλετο. Τοῦτο εἰ
καὶ νῦν γέγονε, μετὰ πλείονος ἂν τῆς ἡδονῆς ἐβιώ-
σαμεν, καὶ πλούσιοι καὶ πένητες. Οὐ τοῖς πένησι δὲ
μᾶλλον, ἢ τοῖς πλουσίοις τοῦτο ᵃ ἔφερεν ἂν τὴν ἡδονήν. Καὶ εἰ βούλει, τέως ὑπογράψωμεν αὐτὸ τῷ λόγῳ, καὶ ταύτῃ καρπωσώμεθα τὴν ἡδονήν, ἐπειδὴ ἐν
ἔργοις οὐ βούλεσθε. Μάλιστα μὲν γὰρ καὶ ἐξ ἐκείνων δῆλον τῶν τότε γενομένων, ὅτι πωλοῦντες οὐκ
ἦσαν ἐνδεεῖς, ἀλλὰ καὶ τοὺς πένητας πλουσίους
ἐποίουν.

Πλὴν ἀλλὰ καὶ νῦν ὑπογράψωμεν τοῦτο τῷ λόγῳ,
καὶ πάντες τὰ αὐτῶν πωλείτωσαν πάντα, καὶ φερέ-
τωσαν εἰς μέσον, τῷ λόγῳ λέγω · μηδεὶς θορυβείσθω,
μήτε πλούσιος, μήτε πένης. Πόσον οἴει χρυσίον συν-
άγεσθαι ; Ἐγὼ στοχάζομαι (οὐ γὰρ δὴ μετὰ ἀκριβείας
δυνατὸν εἰπεῖν), ὅτι εἰ πάντες καὶ πᾶσαι τὰ αὐτῶν
ἐνταῦθα ἐκένωσαν χρήματα, καὶ χωρία καὶ κτήματα

198   JOHN CHRYSOSTOM

καὶ οἰκίας ἀπέδοντο (ἀνδράποδα γὰρ οὐκ ἂν εἴποιμι·
οὐδὲ γὰρ τότε τοῦτο ἦν, ἀλλ' ἐλευθέρους ἴσως ἐπέ-
τρεπον γίνεσθαι)· τάχα ἂν ἑκατὸν μυριάδες λιτρῶν
χρυσίου συνήχθησαν· μᾶλλον δὲ καὶ δὶς καὶ τρὶς
τοσαῦτα. Εἰπὲ γάρ μοι, ἡ πόλις ἡμῖν εἰς πόσον μιγά-
δων ἀριθμὸν νῦν τελεῖ; πόσους βούλεσθε εἶναι Χρι-
στιανούς; βούλεσθε δέκα μυριάδας, τὸ δὲ ἄλλο Ἑλλή-
νων καὶ Ἰουδαίων; πόσαι μυριάδες χρυσίου ᵇ συνε-
λέγησαν; πόσος δὲ ἀριθμός ἐστι πενήτων; Οὐκ οἶμαι
πλέον μυριάδων πέντε. Τούτους δὴ καθ' ἑκάστην
ἡμέραν τρέφεσθαι, πόση ἀφθονία ἦν; Μᾶλλον δὲ
κοινῆς τῆς τροφῆς γινομένης, καὶ συσσίτων ὄντων,
οὐδὲ πολλῆς ἂν ἐδέησε δαπάνης. Τί οὖν, φησὶν, ἐμέλ-
λομεν ποιεῖν μετὰ τὸ ἀναλωθῆναι; Σὺ οἴει δυνηθῆναι
ἀναλωθῆναί ποτε; οὐ γὰρ ἂν μυριοπλασίων ἡ τοῦ
Θεοῦ χάρις γέγονε; οὐ γὰρ πλουσίως ἂν ἡ τοῦ Θεοῦ
χάρις ἐξεχύθη; Τί δέ; οὐκ ἂν οὐρανὸν ἐποιήσαμεν
τὴν γῆν; Εἰ ἔνθα τρισχίλιοι καὶ πεντακισχίλιοι, τοῦτο
γενόμενον οὕτως ἔλαμψε, καὶ οὐδεὶς αὐτῶν πενίαν
ᾐτιάσατο, πόσῳ μᾶλλον ἐν τοσούτῳ πλήθει; τίς δὲ
οὐκ ἂν καὶ τῶν ἔξωθεν ἐπέδωκεν; Ἵνα δὲ δείξω, ὅτι
τὸ διεσπάσθαι ᶜ, τοῦτο δαπανηρὸν καὶ πενίας ποιητι-
κὸν, ἔστω οἰκία, ἔνθα παιδία δέκα καὶ γυνὴ κ. ᵈ ἀνὴρ
καὶ ἡ μὲν ἐριουργείτω, ὁ δὲ ἔξωθεν φερέτω προσ-
όδους· εἰπὲ δή. μοι, οὗτοι κοινῇ σιτούμενοι, καὶ μίαν
ἔχοντες οἰκίαν, [94] πλείονα ἂν ἀναλίσκοιεν, ἢ διασπασθέντες; Εὔδηλον, ὅτι διασπασθέντες; Εἰ γὰρ
μέλλοιεν διεσπάσθαι τὰ δέκα παιδία, δέκα καὶ οἰκη-
μάτων χρεία, δέκα τραπεζῶν, δέκα ὑπηρετῶν, καὶ
τῆς ἄλλης προσόδου τοσαύτης. Τί δὲ, ἔνθα δούλων
πλῆθός ἐστιν; οὐχὶ διὰ τοῦτο πάντες μίαν ἔχουσι τρά-
πεζαν, ὥστε μὴ πολλὴν γενέσθαι τὴν δαπάνην; Ἢ

γὰρ διαίρεσις ἀεὶ ἐλάττωσιν ἐμποιεῖ, ἡ δὲ ὁμόνοια καὶ συμφωνία αὔξησιν. Οὕτως οἱ ἐν τοῖς μοναστη-ρίοις ζῶσι νῦν, ὥσπερ ποτὲ οἱ πιστοί. Τίς ἂν ἀπέθα-νεν οὖν ἀπὸ λιμοῦ; τίς δὲ οὐ διετράφη μετὰ ἀφθονίας πολλῆς; Νῦν μὲν οὖν τοῦτο δεδοίκασιν ἄνθρωποι μᾶλ-λον, ἢ εἰς πέλαγος ἐμπεσεῖν ἄπλετον καὶ ἄπειρον. Εἰ δὲ πεῖραν ἐποιησάμεθα τούτου, τότε ἂν κατετολμήσα-μεν τοῦ πράγματος. Πόσην οἴει καὶ χάριν εἶναι ; Εἰ γὰρ τότε, ὅτε οὐδεὶς ἦν πιστὸς, ἀλλὰ τρισχίλιοι καὶ πεντακισχίλιοι μόνον· ὅτε πάντες οἱ τῆς οἰκουμένης ἦσαν ἐχθροί· ὅτε οὐδαμόθεν προσεδόκων παραμυθίαν, οὕτω δὴ κατετόλμησαν d τοῦ πράγματος· πόσῳ μᾶλλον νῦν τοῦτο ἂν ἐγένετο, ἔνθα τῇ τοῦ Θεοῦ χάριτι παν-ταχοῦ τῆς οἰκουμένης πιστοί ; τίς δ' ἂν ἔμενεν Ἕλ-λην λοιπόν ; Οὐδένα ἔγωγε ἡγοῦμαι· οὕτως ἂν πάντας ἐπεσπασάμεθα, καὶ εἱλκύσαμεν πρὸς ἡμᾶς αὐτούς. Πλὴν ἀλλ' ἐὰν ὁδῷ ταύτῃ προβαίνωμεν, πιστεύω τῷ Θεῷ, ὅτι καὶ τοῦτο ἔσται. Πείσθητέ μοι μόνον, καὶ κατὰ τάξιν κατορθώσομεν τὰ πράγματα· καὶ ἂν ὁ Θεὸς ζωὴν δῷ, πιστεύω, ὅτι ταχέως εἰς ταύτην ἡμᾶς ἄξομεν τὴν πολιτείαν.   [*In Act. Apost.*, 11, 3, *PG* 60:96-98]

AUGUSTINE

Text 1

A   3. Res ergo aliæ sunt quibus fruendum est, aliæ quibus utendum, aliæ quæ fruuntur et utuntur. Il-læ quibus fruendum est, beatos nos faciunt. Istis quibus utendum est,...........................
.... Frui enim est amore alicui rei inhærere propter seipsam. Uti autem, quod in usum venerit ad id quod amas obtinendum referre, si tamen amandum est.

Nam usus illicitus, abusus potius vel abusio nomi-
nandus est. . . . . si
redire in patriam volumus, ubi beati esse possimus,
utendum est hoc mundo, non fruendum .

[De Doc. Christ., 1, 3-4, PL 34:20-21]

B   Ad extremum pecunia, quo uno nomine conti-
nentur omnia quorum jure domini sumus, et quorum
vendendorum aut donandorum habere potestatem vi-
demur.

[De Lib. Arb., 1, 15, PL 32:1238]

C   Totum enim quidquid homines possi-
dent in terra, omnia quorum domini sunt, pecunia
vocatur. Servus sit, vas, ager, arbor, pecus ; quidquid
horum est, pecunia dicitur. Et unde est primum vo-
cata pecunia. Ideo pecunia, quia antiqui totum quod
habebant, in pecoribus habebant. At pecore pecunia
vocatur.

[De Disc. Christ., 6, 6, PL 40:672]

Text 2

A   **26.** Jamvero si prudenter intueamur quod scriptum
est, *Fidelis hominis totus mundus divitiarum est, infi-*
delis autem nec obolus (a); nonne omnes qui sibi vi-
dentur gaudere licite conquisitis, eisque uti nesciunt,
aliena possidere convincimus? Hoc enim certe alienum non est, quod jure possidetur; hoc autem jure
quod juste, et hoc juste quod bene. Omne igitur quod
male possidetur, alienum est; male autem possidet,
qui male utitur.

[Ep. CLIII, 26, PL 33:665]

B   Cernis ergo quam multi debeant red-
dere aliena, si vel pauci quibus reddantur, reperian-
tur : qui tamen ubi ubi sunt, tanto magis ista conte-

mnunt, quanto ea justius possidere potuerunt. Justitiam quippe, et nemo male habet, et qui non dilexerit non habet. Pecunia vero, et a malis male habetur, et a bonis tanto melius habetur, quanto minus amatur. Sed inter hæc toleratur iniquitas male habentium, et quædam inter eos jura constituuntur, quæ appellantur civilia; non quod hinc fiat ut bene utentes sint, sed ut male utentes minus molesti sint :   [*Ep. CLIII*, 26, *PL* 33:665]

C   **Unde**

quisque possidet quod possidet? nonne jure humano? Nam jure divino, Domini est terra et plenitudo ejus (*Psal.* xxiii, 1): pauperes et divites Deus de uno limo fecit, et pauperes et divites una terra supportat. Jure tamen humano dicit, Hæc villa mea est, hæc domus mea, hic servus meus est. Jure ergo humano, jure imperatorum.   [*In Ioann.*, 6, 25, *PL* 35:1437]

Text 3

A   **Communem habetis**

cum divitibus mundum : non communem habetis cum divitibus domum; sed habetis commune cœlum, communem lucem. Sufficientiam quærite, quod sufficit quærite, plus nolite.............................
.... An attulisti huc aliquid? Sed nec vos, divites, aliquid attulistis. Totum hic invenistis, cum pauperibus nudi nati estis.   [*Serm. LXXXV*, 5, 6, *PL* 38:522-23]

B   **Multa** autem superflua habemus, si nonnisi necessaria teneamus : nam si inania quæramus, nihil sufficit..............................

.... Videte quia non solum pauca sunt quæ vobis sufficiant; sed nec ipse Deus multa a vobis quærit. Quære quantum tibi dederit, et ex eo tolle quod sufficit : cætera quæ superflua jacent, aliorum sunt necessaria. Superflua divitum, necessaria sunt pauperum. Res alienæ possidentur, cum superflua possidentur.

[In Ps. 147, 12, PL 37:1922]

C Nihil dives habet de divitiis suis, nisi quod ab illo postulat pauper, victum et tegumentum. Hinc tu quid plus habes ex omnibus quæ habes? Accepisti victum, accepisti necessarium tegumentum. Necessarium dico, non inane, non superfluum. Quid plus de divitiis tuis capis? Dic mihi. Certe omnia tua superflua erunt. Quæ sunt tua superflua, sint pauperibus necessaria ².

[Serm. LXI, 11, 12, PL 38:413]

D Animam enim suam superfluis et nimiis epulis satiare cupiebat, pauperum tot inanes ventres superbissimus contemnebat. Nesciebat pauperum ventres apothecis suis esse tutiores. Quod enim recondebat in illis apothecis suis, fortassis et a furibus auferebatur : si autem reconderet in pauperum ventribus, in terra quidem digerebatur, sed in cœlo tutius servabatur.

[Serm. XXXVI, 9, 9, PL 38:219]

Text 4

A Mundum præstat Deus pauperi, præstat et diviti. Numquid quia dives est, duos ventres impleturus est? Attendite, et videte quoniam de datis Dei pauperes saturati dormiunt. Qui pascit vos, pascit et illos per vos.   [*Serm. XXXIX*, 2, *PL* 38:242]

B   Cur non autem miseri intelligunt, quod apud
Aggæum loquens Dominus, propterea dixerit, *Meum
est aurum*, *et meum est argentum*, ut et ille qui non
vult cum indigentibus communicare quod habet, ...
. . . . intelligat
Deum non de re illius cui jubet, sed de re sua jubere
donari ; et ille qui aliquid porrigit pauperi, non se
arbitretur de suo facere,   [*Serm. L*, 1, *PL* 38:326]

C   *Aurum ejus proprie est*, *qui illo bene utitur, ad-
eoque verius est Dei.* Illius est ergo aurum et argentum, qui novit uti auro et argento. Nam etiam inter ipsos homines, tunc quisque habere aliquid dicen-
dus est [1], quando bene utitur. Nam quod juste non
tractat, jure non tenet. Quod autem jure non tenet,
si suum esse dixerit, non erit vox justi possessoris, sed
impudentis incubatoris improbitas.   [*Serm. L*, 2 and 4, *PL* 38:327]

Text 5

A   Quod est onus paupertatis ? Non habere. Quod est
divitiarum onus? Plus quam opus est habere. . . . .
. . . . .Porta cum illo non
habere, portet tecum plus habere ; ut fiant æquales
sarcinæ vestræ. . . . . .Duo ambulatis viam Dei in pe-
regrinatione hujus sæculi : tu portabas sumptus ma-
gnos superfluos ; . . . . Non vides quantum portes ? Nihil portanti et non habenti da inde
aliquid , et comitem adjuvabis, et te relevabis.

[*Serm. CXLIV*, 7, 9, *PL* 38:899]

B   Audiant nunc di-
vites, qui nolunt esse misericordes ; audiant quia una
omnes nascimur lege, una vivimus luce, unum spira-
mus aerem, una quoque exstinguimur morte : quæ si
non intercederet, nec pauper ipse duraret.

[Serm. CCLXVII, 1, 1, PL 39:1651]

C   *Radix omnium*
malorum est avaritia (I *Tim*. VI, 10) ; si avaritiam ge-
neralem intelligamus, qua quisque appetit aliquid
amplius quam oportet, propter excellentiam suam, et
quemdam propriæ rei amorem : cui sapienter nomen
latina lingua indidit, cum appellavit privatum, quod
potius a detrimento quam ab incremento dictum elu-
cet. Omnis enim privatio minuit.   [De Gen., 11, 15, PL 34:436]

D   Unde inter fratres discor-
dia? unde perturbatio pietatis? unde unus uterus, et
non unus animus, nisi dum curvatur anima eorum, et
partem suam quisque respicit, et parti suæ opimandæ
et exaggerandæ operam impendit, et in possessione
sua vult habere unitatem, qui cum fratre suo possidet
divisionem? . . . .
. . . . Quid tam iniquum quam velle ditescere
alterius paupertate ?   [Serm. CCCLIX, 2, PL 39:1591]

Text 6
                                Qui te fecit,
ipse te pascit ex his quæ fecit, ipse pascit et filios
tuos. Neque enim melius committis filios tuos patri-
monio tuo [2], quam Creatori tuo. . . . .
. . . . Quare non facit elcemo-

synam? Quia servat filiis suis. Contingit ut amittat
unum : si propter filios servabat, mittat post illum
partem suam. Quare illam tenet in sacculo, et illum
relinquit ab animo? Redde illi quod suum est, redde quod illi servabas. Mortuus est, inquit. Sed
præcessit ad Deum, pars ipsius pauperibus debe-
tur .   [*Serm. IX*, 12, 20, *PL* 38:89-90]

Text 7

A   Et tamen Christus dicit tibi :
Da mihi ex eo quod dedi tibi. Quid enim attulisti,
quando huc venisti? Omnia quæ creavi, creatus hic
invenisti : nihil attulisti, nihil hinc tolles. De meo mihi
quare non donas? Quia tu plenus es, et pauper inanis
est. Primordia vestra attendite : ambo nudi nati
estis. Et tu ergo nudus natus es. Multa hic invenisti :
numquid tecum aliquid attulisti?   [*Serm. CXXIV*, 5, 5, *PL* 38:686]

B   Qui autem vult facere
locum Domino, non de privato, sed de communi de-
bet gaudere. . . . . .Intendat
Charitas vestra : quia propter illa quæ singuli possi-
demus, existunt lites, inimicitiæ, discordiæ, belia
inter homines, tumultus, dissensiones adversum se,
scandala, peccata, iniquitates, homicidia. Propter
quæ? Propter ipsa quæ singuli possidemus. Numquid
propter ista quæ communiter possidemus, litigamus?
Aerem istum communiter ducimus, solem communiter omnes videmus. Beati ergo qui sic faciunt locum
Domino, ut privato suo non gaudeant.
                                        [*In Ps. 131*, 5, *PL* 37:1718]

C   **6. Abstineamus ergo nos, fratres, a possessione rei privatæ; aut ab amore, si non possumus a possessione; et facimus locum Domino. Multum est ad me, ait aliquis. Sed vide quis sis²**, facturus locum Domino....
.... In re quam privatam quisque possidet, necesse est superbus sit:............
.... Et tamen caro dives extendit se contra carnem pauperem; quasi aliquid illa caro attulerit quando nata est, aut aliquid auferat quando moritur.**

[In Ps. 131, 6-7, PL 37:1718-19]

D   Verumtamen magister bonus mandata legis ab ista excellentiore perfectione distinxit : ibi enim dixit, *Si vis venire ad vitam, serva mandata ;* hic autem, *Si vis perfectus esse, vade, vende omnia quæ habes,* etc. Cur ergo negamus divites, quamvis ab illa perfectione absint, venire tamen ad vitam, si mandata servaverint, et dederint ut detur illis, et dimiserint ut dimittatur illis (*Luc.* VI, 37, 38)?

[Ep. CLVII, 25, PL 33:687]

E   Cum igitur eisdem rebus alius male, alius bene utatur; et is quidem qui male, amore his inhæreat atque implicetur, scilicet subditus eis rebus quas ei subditas esse oportebat, et ea bona sibi constituens, quibus ordinandis beneque tractandis ipse esse utique deberet bonum: ille autem qui recte his utitur, ostendat qui-............................... sed eis totus superferatur, et habere illa atque regere, ... cum ergo hæc ita sint, num aut argentum et aurum propter avaros accusandum putas, aut cibos propter voraces, aut vinum propter ebriosos, aut muliebres formas propter scortatores et adulteros.

[De Lib. Arb., 1, 15, 33, PL 32:1239]

INDEX OF BIBLICAL REFERENCES

1 Kings

21	61

Job

1:21	49
29:15-16	69

Psalms

14	56
23:1	111, 131
41:1	98
112:9	74, 77

Proverbs

13:8	42
22:28	72

Ecclesiasticus

4:1	84
4:8	67

Isaiah

5:8	62, 63, 72
40:6-8	98
65:21	151, 155

Baruch

3:24-25	73, 142

Haggai

1:6	35
2:8	78, 115

Malachi

3:10	83

Matthew

6:26	72
13:46	37
19:17	120
19:21	67, 120
24	91
25:31-46	71

Mark

10:17-31	43
10:20	50

Luke

1-24	71
6:37-38	120
9:55	74, 139
12:16-21	69
12:18	49
16	83-85
16:1-9	94
16:9	44
16:13	140

John

1-21	110, 111

Acts

4	100-2, 146-48
4:32	87

Romans

1-16	88-90
15:26	40

1 Corinthians

1:9	40
9:11	40
12:12-31	40

2 Corinthians

1-13	76-78
8:4	40
9:9	77
9:10-11	77

Galatians

6:2	118
6:6	40

Philippians

4:15	40

2 Thessalonians

3:10	89
3:13	90

1 Timothy

1-6	94
6:7-8	115
6:9	118
6:10	117

Philemon

v. 17	40

Hebrews

2:14	40

2 Peter

1:4	40

GENERAL INDEX

accessio, 20
Adeodatus, 106
Aelianus, 30
Alexandria, 26, 33-35; Catechetical
    School of, 33-34
almsgiving, 129-30
Amandus, 30
Ambrose, Saint, Bishop of Milan, 10,
    59-80, 114, 130-44, 148, 152
  on avarice, 61-66, 73, 75, 78, 139,
    141
  baptizes Augustine, 106
  Basil's influence on, 61, 71, 162n.6
  *Commentary on the Second Epistle
    of Paul to the Corinthians*, 76-
    78
  eschatology in, 130
  on God as our Debtor, 69-71
  Hexaemeron, 71-72
  on justice, 73-77
  on mercy, 70-71, 73-76
  De Nabuthe Jezraelita, 61-70
  on nature, communality of, 62-80,
    131, 135, 139, 142
  De Officiis Ministrorum, 70, 73-76
  on the poor, 65-70, 132-33
  on private ownership, 62-80, 135,
    139, 144, 152, 163-64 n. 35
  on restitution and redistribution,
    66-69, 77-79, 132-33, 137
  Stoic influence in, 63-64, 67, 70-76,
    78-79
  supports tenant farmers, 31
  on wealth as cause of poverty, 64-
    66
  on the wealthy, 62-70, 132-33
Ammonius Saccas, 33-34
anachorēsis, 149
anankaion and cognates, 38, 41, 86-87
Anthony, Saint, 149
Anthusa, 81

Antioch, 26, 81-83, 88, 91, 94-95
appropriation of common goods, 6-9,
    15-16, 54, 139
appropriation of land, 19-20
Aquinas, Saint Thomas, 115
Augustine, Saint, Bishop of Hippo, 1,
    10, 13, 105-24, 125, 130-46, 149,
    152
  on almsgiving, 114-15, 119-20, 137
  on avarice, 117-18
  City of God, The, 108
  Confessions, 108
  eschatology in, 130-31
  on frui, uti, pecunia, 109-10, 114,
    116, 122
  on God the Creator, 113, 116, 119,
    123
  on God as Supreme Good, 108,
    113, 124
  on God as Supreme Owner, 116,
    121
  on human solidarity, 116-18
  on inherited property and wealth,
    119, 137
  In Ioannis Evangelium, 110-11
  letter to Macedonius, 110-11
  and monasticism, 106, 123, 149
  on nature, communality of, 111,
    113-14, 117, 123, 136
  On Christian Doctrine, 109
  On the Trinity, 108
  on ownership of property and
    wealth
    based on need, 113-16
    communal character of, 115-16,
    120, 123
    destructive aspects of, 119-23,
    133, 137-39
    moral and philosophical aspects
    of, 110-13
    and private property, 116-22

209

Platonist influence in, 108, 115
rejects Roman law on private property, 111-12, 120-24
on restitution, 110-12, 117, 133, 137
on social character of person, 113
Stoic influence in, 115, 118
Ten Commandments, sermon on, 119
theocratic communism in, 110-13
on wealth as cause of poverty, 113-14, 118-22, 145-46
on wealth as good, 121-22, 131
autarkeia, 35-37, 40, 43, 45-47, 50, 52, 54, 133, 144-45, 150, 154-55
defined, 35
auxilium, 18
Bacaudae, 30
baranggay, 4
Basilides, 34
Basil the Great, Saint, Bishop of Caesarea, 13, 47-58, 130-35, 141, 161-62 n. 14
on *autarkeia*, 50-52, 54
on avarice, 49-51, 55, 133
eschatology in, 130
on God as Giver and Provider, 50-55, 57-58
on *ta idia*, 53-54, 135
on inherited property and wealth, 54-55
on *ta koina*, 53-55
Luke 12:18, commentary on, 49-53
and monasticism, 149-50
on Nature, communality of, 51-56, 135
on ownership of property and wealth
limited by one's needs, 49-58
morality of, 49-58, 141
Psalm 14, commentary on, 56
on redistribution, 50-58
Stoic influence in, 57, 71
on usury, 56
on wealth as cause of poverty, 49-53, 55-58, 133-34
on wealth as good, 51, 131
Belloc, Hilaire, 6
bucellarii, 30
Bury, J.B., 81-82
Caesarea, 47-49

Cappadocia, 47, 49, 53
Cardozo, Benjamin, 9
Carpocrates, 34
Carthage, 105-7
Case, Shirley Jackson, 13, 157n.21
cessio, in iure, 20
chrēmata, 45, 53, 86, 88, 144
chrēsima, 45
chrēsis, 45, 93
Christianity, Early
communal aspects of, 87, 100, 128-30, 146-48
as an international movement, 128-31
as a peasant movement, 127-28
socialistic and communistic elements in, 87, 129-30, 152-53
Chrysostom, Saint John, Bishop of Constantinople, 1-2, 29-30, 81-104, 114, 125, 130-149
on accountability, 89, 91-94, 134-35, 140-41
on almsgiving, 84-85, 92-94, 98-100, 132, 137
on avarice, 85-86, 92, 104, 134
commentaries and homilies on
Acts 4, 86-87, 100-102, 146-48
Hebrews, 98
Luke 16, 83-85, 87-88, 94-97
Matthew 24, 29, 30, 91
Psalm 41, 98-99
Romans, 88-89
1 Timothy, 94-96
2 Thessalonians, 89-90
on communal life, 100-102, 146-48
eschatology in, 98-99, 130
on God as Absolute Owner, 86, 91-98
on God as Giver and Provider, 85, 89
on God as Supreme Lord, 84
on human solidarity, 82, 98-103, 143
on idleness, 89, 90
on inherited property and wealth, 84, 88-92, 94, 96, 104, 132, 136-37
and landlords, attack on, 29
and monasticism, 101, 149
on nature, communality of, 85-86, 95-98, 104, 135-36, 140-41

on ownership of property and
wealth, 1-2, 84-87, 91-104
and destructive aspects, 84-86,
90-94
and dispersion of property, 100-
102, 147-48
and land, 94-98
purpose and meaning of, 85-87
and Roman law, 93, 95-97
on the poor, 87-91
on possessions, 87-88
on restitution and redistribution,
91-102, 137, 146-48
on sharing, 83-85, 93, 98-104, 146-
48
on wealth as cause of poverty, 82-
85, 90-95, 132, 135-36
on wealth as good, 87-88, 92-93, 95,
102, 131-32
Church as landowner. *See* ownership
and the Church
Cicero, 63, 73, 76, 105
civitas, 108, 113
Clement of Alexandria, Saint, 13, 33-
46, 85, 88, 129, 131-32, 144-45
on *autarkeia*, 35-37, 40, 43, 45-46,
144-45
Didaskaleion, 34-35
on the Divine Logos, 35-41
on God as Giver, 44-45, 131-32
on human solidarity, 39-40, 145
on *koinonia*, 37-46, 145
on *Koinos Logos*, 39-41
on law, Roman property, 38
on nature, communality of, 37-39,
135
on ownership of property and
wealth, 35-46
Paidagogos, 34-43, 160 n. 10
Protreptikos, 34-35
Quis Dives Salvetur?, 43-45
Stoic influence in, 33-42
Stromata, 34
triadology in, 41
on wealth as good, 43-46, 88, 131-
32
on wealth and its limits, 42-43
clergy, 26-27
coloni. See tenant farmers
common proprietorship of the things
of nature, 5-8, 37-39, 51-56, 62-80,

85-86, 95-98, 104, 111, 113-14, 117,
123, 134-36, 139, 141-42. *See also
res communes*
compensation to landlords, 9-10, 137
concilium plebis, 17
conductores, 107
conformis, 71, 79
consors naturae, 63-64, 71, 73, 75, 79,
142
Constantine, 148
Constantinople, 26, 81, 82, 98, 101,
146
Countryman, L.W., 12, 13
De Laveleye, Emile, 6
despoteia, 93, 103, 140
didaskaleia, 129
Diocletian, 27
dominium, 19-21, 140
dominus, 68-69
domus, 113
doulos, 88
eleēosunē, 129
eminent domain, 8
Emmelia, 47
Epictetus, 36, 63, 70
eschatology, 130-31, 144
Essenism, 129
Eudoxia, Empress, 82
Eusebius, Bishop of Caesarea, 47
exousia, 41
familia, 23, 158-59 n.17
Fénelon, François, 51
First Secession of the Plebs, 18
frui, 19, 109, 114, 116, 122
Galilee, 127-28
George, Henry, 7, 156 n.6
Gnostics, 34
God:
as Absolute Owner, 45, 86, 91-98,
102, 104, 116, 121, 146
the Creator, 52, 113, 116, 119, 123
as Debtor, 69-71
as Giver and Provider, 44-45, 50-
55, 57-58, 85, 89, 131-32
the Supreme Good, 113, 124
the Supreme Lord, 84
See also Kingdom of God
Gratian, Emperor, 60
Gregory I, Pope, 26
heredium, 16
Hippo, 106

Hortensius, 105
humiliores, 61
inheritance, 54-55, 84, 88-91, 94, 96, 104, 119, 132, 136-37
in iure cessio. See cessio, in iure
Italy, 59-60
iugera, 16, 19
ius rerum, 19
Jesus, 127-28
Julius Caesar, 21
justice, 9, 11-13, 70, 73-77, 86, 92, 95-97, 137-38, 155
Justinian, Emperor, 157-58n.1
kathēkon teleion, 41
katorthōma, 41
Kingdom of God, 127-30
Klueber, Franz, 12
koina, ta, 9, 53-55, 104, 134-36, 142-43, 152
koinōnia, 37-46, 100, 129-30, 143-50, 152-55
defined, 39
Koinos Logos, 39-41, 63
ktēmata, 53
labor, 5-10, 19, 22-32, 34, 46, 134-35, 138, 152, 154. *See also* slavery, tenant farmers
Lactantius, 32
landownership:
absentee, 17, 20, 34, 60, 83, 107-8
in Asia Minor, fourth century, 48-49, 53, 82-83
in Carthage, fourth century, 107-8
collective, 4-7, 15-17
in early Roman Empire, 22-25
in Egypt, third century, 34-35
during Patristic Age, 25-32
private, 5-10, 138
in Roman Republic, 16-19
See also Law, Roman, concept of ownership
Laros, Matthias, 12
latifundia, 20, 25, 62, 107, 151, 162n.4
Law, Anglo-American, 15
Law, Roman:
and concept of ownership and property, 8-12, 14-32, 38, 64-66, 93, 95-97, 103, 107-8, 111-12, 120-31, 134, 140, 151-55, 160n.14
and influence on present legal systems, 8-10, 15-16, 151-52

and Licinian Laws, 19
and slavery, 19, 21-30, 128-29, 158-59n.17
and State of Louisiana, 15
Twelve Tables of, 18, 21
See also accessio; cessio, in iure; dominium; ius rerum; locatio-conductio; mancipatio; occupatio; precario; proprietas; res communes; res mancipi; res nec mancipi; specificatio; usucapio; vindicatio
Libanius, 30
Licinian Laws. *See* Roman Law
locatio-conductio, 48
Logos, Divine, 35-41. *See also Koinos Logos*
Longinus, 34
Lumpenproletariat, 23, 31, 126
Macedonius, 110
mancipatio, 20, 21
Marcus Aurelius, Emperor, 38, 72
marriage, inter-class, 18
Marx, Karl, 154
Melania, 26
mercy, 70-71, 73-76
metadidonai, 85
metochos, 39
middle class, 126-27
Migne, Abbé J.P., 61
Mill, John Stuart, 9
monasticism, 101-2, 129, 148-50
Monica, Saint, 105
More, Saint Thomas, 51, 153
Musonius, 36
nature, things of. *See* Common proprietorship of the things of nature; *see also res communes*
occupatio, 20
Origen, 40
Ownership:
and the Church, 10-13, 25-30, 128-31
collective, 4-8, 15-16
defined, 3-4
in early Christian communities, 87, 100-102, 128-30
in English law, 8
in Islamic law, 8
as moral-philosophical phenomenon, 1-2, 61, 133
in Mosaic law, 6

and natural law, 72-73
in patristic thought, 10-13, 25-30, 131-50
and private property, origins, 4-8
as socio-legal phenomenon, 1-2
in South America, 15
among Teutonic peoples, 6, 21
and the Third World, 2, 9, 154
See also Ambrose, Augustine, Basil, Chrysostom, Clement, on ownership; Law, Roman, and ownership
Palestinian movement, 127-28
Panaetius, 73
Pantaenus, 33
patricians, 16-18
Patricius, 105
paterfamilias. See familia
Paul, 40, 63, 118
pecunia, 109-10, 165n.13
Pharisees, 127
Philippines, 4-5, 15, 154
Philo, 34
plebians, 16-19, 21
Pliny, 14
poor, the. *See* Ambrose, Augustine, Basil, Chrysostom, on the poor, and wealth as cause of poverty.
possessio, 62
property. *See* landownership; ownership; Law, Roman, concept of property and ownership; Ambrose, Augustine, Basil, Chrysostom, Clement, on ownership of property and wealth
proprietas, 19
rents, 9, 16, 29-32, 107, 152
res:
   communes, 19-20
   mancipi, 21
   nec mancipi, 21
restitution, 137-38. *See also* Ambrose, Augustine, Basil, and Chrysostom, on restitution
Russell, Bertrand, 10
Ryan, John A., 12, 51, 55, 161nn.11, 12
Schilling, Otto, 12
self-sufficiency. *See autarkeia*
Senate, Roman, *17*
Seneca, 63, 70
serfs. *See* tenant farmers

sharing. *See koinōnia*
slavery:
   decline of, 25, 27
   in Patristic thought, 7-8, 48, 100
   and private ownership, 7-8, 19, 21-27, 31
   in Roman history, 19, 21-25, 29, 107, 126-27
   under Roman law, 19, 21-30, 128-29, 158-59n.17
   See also doulos, ius rerum
socii, 129
socio-economic conditions:
   in Asia Minor, fourth century, 48-49, 53, 82-83
   in Carthage, fourth century, 107-8
   in early Roman Empire, 22-25
   in Egypt, third century, 34-35
   in Italy, fourth century, 22-25
   in Patristic Age, 25-32, 162n.4
   in Roman Republic, 16-19
specificatio, 20
Spencer, Herbert, 9
Stoicism. *See* Ambrose, Augustine, Basil, Clement, Stoic influence in
sundouloi, 84, 103, 141
Sylvester I, Pope, 153
Synod of the Oak, 82
Tacitus, 21
Tagaste, 105-6
Tasadays, 4
taxation, 5, 27, 31, 48-49, 107
tenant farmers, 20, 27-32, 48-49, 60, 107-8, 126-27
   resistance by, 30-31
   status legalized, 27, 28
   See also locatio-conductio, rents
theocratic communism. *See* Augustine
Theodosius, Emperor, 28, 60
Tiberius Gracchus, 14
tribuni, 18
Twelve Tables. *See* Roman law
Universal Reason (Logos). *See Koinos Logos*
usucapio, 20
usurpatio, 76
usurpation, 8-10, 76, 139
usury, 56
uti, 19, 109, 114, 116
Valentinian, Emperor, 28
Valentinus, 34
Valerius, Bishop of Hippo, 106

Varro, 63
vectigal, 107
Veii, subjugation of, 17
vindicatio, 95
wealth:
    as cause of poverty, 132-36

as a good, 131-34
See also Ambrose, Augustine, Basil, Chrysostom, Clement, on ownership of property and wealth, restitution, wealth as cause of poverty, and wealth as a good

Other Orbis Books . . .

James Armstrong
FROM THE UNDERSIDE
Evangelism from a Thirld World Vantage Point
Foreword by José Míguez Bonino
"This is not the usual book on evangelism. The author has the
insight and courage to relate a biblical view of evangelism to
such issues as military oppression, human rights, justice, conditions of the poor, U.S. foreign policy and—through all—to the
inner work of the Spirit in the lives of Christians today."

Concern

"A remarkable blending of a deeply biblical view of evangelism
as personal conversion with a vivid portrayal of the compassion
for those on the 'underside' which must result from such conversion. As a critique of much of the popular religion of today it
is superb." *Cynthia C. Wedel, former president,*
National Council of Churches
ISBN 0-88344-146-2 *112pp. Paper $4.95*

Rafael Avila
WORSHIP AND POLITICS
"These pages are written from the perspective of political oppression in the South American country of Colombia. And like
much theology written under the dominant motif of liberation,
they are both historically informed and contemporary. Avila is
primarily concerned with showing how in the history of Israel
and the church, and in contemporary practice, worship (and
especially the eucharist) has profound political significance.
For in worship we celebrate the reality and presence of One
whose purpose is liberation from all forms of oppression and
bondage. The publication of this work in English is welcome for
it will remind us who grow comfortable in middle-class piety
that we need to examine our own worship practices to determine whether they are, in style and content, self-serving or liber-
ating." *The Clergy Journal*
ISBN 0-88344-714-2 *144pp. Paper $6.95*

Tissa Balasuriya
THE EUCHARIST AND HUMAN LIBERATION *(2nd Printing)*
Balasuriya, one of Asia's most productive Christian theologians, is now at the Centre for Society and Religion in Colombo,
Sri Lanka. In this disarmingly straightforward and profoundly
disturbing book he makes a bold contribution to the contemporary debate about what roles Christians and the Church
should play in the struggles for universal justice, equitable distribution of the world's goods, and the liberation of oppressed
nations and social classes. Balasuriya shows how the chief
liturgical service of the Church, the celebration of the Eucharist
(Holy Communion) could become a major revolutionary force,
challenging and empowering millions of people to contribute to
the birth of a new world order.
ISBN 0-88344-118-7   *184pp. Paper $6.95*

John Eagleson & Sergio Torres, Eds.
THE CHALLENGE OF BASIC CHRISTIAN COMMUNITIES
(2nd Printing)
Preface by Jorge Lara-Braud
"A grass-roots 'people's church' movement has emerged in the
last two decades, especially in Latin America among Roman
Catholics. The fourth meeting of the Ecumenical Association of
Third World Theologians attempted to evaluate this development. The addresses, papers, and reports of the meeting in São
Paulo, Brazil are published in this book. The significance of this
new form of church life is analyzed, along with the challenge it
poses to historic churches—especially in light of the formal
declarations of many Christian assemblies of solidarity with the
poor and oppressed."   *The Disciple*
ISBN 0-88344-503-4   *352pp. Paper $9.95*

Joseph Gremillion
THE GOSPEL OF PEACE AND JUSTICE *(6th Printing)*
Catholic Social Teaching Since Pope John
"This source book and survey of social problems contains
twenty-two documents—encyclicals, conciliar decrees, and
papal and episcopal addresses—which have appeared during
the reigns of Popes John XXIII and Paul VI. Msgr. Gremillion, a
diocesan priest from Louisiana and the first secretary of the
Pontifical Commission for Justice and Peace, introduces them
with a 140-page outline of the world situation today, the role the

Catholic Church has played and should play in promoting justice and peace, and the development of papal thought on these questions."   *Theology Digest*

"Trying to locate the various official documents of the Church —even those of recent vintage—has always been a problem for the scholar. We are indebted to Msgr. Gremillion for gathering all the significant statements made by the Catholic Church during the past 15 years that have definite social significance and relevance. This compilation for many reasons is most valuable and a striking witness to the current social concerns of the Catholic Church throughout the world."

                                                          Worldmission
ISBN 0-88344-165-9   *637pp. Cloth $15.95*
ISBN 0-88344-166-7   *Paper $12.95*

José Porfirio Miranda
COMMUNISM IN THE BIBLE
"A scholarly study in biblical teaching—brief, direct, powerful—which puts the burden of proof on those who would deny that original and authentic Christianity is communistic (*not*, to say, Marxist). This is vintage Miranda—erudite, passionate, persuasive, and above all, disturbing."
                               Prof. Robert T. Osborn, Duke Univ.
ISBN 0-88344-014-8   *96pp. Paper $5.95*

George V. Pixley
GOD'S KINGDOM
A Guide for Biblical Study
Foreword by Harvey Cox
"This is a book that analyzes the vital connections between political economy and religious faith in all the major periods of biblical history. Compactly and clearly written, with abundant biblical references, Pixley's work will be a tremendous asset for study groups that want to grasp the Bible as a resource for social change."   *The College Store Journal*

"There is no pie-in-the-sky theology here. Rather the author has initiated a real consideration for the Bible serving as a resource for social change."   *Today's Parish*

"This is a thoroughly provocative study of the motif of the Kingdom of God, presented not in an abstract fashion but against the backdrop of the liberation issue in Latin America. Pixley, a professor of Old Testament at a Baptist seminary in

Mexico City, is well aware of recent studies on this theme, and he deftly outlines the various stages of Kingdom theology against the political and religious contexts of Israel, Jesus, and the early Church."   *The Bible Today*

"This is a scholarly and disturbing book, which is also fortunate in its clear translation from the original Spanish. It is both exceptionally well-written and well-produced, using diagrams and short passages of the Old Testament to useful effect. It can be warmly recommended to the wide readership it seeks to serve."
                                                Search (Church of Ireland)

ISBN 0-88344-156-X   *128pp. Paper $5.95*